SHOUTING
IN THE EVENINGS

JAMES HAYES
50 YEARS ON STAGE

Matador
9 Priory Business Park,
Wistow Road, Kibworth Beauchamp,
Leicestershire. LE8 0RX
Tel: 0116 279 2299
Email: books@troubador.co.uk
Web: www.troubador.co.uk/matador
Twitter: @matadorbooks

ISBN 978 1785892 660

British Library Cataloguing in Publication Data.
A catalogue record for this book is available from the British Library.

Printed and bound in the UK by TJ International, Padstow, Cornwall
Typeset in 11pt Minion Pro by Troubador Publishing Ltd, Leicester, UK

Matador is an imprint of Troubador Publishing Ltd

For my grandsons,
Stanley and Eddie Monaghan

"Guest: What do you do for a living?
Troughton: I shout in the evenings."

– An exchange between a party guest and the
actor Patrick Troughton

* * *

"Oft in the stilly night,
Ere Slumber's chain has bound me,
Fond Memory brings the light
Of other days around me."
Irish Melodies – Thomas Moore (1779–1852)

ACKNOWLEDGEMENTS

My publishers and I would like to thank the following for permission to use copyright material:

Nick Hern Books for permission to quote from *Written on the Heart* by David Edgar.

Alan Ayckbourn for a quote from *A Chorus of Disapproval*. Peter Terson for quotes from *Zigger Zagger* and *The Knotty*. Gillian Brown for her song "Railway Lines" and Jeff Parton for his song "Goodbye To Days" from *The Knotty*.

Macnaughton Lord Representation for permission to quote from *Amadeus* by Peter Shaffer.

Michael Bogdanov for permission to quote from an article by him, and a piece by me, for the English Shakespeare Company Magazine.

The Open University for permission to quote from an article I wrote for their magazine *Sesame*.

Taylor and Francis Group for permission to quote from Jim Hiley's book *Theatre at Work*.

I would like to thank the following newspapers for permission to quote from various theatre reviews and articles:

The *Sunday Herald* (Scotland).

The Irish newspapers, *Irish Independent, Sunday Independent* and *Irish Times.*

The *Evening Standard.*

News UK for permission to quote from *The Times* and

Sunday Times for reviews by Irving Wardle, James Fenton and John Peter. The *Daily Telegraph* for a 1980 editorial on *The Romans in Britain*.

And especial thanks to Guardian News and Media Ltd. for permission to quote from the *Observer* and the *Guardian* for a number of reviews by Kenneth Tynan, Robert Cushman and Michael Billington.

The archivists at the RSC (Shakespeare Centre Library, Stratford) and Erin Lee and her team at the National Theatre Archive went to a great deal of trouble to provide me with invaluable material and were very generous with their time and help. I thank them.

I would also like to thank Jim Hiley, the author of *Theatre At Work: The Story of the National Theatre's production of Brecht's Galileo.* Jim's excellent book followed the progress of the production from the commissioning of the translation to the opening night and has proved an invaluable aide-mémoire.

I owe an especial thanks to Lyn Haill at the National Theatre for her constant support, indispensible advice, help with factual accuracy and editing suggestions over the many months of the writing of this book.

I am extremely grateful to my friends and theatre colleagues Sean Gilder, Christopher Hunter and Mark Lockyer for their support and encouragement.

Finally, three people who feature little in this book, but feature greatly in my life. I'm deeply indebted to my ex-wife Jackie Hayes, to my daughter Abigail and to my son Séamus. Throughout the gestation of this book they have given me tremendous support, vital help, telling suggestions and much encouragement. I would particularly thank Abigail, who, at the end, and despite her busy working and family life, helped shape and edit this work. To all three, much love and thanks.

Every effort has been made to contact copyright holders, but, should there be any omissions in this respect we apologise and shall be pleased to make acknowledgement in any future editions.

ILLUSTRATIONS

Playing Razor, the impudent valet, in Vanbrugh's The Provoked Wife at Guildhall in 1964.

Tremendous use of the Leichner greasepaint sticks – No. 5, 9, 7 and 'Lake' in Webster's The White Devil.

Spotlight mugshot 1966.

As the gardener, Hodgson in Agatha Christie's Love From A Stranger, Barrow in Furness – a personal triumph!

With Jane Wood in Tony Perrin's Get Out In The Green Fields – Stoke on Trent 1967.

Darius Clayhanger in Arnold Bennett's Clayhanger adapted by Peter Terson and Joyce Cheeseman – Stoke 1967.

The huts at Aquinas Street – National Theatre (NT) Old Vic Headquarters 1963–75. (Photo: Chris Arthur)

Rose and Nellie in the kitchen at Aquinas Street, 1968. (Photo: John Haynes)

Sir Laurence Olivier in Strindberg's The Dance of Death, NT Old Vic 1967. (Photo: Zoe Dominic)

The second cast of The Front Page NT Old Vic, 1973.(See List of Illustrations for the actors names)

With Desmond McNamara in The Front Page in Australia.

Michael Gambon and John Dexter at the first rehearsal of Brecht's The Life of Galileo, with Michael Beint behind. NT, 1980. (Photo: Zoe Dominic)

Michael Gambon in foreground with John Dexter, Simon Callow, Michael Thomas and myself. Rehearsing Galileo. (Photo: Zoe Dominic)

Playing a Celtic Envoy in The Romans in Britain. NT, 1980.

The Great Paul Scofield. (Photo: John Haynes)

The Oresteia cast and Peter Hall in Epidavros 1982. (Photo: Nobby Clark))

A Horde of Unemployed Ventriloquists my one-man-show at the NT Cottesloe Theatre, 1982.

Ian McKellen, Coriolanus in Athens. (Photo: John Haynes)

Peter Hall rehearsing in Athens, 1985.

Alan Ayckbourn's Company at the NT, 1986. (Photo: John Haynes)

Adrian Rawlins and Michael Gambon in A View From The Bridge, NT Cottesloe Theatre, 1987. (Photo: Nobby Clark)

As Autolycus in Michael Bogdanov's production of The Winter's Tale for the English Shakespeare Company, 1990. (Photo: Laurence Burns)

With Jenny Quayle in Brendan Behan's The Hostage at the RSC Barbican Theatre, 1994. Can't beat a comb-over. (Photo: Laurence Burns)

NT Othello group on the Great Wall of China, 1998. (Photo: Michael Owen, Evening Standard)

Finbar Lynch, Ariyon Bakare, Rob Carroll, me as Julius Caesar, John Light and Keith Osborn in Julius Caesar at the RSC in Stratford, 2006. (Photo: Tristram Kenton)

Messin' with Donald Sutherland in Budapest

The company of David Edgar's Written on The Heart onstage in the Swan Theatre RSC, 2011.

The company of All That Fall at the Jermyn Street Theatre, 2012.

Myself, Rory Keenan and Paul Reid in Friel's Philadelphia Here I Come at the Donmar, 2012. (Photo: Johan Persson)

Carla Langley, Rory Keenan and myself in Liola, NT Lyttelton Theatre, 2013. (Photo: Catherine Ashmore)

Messing around with Michael Gambon in New York.

GROUP PHOTOGRAPHS

THE FRONT PAGE COMPANY

Front Row: John Shrapnel, Gawn Grainger, Richard Howard, me.

Second Row: Harry Lomax, David Bradley.

Third Row: Mary Griffiths, Paul Gregory, David Graham, Paul Curran, Alan MacNaughton, Anna Carteret, Denis Quilley, Sarah Atkinson, Clive Merrison, Benjamin Whitrow, David Healy.

Back Row: Stephen Williams, David Kincaid.

ALAN AYCKBOURN'S NT COMPANY

Front Row: Simon Cadell, Polly Adams, Marcia Warren, Michael Gambon.

Second Row: Elizabeth Bell, Ron Pember, Diane Bull, Russell Dixon, Barbara Hicks.

Third Row: Mary Chester, Myself, John Arthur, Michael Simkins, Adrian Rawlins, Suzan Sylvester.

Back Row: Kate Dyson, Lewis George, Simon Coady, Allan Mitchell, Tel Stevens, Paul Todd.

OTHELLO CAST ON
THE GREAT WALL, CHINA

Impossible to name everyone in this photo. In the back row are Myself, Crispin Letts, Clifford Rose, Trevor Peacock, Colin Tierney, Jamie Leene, Roger Chapman, Simon Russell Beale, Ian Williams and at the end, the moustachioed John Caulfield. In the centre is Maureen Beattie. Along the front are Garth Kelly, Stephen Ashby, David Harewood (Othello), Judith Thorp, Jane Suffling and Ken Oxtoby.

THE ORESTEIA COMPANY
IN EPIDAVROS

Front Row: Alfred Lynch, Roger Gartland, Kenny Ireland, John Normington, Pip Donaghy, Michael Thomas.
Second Row: Peter Hall, Peter Dawson, Barry Rutter, Tony Robinson, Tim Davies, Myself.
Third Row: Greg Hicks, Sean Baker (standing) David Bamber, David Roper, Jim Carter.

WRITTEN ON THE HEART COMPANY

The cast, assistant director, singers, and stage management on the Swan Stage RSC, 2011.

Bruce Alexander, Jim Hooper, Oliver Ford Davies, Stephen Boxer, Joseph Kloska, Paul Chahidi, Jodie McNee, Annette Mc Laughlin, Daniel Stewart, Mark Quartley, Sam Marks, Simon Thorp, Youssef Kerkour, Jamie Ballard, Ian

Midlane, Tom King, Suzanne Bourke, Lorna Seymour, Chris Priddle, Anna Bolton, Alexandra Saunders, Mitesh Khatri, Matthew Spillett, Lewis Jones, and, of course, my good self, praying for my career.

ALL THAT FALL COMPANY

Anthony Biggs, Ian Conningham, Catherine Cusack, Aidan Dunlop, Michael Gambon, Eileen Atkins, Frank Grimes, Gerard Horan, Trevor Nunn, Ruairi Conaghan, and me.

PREFACE

NATIONAL THEATRE 2013

ONE OF THOSE WEEKS

On the 22nd October 1963, the National Theatre's inaugural production of Shakespeare's *Hamlet* opened at the Old Vic. It was directed by Laurence Olivier with Peter O'Toole in the lead.

Fifty years later in October 2013 I am coming to the end of a run of Pirandello's *Liolà* in the Lyttelton Theatre at the National. The play is set in rural Sicily in 1916. I am playing a rich old landowner of peasant stock with a beautiful young wife. After five years of marriage they are still childless. Desperate for an heir, he blames her for the lack of children. He is violent, mean and dominating. It is a very good part in a beautifully directed production by Richard Eyre.

In the building, plans are well advanced for a number of celebratory events, culminating in a special gala performance on Saturday 2nd November in the Olivier Theatre to mark the fifty years. It will consist of extracts from twenty-six memorable productions performed over the five decades. The extracts will cover productions from the reigns of the five NT Directors: Laurence Olivier, Peter Hall, Richard Eyre, Trevor Nunn and Nicholas Hytner. It will be broadcast live on BBC2 and in cinemas worldwide. The cream of the acting profession will be involved. It's a big deal.

Nicholas Hytner is very keen for me to take part in the gala performance. He informs me that I have appeared in fifty-six NT productions over the fifty years. Only the great Michael Bryant has come near to that figure, he tells me. *I* had no idea how many plays I had done at the National. I had played in a production in that inaugural season. Where has Nick found this statistic? Somebody told him.

He asks me to appear in a short four-minute extract from a 1971 production of Peter Nichols' play *The National Health* where I will play a dying patient in a hospital scene. I am very keen to be involved. Nick then tells me there is a small problem, but it *can* be overcome. The gala will begin at 9:10pm to suit the TV schedules. Unfortunately, he says, I will be playing in *Liolà* in the Lyttelton that evening – *but* – as it is a short play and has no interval, the curtain will come down at *about* 9:10pm. He reckons I will need to appear in *The National Health* extract on the Olivier stage at 9.15pm. So I'll have *five* minutes to get there. 'Easy!' he says.

Now, *if Liolà* goes up late, *or*, the performance is a slow one – *or both* – my five minutes could be drastically reduced. Then we will be in what Sir Alex Ferguson calls "squeaky bum time".

'Of course I'll do it,' I tell Nick.

So, at the most, I'll have five minutes to flee from the Lyttelton stage to my dressing room on the ground floor, where, with the help of my dresser, Ralph, I'll fling off my three-piece woollen suit and shirt, untie and pull off my heavy lace-up boots and socks and then jump into a pair of wynceyette pyjamas. At the same time two make-up girls will attempt, with the aid of moist baby wipes, to rub off my heavy Italian peasant "suntan" and remove the black make-up from my specially grown *Liolà* moustache restoring it to its natural grey. They will then, very swiftly, apply to my face the pallor of a dying hospital patient. All this will be supervised by Fi Bardsley, the stage manager of the gala, who, with her radio mike, will be monitoring the progress of the Olivier proceedings upstairs. We will then exit the dressing room, leg it along the corridors, dash up six flights of stairs, hare along more corridors to the stage left wing of the Olivier where, with a bit of luck, I will have a few seconds to catch my breath before I walk on in a blackout to my hospital bed.

In the couple of weeks leading up to the big night the many extracts are rehearsed. The walls of the large Rehearsal Room 2 are covered in photocopies of the twenty-six sets. The logistics of the project are mind-boggling. Two dozen sets have to be constructed. Hundreds of costumes have to be made or found and then fitted. There are nearly a hundred actors involved. Nick is directing almost all the extracts. He is totally in command and supercool.

So, here is the week's schedule:

Friday: We 'tech' the whole production, which, along with the twenty-six extracts and their dozens of actors, sets, lighting and sound plots, is interspersed with a lot of BBC filmed interviews, archive material, etc. We then do a dress rehearsal that magically glides along with ne'er a glitch or hold-up. Unprecedented.

Saturday: The big day arrives. Our *Liolà* stage manager, Jane Suffling, manages to get the play started at 7:30pm on the dot. This is good news. Throughout the show I am constantly concerned about the running time and whether we are giving a "slow" performance. The whole cast are onstage for the final scene, which ends with a song. Blackout. The lights come up and we start the curtain calls with a company bow, which will be followed with further bows for the actors, band etc. But after the first company bow, and accompanied by encouraging cheers from my fellow actors, I run offstage and head for my dressing room, frantically undoing buttons as I go. In the dressing room, Fi Bardsley tells me we have four and a half minutes. Good news. With all the help my change goes like clockwork. We're away up the stairs. As I enter the Olivier wings I see Maggie Smith. Her extract is a solo speech from Farquhar's *The Beaux' Stratagem,* which immediately precedes our *National Health* scene.

'Have you been on yet?' I gasp.

'Just about to,' she whispers. A technician fits me with a radio mike and transmitter for the BBC coverage. I watch Dame Maggie do the speech from the wings. I appeared in the production with her in 1970. More of that later. Dressed in stylish black shirt and trousers she delivers the speech beautifully. Ecstatic applause, blackout, she exits past me.

'Terrific,' I mouth to her and walk on to my bed. Our scene goes well. Lots of laughs.

Under the Olivier stage, Rehearsal Room 3 has been converted into a make-up room and radio mike area. It is crowded with people. There are two large television monitors with a few rows of wobbly benches where the actors can watch the show. Throughout the evening performers come and go, sit and watch. Encouragement and praise are warmly given. The company is very, very impressive. Dames and knights in profusion: Dench, Smith, Gambon, Jacobi, Mirren. Big stars –

Wilton, Fiennes, Bennett, Cumberbatch, Wanamaker, Russell Beale, along with an amount of fantastic supporting actors. In the filmed extracts we watch Olivier, Gielgud, Richardson, Plowright, Scofield, Smith, McKellen. Fifty years of outstanding work rolls by. I find the whole experience deeply moving. Michael Gambon, sitting next to me, whispers, 'Christ, it's extraordinary.' He has a tear in his eye. He "walked on" in that first production of *Hamlet* at the Vic. Along with Michael, my connection with the National, goes back the full fifty years.

The curtain calls at the end, with the actors grouped within the decades they first worked with the company, is deeply affecting. Finally, a wonderful touch, all the crew, technicians, stage management, dressers, make-up people, all take a call. An unforgettable night. And all the better for having no boring, backslapping speeches. Nick Hytner has done a superb job.

- Sunday: Performance of *Liolà*
- Monday: Performance of *Liolà*
- Tuesday: Performance of *Liolà*
- Wednesday: Last two performances of *Liolà*
- Thusday: Up at 6.00am. Taxi to Heathrow. Fly to New York. Then at 4.00pm US time, make my way to 59E59 Theatre where I have a very quick rehearsal of Samuel Beckett's *All That Fall*. 7.00pm do the press night performance of that play.

One of those weeks.

(*All That Fall* was a production I had done in London the previous year. It was directed by Trevor Nunn and starred Michael Gambon and Eileen Atkins and had been very successful. But… more of *that* later.)

MY FIFTIETH YEAR AS AN ACTOR
BLOGGING FOR THE RSC 2012

2012 marked my fiftieth year as an actor; it was a very good year for me. In the spring, while preparing to transfer David Edgar's fine play *Written On The Heart* from the Swan Theatre in Stratford to the West End, I was asked to write a blog for the Royal Shakespeare Company website about the production and its transfer.

From this sprang the ludicrous idea to write a loose memoir about my fifty years in the theatre. Just that. Fifty years in the theatre. No personal or private stories. Nothing on film, television or radio work. Just theatre.

Actors are very good at bitching, complaining and moaning, and I am as guilty as most. So, I have determined from the start that this book will only celebrate the work that I have have been involved in. I will attempt to dwell on the good. I may fall from my perch occasionally, tell some indiscreet stories, reach for the laugh. But all I write, all of the characters I write about, all, will be done with affection and admiration.

Who would publish it? Who would read it? Who would *buy* it?

The five decades I have worked as an actor have seen vast changes in the theatre. I figured an account of the journey through these decades might prove an interesting read.

When I started in 1963 there were only a handful of drama schools. Repertory theatre was very much alive in many towns and cities over the land. Weekly rep, where a company of actors rehearsed, learned and performed a new play every week for a year, was still going – on its last legs, but still going. Actors leaving drama school were not allowed to work in the West End or in television without doing an apprenticeship in the reps. The National Theatre at the Old Vic had not yet opened, the Royal Shakespeare Company at Stratford was two years old. The word "Fringe" was only associated with hairdressers.

Here is an edited version of that RSC blog, as well as a chronicle of all the plays I did in 2012.

WRITTEN ON THE HEART

On the 16th of April 2012 we move David Edgar's play *Written On The Heart* from The Swan Theatre in Stratford into the Duchess Theatre just off the Strand. We are just around the corner from the Lyceum Theatre where *The Lion King* is currently playing. (In 1964 the Lyceum was a Mecca Ballroom and it was there I washed dishes in the evenings to help pay my way through drama school.)

Written On The Heart marks the four-hundredth anniversary of the King James Bible. The play explores how, across an eighty-year divide, two men translated the word of God. One, William Tyndale, died for it. The other, Lancelot Andrewes, was in line for an archbishop's mitre.

My name is James Hayes and I play two parts in the production. The first, Laurence Chaderton, Master of Emmanuel College, Cambridge, is one of the scholars who, in 1610, is working on the translation for King James' new Bible. The second part, the Archdeacon in the Yorkshire Church Scene, who in 1586, twenty-four years earlier, is there to remove all traces of idolatry and superstition and to see to the destroying of the stained glass windows.

* * *

DAY ONE – MORNING

On Monday 8th August 2011, I set out from my home in South West London for the first day's rehearsal of *Written on the Heart*. The RSC has a number of rehearsal rooms dotted along Clapham High Street where I have worked on numerous occasions. I arrive at St Peter's Church Hall on time, only to discover I have gone to the wrong room. The building is deserted and I soon realise I should be at St Anne's Hall three hundred yards away. Three minutes later – and three minutes late – I enter the thronged rehearsal room. I am immediately confronted, foully abused and admonished for my tardiness by the company manager, Jondon. He and I have worked together for over thirty years. His default position is attack dog, so naturally there is only one course of action: I immediately insult and abuse him back. Jondon is Turkish, shaven-headed and built like a boxer. When I first worked with him in the eighties he was Jondon Gourkan. But, for some unknown reason, the surname has been dropped and like some fabled rock star he is now referred to – even in print as – Jondon.

So begins the first day's rehearsal. The hall is full of that loud buzz that attends the early rehearsals of any play. A mixture of nervousness, excitement and apprehension, which soon dissipates and, within a couple of weeks, is replaced by relaxed banter, irreverence and insult. On the first day every actor hopes to know another actor in the room – it helps relieve the tension. If we do, we greet each other like long-lost comrades. I greet Oliver Ford Davies, Stephen Boxer, Jamie Ballard, Paul Chahidi, Annette McLaughlin, all of whom I have worked with over the decades.

The director, Greg Doran, comes over to welcome me. He is a handsome man with the best head of hair in the business. With his flashing smile, long curly locks and neat beard he looks like a recently retired Dumas Musketeer. I have worked on three productions with him – *The Winter's Tale*, *Sejanus* and *Antony and Cleopatra*. His love of Shakespeare, of the Elizabethan and Jacobean playwrights, together with his knowledge of that extraordinarily fertile period is encyclopaedic. His ability to articulate, use and share this knowledge enriches all his work.

We all drink coffee as Greg welcomes the company. After introductions from actors, designers, composer, stage management, the press office, the education department, development people, and so on, the cast gathers around a number of large tables pushed together and the work begins.

* * *

DAY ONE – AFTERNOON

Greg has been talking about the play, and now he and the designer, Francis O'Connor, show us the model of the set. We are introduced to a miniature version of the physical world we will inhabit in the coming months. We all crowd around the model-box, as Greg and Francis, with tiny scale models of the actors, furniture and props, explain the settings for each scene. The design is excellent. At the end of the presentation we all show our appreciation with loud applause. I have been going through this ritual for decades, we *always* applaud the design. Sometimes the design is dull, sometimes the actors can quickly see how difficult the set will be to work on. It may have tricky entrances or a very steep rake [a heavily tilted stage], perhaps with an uneven surface hard to walk on, etc. etc. But we *always* applaud and *always* murmur appreciative comments.

Greg suggests a little competition. He asks us to name all the books of the Old Testament in order. We are hopeless. He asks us to name the Seven Sacraments: we manage five. He asks about the Articles of Faith, we are totally flummoxed. We have a lot of research to do.

We are suddenly interrupted by Jondon, who tells us that he has been advised by the police to send us home early. There is a serious threat that the riots of the previous night in Tottenham, where there was much looting and a number of buildings were set alight, will spread to Clapham and other areas this evening. We all think this is an overreaction but Jondon insists. So, we reluctantly break and make our way homewards past shops being shuttered and barricaded. People look worried and there is a mild sense of foreboding in the streets.

* * *

Next day, as I arrive at Clapham Junction Station, I can see smouldering buildings being hosed down by the fire brigade.

St John's Road, where I get my bus to rehearsal, is closed. We are all diverted round the backstreets. As our group come round a corner we are passed by a large crowd of mostly young people carrying numerous brushes and buckets on their way to help with the clear-up. St John's Road, a street full of phone shops, sportswear outlets, white-goods stores etc. has been badly damaged. It is heartening to see this public-spirited group. How they got together I have no idea – the Blitz comes to mind. A small ray of sunshine on a gloomy day.

For some days after, as my bus takes me up and down St John's Road to and from rehearsals, I notice virtually every store in the road is damaged and boarded up with large sheets of plywood. It is both funny and sad to observe that virtually the only shop untouched is a large branch of Waterstones.

* * *

Over the next twelve weeks, we rehearse *Written* in St Anne's Hall. Very quickly this high, timber-beamed Victorian room fills with tables bearing history books, biographies, documents, photographs and DVDs relating to the world of the play. They contain much biographical information on the "real" characters we will be playing. I noticed Adam Nicolson's very useful *God's Secretaries*, which I had read a few years earlier. As the play shifts historically back and forth from 1610 to the fictional meeting between William Tyndale and the young Jesuit priest in 1536, then forward fifty years to 1586 in the Yorkshire Church, we become very aware of the physical and doctrinal changes that occurred in the Church along the way. All this demands much research and reading to familiarise ourselves with these very different decades. The walls of the rehearsal room are soon covered with Bayeux-style rolls of lining paper with the dates, pictures and illustrations of important rulers, clerics, gunpowder plotters etc.

Tom King, our assistant director, through much internet delving, unearths copies of engravings and paintings of some of the main protagonists. Actors can find these useful in helping to imagine and flesh out their characters. Tom finds one of my characters, Laurence Chaderton, depicted in a stained glass window in Emmanuel College, Cambridge. Although attractive it is a very anodine portrait. No sense of character in the picture.

* * *

After a number of days we reach the momentous occasion when we "stand up". No more reading of the play, no more discussion, no more delay. It is time to put the play on its feet. The set design is beautifully simple. The main feature and background to the action is a wonderfully ornate wooden rood screen. This, on the Swan's thrust stage with its surrounding wooden galleries and balustrades, will look very beautiful. The floor will be of rough wooden boards. The furniture, simple refectory tables and chairs.

But for now in the rehearsal room we work with a semblance of a "rood screen": it is a strange steel and wire mesh structure, six foot high on concrete feet. It looks like the set of a gritty sixties prison drama at The Royal Court.

Our play has a prison scene. It takes place in Flanders,

in 1536, between Tyndale, his Flemish jailer and the young Jesuit priest who smuggles Tyndale's translation out. It is set in a tiny six by six-foot cell on the eve of the translator's execution. The scene, which also calls for a practical wood-burning stove in one corner, is rehearsed on a small raised platform that will rise smoothly through the stage. Watching three actors rehearse in this "dark, tiny cell" where they share the space with a small table, two stools and the forementioned stove is fascinating. It is the smallest acting area I have ever seen. But it works extremely well, and in performance, with subdued lighting, will convey claustrophobia, and a sense of cold, dirt and fear. It will also be greatly helped by the playing of Stephen Boxer, Mark Quartly and Youssef Kerkour.

I believe eighty per cent of the King James Bible is based on Tynedale's work and a substantial proportion of that text is word for word Tyndale.

* * *

Rehearsals are moving fluidly now. The opening scene takes place in Ely House, Holborn, the London home of Bishop Lancelot Andrewes and starts with the entrance of the various translators. Greg has decided that it is raining outside and we should enter wet from the rain. My character, Chaderton, rushes in late, wearing a very, very wet floor-length cloak with the line, 'Masters, forgive me, I have ridden here from Cambridge in the rain.' I then remove the cloak and selfishly shake a lot of water off it on to the other characters around me. It is suggested by some that this is a bit of "cheap business" and inserted for the purpose of getting an easy laugh. I have to assert loudly that the idea came from our distinguished director and not me. Obviously I am an actor who looks down on such low comic tricks.

This opening scene is autumnal and is followed by the prison scene, which takes place at night and is suitably gloomy. The sun does not intrude until the "Yorkshire Church scene" when light comes through the stained glass windows high above the Swan stage, throwing coloured patterns on to the plain floor.

The dream-like meeting between Andrewes and the ghost of Tyndale in Ely House is the climax of the play. The two debate and squabble over the wordings and meanings of certain passages in their translations. Oliver Ford Davies is the highly intellectual Launcelot Andrewes debating, arguing, often in great frustration with the radical, earthy and obdurate William Tyndale of Stephen Boxer.

> *Tyndale: (quoting) "'Verily, verily, I say unto you"* ...
> *Why translate into an ancient tongue?*
> *Andrewes: What, you would have us ape the blabber of the town?*

As they argue, the two men delve eagerly into the many other versions of the Bible – the Coverdale, the Bishop's, the Geneva – which are on the tables and floor around them. They consult large rough-printed early proofs of the latest translation. The intellectual ferment is blistering to listen to and a joy to watch. In performance, being the RSC, all of these "ancient" books, documents and papers will be lovingly researched and manufactured. Even on close inspection they will have a truly authentic look and feel, with heavily embossed leather covers and gold lettering. Thick paper will be dyed, aged and covered with handwriting in sepia ink. There will be red ribbon and waxen seals. This period detail and ornamentation is important, as the Swan audience will be sitting close to the action and able to see it all. An added bonus for the actors is how much these books and documents, not to mention the beautiful, painstaking work that goes into the set, furniture and props, determine the solid and tangible world of the play. It is the same with the quality of costume the RSC provides. The actor walking on stage each night is assured that he looks perfect. Of course, his performance may be terrible.

* * *

I notice that the front page of the text we are using says "Sixth Draft, first version". David Edgar is continually making changes to the play, not unlike the many clerics in the script toiling over the wording of the new Bible. Sometimes we are given new speeches, sometimes tiny alterations. David realises that characters using the phrase "of course" is too modern and he substitutes it with "indeed". He makes small cuts, but nothing so big as to depress the actors; cuts unsettle an actor and break his rhythm. In fact, even as we near the opening night, I found myself saying under my breath, 'Enough, David. Enough!'

* * *

We are rehearsing the opening scene and having a lot of bitchy fun. We have three older and heavily bearded clerics in long black cassocks, white surplices and a profusion of ruffs. Jim Hooper is John Overall, the Dean of St Paul's. Bruce Alexander is George Abbot, the Bishop of London. I am Laurence Chaderton, the Master of Emanuel College, Cambridge. Waiting for the arrival of the Bishop of Ely (Andrewes), we argue heatedly over particular wordings in the new translation.

* * *

At the end of the prison scene, mentioned earlier, the Young Priest exits the cell. There is now a tricky transformation to be executed.

Before us, he changes from the twenty-year-old Catholic priest to a seventy-year-old, Anglican archdeacon. Behind this, the prison cell changes into a small church in Yorkshire, on a summer morning in 1586.

The archdeacon I play is not a new character. He is the Young Priest as an older man.

Greg Doran, Mark Quartly (who plays the Young Priest) and I spend a number of rehearsals trying to bring this transformation about. We will be dressed similarly and will have the same leather satchels. In one version we glided together onstage, looked significantly into each others' eyes and circled one another. He then exited while I remained to play the new scene. Mark and I thought this wasn't bad, but Greg said we looked like a couple of gay men in search of a bit of hanky-panky. It was hard to look at each other after that. Eventually, we found the right solution.

16

The Archdeacon, which is a very good part, is a very strong contrast to the extrovert and eccentric Chaderton. He is a man on a mission, reticent, watchful, implacable. I decided to play him as a very still man with few gestures, and vocally very measured. Stillness doesn't come naturally to me. While implacable in his quest to destroy the church's stained glass and "all feigned images of wood or stone... all tunicles, albs, stoles, pixes, paxes, sacrine bells, chalices... all popish trumpery", the Archdeacon surprises us at the end with a speech extoling the need for humility, love and mercy.

> *'For, truly, only love and mercy truly comprehend the law. And he who has not that written on his heart, shall never truly come to Christ, though all the angels taught him. And God forbid it should be otherwise...'*

* * *

Rehearsals are now in full swing, the production takes shape. We break now and again to watch TV drama documentaries related to the world of the play. All the music our composer, Paul Englishby, has written for the production is for the voice. It is sacred music in the style of Tallis and Byrd and we are lucky to have a small choir of five singers. When they first come to sing at rehearsals the sound they make is astonishingly beautiful.

The full company is to sing a three-part Catholic "Gaude Gloriosa" for the Virgin Mary, which Paul has composed. Unlike the professional singers, it takes us many rehearsals to learn the harmonies.

We watch an episode of an excellent documentary series in which actor and former chorister Simon Russell Beale explores the flowering of Western sacred music. I have worked with Simon who is a terrific actor and extremely intelligent. Here he is now effortlessly and knowledgably presenting this series. My God, he'll be compiling cryptic crosswords for the *Guardian* next.

* * *

Greg has arranged a tour of St. Paul's Cathedral for us. We are met by the canon chancellor Giles Fraser, a warm, open-faced, balding man, fizzing with knowledge. Very down to earth, he is the exact opposite of the kind of cleric I had expected to meet. (He later resigned with much controversy, in October 2011 in protest at plans to forcibly remove the Occupy protesters from the cathedral steps.) He gives us a short talk on the history of the building and provides some lighthearted gossip about the rivalry between the St. Paul's and Westminster Abbey clergy. He then leads our group of about twenty up many internal steps to the Cathedral Library. Designed by Wren it is not open to the public. It has a high ceiling and the large windows have the blinds permanently drawn for conservation reasons. The walls are covered with massive mahogany bookcases groaning under weighty tomes. All available surfaces are covered with busts, bibles, ledgers, liturgical texts and documents. There is some dust. We are introduced to the Librarian Joseph Wisdom, a name that comfortably suits his occupation. He shows us a very rare edition of a Tyndale Bible, there are only three left in the world. As we huddle round, Stephen

Boxer, our Tyndale, reads a few lines from it. It is a quietly moving moment.

We are then taken up some more stairs to see Wren's original model of the cathedral. This is a huge structure made of oak and plaster. It was rejected for political reasons for appearing a little too Catholic. Giles tells us this model cost £600 to complete, the equivalent at the time of a good London home.

Afterwards we gather in Paternoster Square and Greg takes us on a short local tour. We visit the site of Stationers' Hall where the twelve scholars revised the final version of the King James Bible (KJB) and where Shakespeare would have registered his plays. Sadly, though the present Hall is very attractive, the original was destroyed in the Great Fire in 1666.

We then walk to what was the former site of Launcelot Andrewes' Ely Place, the London home of the Bishop of Ely and where most of the play is set. Again, little remains of the original, though the chapel houses some simple statues of local people martyred for their beliefs. We then move on to Smithfield Market in the ward of Farringdon Without. Along with Tyburn, Smithfield was for centuries the main site for public executions of heretics and dissidents. Fifty Protestants and religious reformers known as the Marian Martyrs were executed here during the reign of Queen Mary, earning her the nickname "Bloody Mary".

As we stand in tight groups at these sites, Greg, without notes, regales us effortlessy with myriad stories of topical historical information. I really envy him his scholarship. I can barely name all the London clubs in the football premiership.

* * *

Greg employs a much used RSC practice. He asks us to each pick some aspect of sixteenth and seveneeth century historical interest relevant to our production. We then research it and give a fifteen-minute presentation to the company. These prove very valuable and enhance our knowledge of the period.

Jodie McNee speaks passionately about the female martyrs and introduces us to Foxe's *Book of Martyrs*. Annette McLaughlin tells us of the way the English Reformation, ineffectually opposed by a population cowed by the new and crushing force of the monarchy, eradicated a thousand years of tradition and ritual. She draws heavily from Eamon Duffy's magisterial work *The Stripping of the Altars*. The man himself, Eamon Duffy, Irish Professor of History at Cambridge University, also comes and gives us a fascinating talk on English Catholicism in the late Middle Ages. Jim Hooper gives us fifteen minutes on the Separatists, who wished to split from the Church of England and form independent local churches. Bruce Alexander speaks very eloquently on the context of the Catholic Threat in the years up to 1610. I choose the Hampton Court Conference convened by King James at Hampton Court in 1604 to commission the new translation of the Bible. A conference at which Chaderton and his followers were hotly abused by the King. Coincidentally, my home is only a mile across Bushy Park from Hampton Court. On a Sunday afternoon I take my script to the park and run through some lines as I walk. Deep in concentration I happen to look up as I repeat some lines about the Conference, and, past a small herd of deer, I can just see the chapel and roofs of the palace through the trees. The sight brightened what had until then been a rather dull learning slog.

One Sunday in October we move to Stratford, which will now be our home until March the next year. I rent a small Victorian cottage from the RSC, a mere six-minute walk from the theatre. In London, it took me forty minutes to get to rehearsals. I always enjoy my seasons in Stratford and love the fact that the countryside is just a few minutes walk away. I grew up in Mitchelstown, a small town in County Cork, where the highlight of the weekend was going for long family walks.

Next day, Monday, we rise early. We get dressed, we go to the theatre and we undress. We don costumes, boots, wigs and beards. Waiting to start, we spend a lot of time looking at ourselves in mirrors. We hope to see the characters we have been working on for all these weeks looking straight back at us. Yes, he's there. A little strange and awkward, but definitely there. I try on the Archdeacon's hat. I hate it. Here's a fact. Actors do not like wearing hats onstage. Why? The brims cast shadows on our faces. Other actors in the scene don't have hats. Those of us with hats plot to get rid of them. This starts with not wearing them in the Tech. The designer notices. Wardrobe remind us to wear the hats. We "forget". The designer insists.

Here's another fact, techs never start on time. As we wait to begin, we walk the corridors getting used to the long cassocks, soutanes, vestments, cloaks. We put life into them. We twirl, we gesture, we do sudden one-eighty-degree turns. We discover how to "use" them. It is exciting. We older actors try make-up. A little, under the eyes, to "bring them out". The younger actors notice and scoff. Make-up is rarely used in the theatre by young actors, but we know it works. We were taught how to apply it at drama school. My God, we've been using it for decades!

We go on stage. We pace about, inhabiting, claiming the space. We explore the entrances and exits. We go through pass doors and are told where to wait when we make entrances from front of house. We clock the lighting. We are shown our cue lights. We go and handle the books, props etc. The furniture looks great, so authentic. We love it. Suddenly I am aware that I do not sit down in this play. But then one rarely sits down in period plays. Over the decades, in countless coronations, trials, entertainments, depositions, speeches from monarchs, have I ever sat down? Never. Stand, stand, stand. They did have furniture in those days, they probably sat down all the time. We are called for the first scene. The tech begins.

* * *

I don't enjoy techs. Some actors say they love them. We go over entrances, exits, technical business again and again and again. We can spend an hour changing from one scene to another. As a scene ends, the lighting dims, furniture has to be removed, a trap in the floor opened, a platform has to rise through the trap, a piece of set "flown in"; the singers have to sing, actors have to time their entrances. Dozens of lights have to change. If one tiny element of this incredibly complicated manoeuvre is slightly out of time, the whole shebang has to be done again. The platform has to go back understage, the trap close, the flying piece go out, the lighting change, the singers and actors retreat etc,

etc. It can take a day to stage an hour of the play. Acting takes a back seat, technical work is all. Hence 'tech', of course. We usually work for twelve hours on these four days and everyone is exhausted. A comic hysteria sometimes breaks out. Fantastical and very funny repartee prevails, discipline falters. We are admonished, told to focus. "Focus" is a theatrical term I first noticed in the eighties, but it has now been commandeered by football managers, city businessmen and politicians. I have often thought that Hell would be an eternal tech; days, months, years, centuries, spent going over and over and over the minutest theatrical details.

Suddenly the dress rehearsals are upon us. Sometimes reduced to *the* dress rehearsal. And sometimes in my experience, due to the tech proving fiendishly complicated and overrunning, we face an audience for the first time *sans* dress rehearsal. But, dress rehearsals, I'll secretly confess, can be both bowel-loosening and fiercely exciting at the same time; we step forward into the light to fly by the seats of our trousers, or sometimes, our breeches.

I got rid of that hat by the way.

* * *

Like no other night of the run, the press night is nearly always edgy. Nerves emerge. Big displacement activities are put in motion to assuage them.

1. Usually we get a speech from the director exhorting us to forget/ignore the press. 'Don't read the notices,' they say. 'We've worked hard, we now have a show we can all

be proud of.' Good or bad press can influence the future performances.

2. We do a *big* warm-up.
3. We have bought or made "Good Luck" cards. We have written individual messages to our colleagues in them. No matter the relationships, the jealousies, the lack of respect for their work, we write warm wishes. We deliver them.
4. Flowers and gifts from loved ones and agents clog the stage door.
5. Suddenly it is time to prepare. Despite the fact that these nights invariably start late we are ready far too early.
6. Knocks on doors. Strong hugs. 'Best of Luck!' The powers that be flit through.
7. Another visit to the loo, just in case.

Then, long silent minutes until, 'Act One beginners please.' Eyes brighten, the corridors throng, 'Have a good one.' We are in the wings. The buzz from the "house" seems so much louder than in any of the previews. The lights begin to fade, the beautiful voices with their sacred music start. Quiet, though fiercely emotional admonishments and affirmations rattle around one's head. The door opens and you're on!

A very, very good performance. Terrifically warm applause. Huge relief. Backstage and dressing-room corridors are very noisy and full of 'We've done it.' 'We got away with it!' 'Thank God, that's fucking over!' More hugs, sincere handclasps and eye contact. Faces in and out of dressing-room doors. The ban on alcohol backstage is blatantly ignored – at least in my dressing room it is, as roommates Paul Chahidi and Jamie Ballard and I begin a celebration, which within a few nights, becomes a ritual on most *Written* performances. Once the play is finished – and never before or during – we explore some of the finest wines and spirits Stratford can provide. We change out of costume. Glasses, limes, even ice appears and we sit and laugh and talk for twenty minutes. It is civilised, it is comradely, it is a fine full stop to the evening. Then we go to the pub.

* * *

At the after-show party Thelma Holt, a highly respected West End and RSC associate producer, is extremely enthusiastic about the play and says she wants to "take it into town".

'It must be seen in London,' she says. Very flattering, great to hear.

'Fat Chance!' we all say to each other. 'A play about the making of the King James Bible, with a large cast of mostly bearded old men? Yeah, backers will be queuing up to snap this one up.'

The notices appear. Some of us try not to read them. We will wait until the run is over. I have got better at this as the years have gone by. But within a few hours the word is out. They are extremely good, four and five stars. I don't look. Then I get a text from a friend. It tells me that not only does the *Guardian* love it, but I "get a very nice mention". The *Guardian* is probably the paper we all want to be noticed in. Michael Billington is the most respected and knowledgable critic in the country. Do I rush out to buy a copy? I do not. But four days later browsing the net, I surrender and read Mr Billington.

I believe most actors read reviews. We are an insecure bunch and ever on the lookout for a boost to our egos, but we also read them to see what thoughts the critic had on the play; to see if he/she admired the production, thought it served and illuminated the play and if the performances one admired oneself – including one's own – were recognised. Good personal reviews can help promote one's career. But sometimes they can be personal, occasionally savage and can damage the actor's confidence. That said, for most of my life in the theatre, I *have* read reviews.

* * *

THE ARCHDEACON AND THE DUCHESS

On the 16th February 2012 before a performance of *Written* we are called to a meeting in the Swan with Greg Doran and Thelma Holt. We are going to London. Given the subject matter of the play, the large cast of seventeen and the costs, Greg introduces Thelma as "a certifably insane woman". Thelma, with her great cheekbones, red hair wrapped in a turban, then speaks fervently about the play. We are, if we all agree, going to the Duchess Theatre, which has a 482-seat auditorium for a twelve-week run, with an option for a further couple of weeks. However, unlike the subsidised theatre, if we do poor business the management has the right to close the show at any time giving us two weeks' notice. The Duchess has a different configuration to the

Swan. It is a small proscenium arch theatre, therefore the production will retain the same intimacy as at Stratford. Nica Burns, "our generous landlady", has given us a very good deal. Bill Kenwright, former *Coronation Street* actor, current Chairman of Everton Football Club and a very successful West End producer, is Thelma's co-producer. Thelma warns, 'We can't make any money on this project and will be very lucky to get back what we put in.' We will rehearse on Monday 16th April and do our first preview on the Thursday. We are all extremely pleased with the news and I thank Thelma for making the transfer happen. Without her passion, drive and commitment the play would be finishing at Stratford in three weeks. Afterwards one of the actors takes the mickey out of me for "arselicking". I ignore him. What Thelma has brought about for our play, given the current state of West End theatre, is astonishing and should be celebrated.

* * *

On Monday 16th April we gather at the RSC rehearsal rooms back in Clapham where we started work on *Written* over eight months before. My bus journey takes me to rehearsal along St. John's Road in Clapham Junction where I witnessed the damage the rioters had caused back in August. There is now no evidence of the broken windows and fire damage along the length of that street. All is back to how it was.

In the company, two large events have happened since we last met. Greg Doran has been appointed the new artistic director of the RSC. I, among many others, am extremely pleased at this. He is hugely talented, a great Shakespearian, and a man with deep commitment to, and long experience of, the RSC. A very popular and wise decision by the Board.

The second event is that our writer David Edgar has got married. Lots of congratulations all round. At the tea break David presents us with slices of the delicious wedding cake. Then Jim Hooper unwraps two cakes he has baked for us all. I love cake. A great tea break.

It is five weeks since we left Stratford. Owing to the rare luxury of continued employment, most of the actors have been globetrotting. There are stories of visits to New York, Vietnam, Seville, Turkey, Morocco and Southwold. We have been emailed some alterations to the text, which we now rehearse. There are some small changes to clarify some confusions that became apparent in performance. The Duchess is a wider but much shallower stage than the Swan, so we begin to alter the entrances, moves and positions accordingly.

* * *

Tuesday, we move to the Duchess, one of the youngest and smallest of the West End theatres, to tech the show. Our first preview is on Thursday. The Duchess was built in 1929. In the following year it hosted the shortest run in West End history. The show was titled *Intimate Revue* and it closed without completing its first performance. Must have been a shocker. I remember when I first went to the theatre in London in the late sixties, it was not unusual for displeased audience members at many a new play to cry out, 'Rubbish, tosh, terrible!'

The set looks terrific in the new space, but it is a

different story backstage. The wing space is almost non-existent. I am told when the playwright J B Priestley was shown the new theatre in 1929 he expressed his admiration for the building and then enquired, 'Where are the dressing rooms?' There were none. The auditorium is below street level and the dressing rooms are in the roof, approached up a narrow and extremely shabby brick staircase. I count the interminable steps up to my dressing room. There are sixty-nine. The whole backstage area is badly run-down and more than mildly depressing. Welcome to the West End. We moan a lot, but within a day we've adapted to the building. Despite all the discomfort, *Written On The Heart* will work very well here. The younger actors, for whom this is their West End debut, are really excited.

* * *

Wednesday, we tech the whole show. Thursday, we do another dress rehearsal and then our first preview. It's a very good performance to a very good and sizable audience. Strong applause at the end.

We are adapting to the space, and in the proscenium arch we all now "play out front". Perhaps in a drama of such rich language, exciting ideas and torrid argument, the fact that every word is now going in one direction means it impacts more effectively on the audience.

Backstage, all are making the dressing rooms more cosy. Actors bring in pictures, lamps, cards. Bill Kenwright has sent each of us some exotic orchids, which are much appreciated. Joe Kloska, in our dressing room, fixes a Vietnamese propaganda poster attacking Richard Nixon to the wall. Paul Chahidi unpacks a cafetiere and some coffee. I bring some chocolate fingers. Fruit appears. We purchase wine and beer for after the show. Things are looking up. Dammit, the place is looking miles better.

Monday, we face the press – again.

* * *

Monday is a wet April day. We are invited to a post-show dinner hosted by Bill Kenwright at the Waldorf Hotel and can bring a guest. We are told to dress up a bit. Tonight we will be reunited with the people who have left the show since Stratford. For economic reasons we have had to lose our hugely talented quintet of singers. Their work is now a recorded part in the show. It is still terrific. Gifts, cards, champagne and flowers arrive from friends and agents. A wooden heart, carved with best wishes from Thelma, a framed poster of the show from Bill. The performance went really well. Cheers at the curtain calls, though these always seem false, partisan and a bit frenetic on these special nights.

I go to the Waldorf Hotel with my daughter Abi, and her mother Jackie, for a late supper hosted by Bill Kenwright in the spectacular ballroom. This is a stunning, high-ceilinged, pillared room on two levels. One of the staff tells me that scenes from the film *Titanic* were shot here.

Bill makes a very good speech, remembering to thank all the right people. He lavishes much praise on the play, cast, design and direction. Then, some surprising facts. He tells us that in order to bring this costly production to the West End, Nica Burns the theatre owner has charged no rent to the production, that David Edgar has taken no writing fee, likewise the RSC. He speaks warmly of Thelma and her enthusiasm for the piece and how she can always persuade him to get involved with her projects. A great evening. I get home at 1:00am, very tired, but end up watching the second episode of the new Scandinavian thriller *The Bridge*.

* * *

On Wednesday, Thelma, who drops in most evenings during our company warm-up, informs us that Bill is very worried. We interpret this to mean that the bookings are not very good. On Friday, Thelma states, 'We are haemorrhaging money.' Now, actors who had been hoping for a twelve-week run that would help pay mortgages and fill depleted bank accounts, begin to think about finding their next job. The notice is put up on the board ten days later. Our run will only last five weeks.

* * *

On one very hot evening backstage, I visited two of the actors in a dressing room along our corridor. As I entered I happened to glance down and noticed the door was being wedged open with a book. Now, I hate to see a book used in this way. As I leant down and saw what it was, I gasped and giggled simultaneously. It was a copy of the Gideon Bible which, along with many hotel bedrooms, most theatre dressing rooms are supplied. Actors!

* * *

Finally, we learned that the show that was to replace *Written On The Heart* was a piece titled *The Hurly Burly Show*. It was a burlesque that promised much naked skin and a profusion of large feathers. Its publicity advised audiences to "leave their inhibitions at the door". I suspected it would be more to the liking of West End audiences. I was proved wrong. A few weeks later it suffered the same fate as *Written* and was taken off.

(End of blog for the RSC website)

PHILADELPHIA, HERE I COME

During the last week of the run of *Written*, Anne McNulty, the casting director for the Donmar Warehouse – a lovely woman I have known for years – invited me to meet a young director called Lyndsey Turner who was about to direct the Donmar's next production, the great Brian Friel's 1963 play *Philadelphia, Here I Come,* set in rural Donegal. Lyndsey, who looked all of eighteen, was having a big success with the play *Posh* which she had directed at the Royal Court, and had now transferred to the Duke of Yorks. *Posh* offered us an evening in the company of a fictional Bullingdon Club with a terrific cast of somewhat obnoxious young Oxbridge upper-class students, most of whom conformed to the images we have been fed of the student days of our present Prime Minister, our Chancellor of the Exchequer and our yellow-mopped London Mayor. Lyndsey and I talked for an hour about *Philadelphia* and I read the part of S B O'Donnell.

Philadelphia, Here I Come is set in the small fictional town of Ballybeg in Donegal. The action takes place over one evening, and concerns the emigration of a young man to, yes, Philadelphia.

Unhappy both at home and in love, and with few prospects, the young Gar O'Donnell decides, like hundreds of thousands of Irishmen and women before him, to seek a new life in another country. In *Philadelphia,* Friel had the brilliant idea of using two actors to portray the young man. Dressed alike, one plays the public Gar, the other the private Gar. Public Gar acts and relates naturalistically to the other actors in the drama, while Private Gar is "unseen" and comments on the behaviour of his outer self. He also reflects on his own inner turmoil and has a lot of fun satirising some of the play's other characters. We get all aspects of this complex character presented simultaneously. I can think of no other play that adopts this device.

I played Gar's elderly father, S B O'Donnell, who, twenty-five years previously at the age of forty, had married the nineteen– year-old Maire, who died three days after giving birth to Gar. S B runs the shop where Gar is employed. Soberly dressed and never without his hat, S B is cold and uncommunicative. The relationship between father and son, despite working and living together in the same building, is very distant. On the eve of Gar's departure to America their lack of communication and the distance between them shows no sign of changing. The boy is desperate for some genuine contact, some love. Then, in the small hours of the morning, just before Gar's departure when all hope seems lost, the two men, unable to sleep, meet in the sitting room behind the shop. Public Gar, urged on by Private Gar, makes a huge effort to break through the old man's reserve by reminding him of a small event that took place in a boat – a blue boat – on a fishing trip many years before. It rained, he said, and the father put his jacket round the boy's shoulders and gave him his hat and sang a song:

"For no reason at all except that we – that you were happy. D'you remember? D'you remember?"

S B does not remember. He gets sidetracked, talks of having no knowledge of that song, and then in trying to recall the "blue boat" rambles on about other boats. The moment is gone; Gar has slipped away out of the room and S B stares at the dark doorway he has disappeared through.

Then Madge, the old housekeeper, comes in from visiting her niece and S B suddenly unleashes a memory of his own. He asks her if she remembers the trouble they had keeping the boy at school just after he turned ten. He then describes the morning when Gar was wearing "this wee sailor suit" and went behind the shop counter and said he was not going to school – "I'm going into my daddy's business". Madge insists the boy never *had* a sailor suit. S B insists he had and then describes that morning when *he* took the boy to school himself – "and him dancing and chatting beside me". Shortly after and one minute away from the end of the play, S B leaves the stage still thinking on that long ago memory. It is an unbearably moving piece of writing.

S B is a fantastic part. This closed-in and reticent figure was a long distance from any part I had previously played. In rehearsal, remembering my own father and the lack of any demonstrative show of love between us, I tried to use these memories to "find" S B. Once or twice I filled up with emotion and needed to take a little break. Somewhat smugly I thought the expression of this deep emotion in the scene would be very effective. Wrong. I was falling into the actor's trap of doing the audience's job for them. The secret to playing the scene, which Lyndsey constantly, doggedly and brilliantly pushed me towards, was to maintain S B's locked-in emotions. The man cannot, will not, does not know how to let his feelings show. On most nights the scene had a deeply moving effect on the audience.

Philadelphia, Here I Come is a very fine play, with the most richly rounded and realised characters. Actors fall on this kind of material with a huge recognition and a hunger to be involved. I loved playing S B and I think it was one of the best performances I have given.

Lyndsey cast the play extremely well. In rehearsal a real sense of ensemble was created, out of which a complex and beautifully characterised small town community emerged. The two Gars were brilliantly played by Paul Reid (Public) and Rory Keenan (Private). Valerie Lilley was outstanding as Madge the old housekeeper who held the family together. On that shallow Donmar stage the designer, Rob Howell, stunningly managed to create two very distinct acting areas: a bedroom and a sitting room, as well as hinting at the shop next door. Tim Lutkin did something unfashionable with the lighting; he created wonderful atmospheres, but also and importantly lit the actors beautifully. Sometimes in the theatre these days, lighting can be so subtle it fails to let the audience see the actors' faces properly.

Lyndsey Turner's production was exceptional. She captured the world of the play and more importantly the tone of the play perfectly. The research we did with her on the small town life of sixties Donegal was extensive. Rehearsal tables filled up with books on the period. The walls of the rehearsal room, with the help of Hannah Price, Assistant Director, were soon covered in photographs of village streets, shop interiors, people's sitting rooms, dozens of crowd pictures, of market-day farmers, important looking political and professional figures, characters from all walks of Irish life. One particular exercise Lyndsey gave us was to scrutinise these pictures and put post-it notes on the portraits of the people we thought might be 'related' to the play's characters. The actors soon had a lot of fun finding fathers, mothers, teachers, girlfriends, employers from the pictures. Exercises like this help and enrich each actor's preparation.

I have kept a closely typed document numbering all of sixty-one pages, full of questions, which we all researched and contributed to, relating to all of our characters' backgrounds, habits, important personal events, even those outside the action of the play. Here are a few of the many questions we explored and found answers to:

- *What are the sums of money mentioned in the play worth today?*
- *I.e. £3.15 shillings (Gar's measly weekly wage)*
- *What is a boss of the Teamsters Union?*
- *What is the form of the Rosary?*
- *Who was Martin de Porres?*
- *Has S B any other family relatives apart from Gar?*
- *What is the political make-up in the 1960s of Donegal County?*
- *What is a 'halfpenny place'?*
- *Have S B and the Canon had any conversation about Gar leaving?*

- *Why does Madge call S B 'Boss'?*
- *How did Gar tell S B he was going to America?*
- *Is Kate Gar's first girlfriend?*
- *What's a two-pound poke?*
- *How long does it take to salt pollock?*
- *What are men's hose?*

There is one passing mention in the play that S.B is a County Councillor. I spent half an hour on the net researching Donegal County Councillors in the 1960s. I checked their political affiliations, how they were elected, the different areas they covered, their "Reserved Functions": adoption of annual budget; making/revoking bylaws; control of quarries; housing grants; social housing; maintenance of roads, bridges, historic graveyards; building regulations, etc, etc. I then decided that S B, being a major shopkeeper in the area, had shrewdly come to the conclusion that being a Councillor would help his business. Consequently, and in order not to alienate any of his customers, he decided not to affiliate himself to any political party but stood as an independent candidate.

This is a small example of the background and research all the actors carried out. It may seem inconsequential but a village life, and a world around it, can, with this method, be explored and assembled brick by brick. All questions and uncertainties thrown up by the script can be clarified and answered. Over the rehearsal process this work seeps into the bones of the company and enriches the production in a truly creative way.

With a six-week rehearsal period we spent the first three weeks of this sitting round the tables, reading and exploring the life of the play and the characters. Very creative, useful and exciting. But as the weeks went by and, this being the company's first experience of working with Lyndsey, we began to get vaguely twitchy wondering when we would "stand up" and "move" the play. I was personally concerned because, apart from the acting, I had a lot of complicated 'business' to do – some of which had to be carefully timed to speeches by Private Gar. I had a meal to eat which had to be timed to other characters speeches, cups of tea to be poured and drunk, clocks to be wound, a games table and chairs to be set up and a longish game of draughts to plot and play with Benny Young as the Canon. But once up, Lyndsey proved fast and incisive in giving the play movement and action. Her pacing of the scenes was spot on. Almost by magic, all the hours, all the work done around the tables, all the questioning, the researching, the inventing of the characters' backgrounds and relationships now fruitfully flowed into every rehearsal and informed every second of the work. They were exciting days. Soon the amalgamation of rehearsed individual scenes led to runs of the complete play. As ever, each scene is informed and enhanced by what has gone before. Missing, believed lost, pieces of the jigsaw are suddenly and effortlessly found and put in place. A beautiful picture emerges from the jumble. The trees disappear, the wood is plain to see in all its glory.

The tech went very well. These are inevitably long and hard days. One tired evening during a twelve-hour day, Josie Rourke, Artistic Director of the Donmar, appeared in the auditorium with a large bag full of chocolate Magnum ice-creams, which she passed out among the company. A small but telling gesture and much appreciated.

The production opened to almost universal five-star reviews and the Donmar run quickly sold out.

Lyndsey Turner is one of the most talented directors I have worked with. She is highly intelligent and perceptive. She pulls no punches, she goes right to the bone. But, I'm not sure that she has yet learned to trust actors, she micro-manages every moment. The actors' input and creativity have to align with her vision. There is throughout the process a strong steely hand on your shoulder.

Unlike some directors I have worked with, Lyndsey kept a very sharp eye on the production during its entire run. Sometimes a director will pop in a couple of times over the run and give the odd nudge to rectify moments where perhaps the pace has slowed down, or actors are not playing their objectives strongly enough. Sometimes you never see them again 'til the last night. Not Lyndsey. Despite its huge success she watched the show at least once a week. She didn't give her notes personally after the performance. I don't know why. She texted them to us. A vast screed would arrive containing everybody's notes. We all found this annoying. To find one's own notes took a bit of scrolling. 'She's not giving us the play,' could be heard on occasion. In bed one night, after Lyndsey had seen the show, I awoke very dry-mouthed, having consumed a little too much red wine. I made my way to the kitchen to get a drink of water. Suddenly I heard a loud ping. It was my mobile. I looked at the cooker clock. It said 2:17am. Who would be contacting me at this mad hour? I checked. Yes, it was Lyndsey's notes arriving. She must have just finished them. I decided sleep was the more important option at that moment. But, balanced against the plaudits we received from audiences and friends, as well as the deep satisfaction we got from performing this fine play, in this very fine production, dealing with Lyndsey's copious notes was a small inconvenience. She is a major talent and I have no doubt that within a few years, if she wants it, she will be running one of the major theatres in the country. I would work with her again at the drop of a hat.

Frank McGuinness came to a performance and we all had a drink afterwards. I had played in his wonderful *Observe The Sons Of Ulster Marching Towards The Somme* at Hampstead Theatre three years earlier. He spoke of *Philadelphia* with tears in his eyes. His love and admiration for Brian Friel and his work came shining out of him, along with his high opinion of Friel's place in the pantheon of Irish drama. He spoke warmly of Lyndsey's production and how well she had caught the tone of the play. A large, generous, red-faced bearded man brimming with enthusiasm for a fellow writer's work, for the production and the talent of the company.

Brian Friel himself came to one of the last performances. He was very pleased. Eighty-three years old, small and frail, with his high cheekbones, purple knobbled nose and melancholy eyes. I felt it was a great honour to not only have appeared in his play but to have been given the opportunity to speak to the man and express my deep admiration for his work.

[A small footnote. Or three. One night at the curtain call, when audiences often cheered and did that clapping with their hands above their heads to show real appreciation, a small frail old lady in a blue dress in the middle of the front row, with much effort stood up and very shyly clapped the cast. She looked

slightly embarrassed, but her face, indeed her whole body language, expessed the need to show us her appreciation of the evening's work. As we left the stage I tried to catch her eye to express in some small way my awareness and appreciation of her gesture, but by then she was, with no small effort, retaking her seat.

Paul Gambaccini, the disc jockey and general music buff, nodded along to the fifties and sixties soundtrack in the play and at the end of the show climbed on stage to look at the Dansette record player in the bedroom.

Jeffrey Archer was in the audience one night and after the performance someone in the dressing room joked, asking if the spoons had been counted after the tea scene.]

ALL THAT FALL
OR
TWO KNIGHTS AND A DAME IN A BASEMENT

– and a Princess, a Deputy Prime Minister, a Famous Wizard, a Russian Billionaire, some famous writers and an Australian Legend.

During the run of *Philadelphia* I received an offer I couldn't refuse. Sir Trevor Nunn asked me to appear in his production of Samuel Beckett's play *All That Fall*. The cast he told me would include Dame Eileen Atkins and Sir Michael Gambon. It was to be staged at the tiny Jermyn Street Theatre in Piccadilly. It would rehearse for two and a half weeks and play for four.

Now, *All That Fall* is a Samuel Beckett *radio* play and is about one hour and fifteen minutes in length. Since it was first produced on radio, many theatre directors have tried unsuccessfully to get the rights to stage it in a theatre. Laurence Olivier flew to Paris to try and persuade Beckett that it could work as a theatre piece. Despite all his efforts, Beckett was not convinced and refused the offer. Olivier felt he lost the bid when he, very enthusiastically, said to the writer, 'But Sam, Sam, it would make a fantastic show!' The use of the word "show" followed by the pained look on Beckett's face told him he had blundered badly.

Ingmar Bergman also tried, but was also refused.

Trevor had tried a number of times after Beckett's death to persuade the writer's estate to let him stage it. To no avail.

Finally, in a last effort, and with little hope of success he approached them again. If, he suggested, he "staged" it in a theatre, but on a "set" of a radio studio with microphones and a cast of actors apparently recording the piece with scripts in their hands would that be acceptable? To his great shock and surprise they said yes.

So here we are. The Jermyn Street Theatre has seventy seats. Within hours of the announcement of this historic production the whole run was sold out. Mind you, who wouldn't rush to see a little known play by Samuel Beckett, directed by the legendary Sir Trevor Nunn starring Dame Eileen Atkins and Sir Michael Gambon?

The budget was miniscule, so we would all be paid £300

a week. Without the money to hire a rehearsal room, we gathered to rehearse in the theatre, which was down one flight of stairs in a basement and had in a previous life been a gentlemen's club, whatever that means. The stage is oblong and very shallow. The current production was titled *Kissing Sid James*. Its stage setting had two locations. On one side a small, slightly shabby hotel bedroom, and on the other, in front of a brightly coloured backcloth painted in the style of a 1940s McGill seaside postcard, were some white promenade railings. With the bed propped up against the wall it was in this bizarre setting we worked on Mr Beckett's play. On the back wall of the stage a large sign was projected. It said "TOILETS". I will return to this small mystery.

The import of a lot of heavy equipment and scaffolding in the street outside soon became obvious. We spent most days rehearsing to the sound of pneumatic drills coming through the walls. Trevor stated that these drills had followed him around from rehearsal room to rehearsal room for a great deal of his career.

All That Fall was written in 1956 and first performed on BBC Radio in 1957. The story of the play is on the surface very simple. It is set in a small community half an hour outside Dublin. It concerns an old lady called Maddy Rooney who sets out on foot to meet her blind husband Dan. We learn that the Rooneys had a daughter, Minnie, who died at a very young age. Dan is returning from work by train on a Saturday morning. Most people in Ireland worked a half day on Saturdays in the fifties – I had done so myself. Along the way she encounters various seen and unseen neighbours: an unseen troubled old lady locked in a large house who continually plays a recording of Schubert's *Death And The Maiden*; a man with a cart pulled

43

by a hinny (the offspring of a male horse and a female donkey) who tries to sell her some "sty" manure. She meets a retired bill broker on a bicycle whose offer of assistance she refuses. She meets an ex-admirer, the clerk of the racecourse, who offers her a lift in his "limousine" and then takes her to the small railway station. Here she encounters the stationmaster, Mr Barrell, the part I played, and Tommy his assistant whom he bullies. Miss Fitt, a Protestant spinster, helps Mrs Rooney up the steep stairs to the platform. The train is very late. I inform the waiting customers "there has been a hitch. All traffic is retarded". Eventually the train arrives and the blind Mr Rooney comes along the platform assisted by a young local boy, Jerry, who normally guides him home for a few pennies. The Rooneys then set out for home. Along the way she asks him what was the cause of the train delay. He is annoyed. He says he knows nothing. He asks her, "Did you ever wish to kill a child?" He then tells her how once, on the black road home, he nearly attacked the boy, Jerry. On they walk. Soon Jerry comes running up and says Mr Barrell has sent him to return something Dan dropped in his compartment of the train.

Mrs Rooney: It looks like a kind of ball. And yet it is not a ball.

Mr Rooney: Give it to me.

Mrs Rooney: (Giving it) What is it Dan?

Mr Rooney: It is a thing I carry about with me.

Mrs Rooney: Yes, but what—

Mr Rooney: (Violently) It is a thing I carry about with me!

As Jerry runs back to the station Mrs Rooney calls out to him.

Mrs Rooney: Jerry! Did you hear what kept the train so late?
Dan tries to distract her and move her on. She persists. The
*   boy replies:*

Jerry: It was a little child, ma'am.

(Mr Rooney groans)
Jerry: It was a little child fell out of the carriage, ma'am.
*   (Pause) On to the line, ma'am. (Pause) Under the wheels,*
*   ma'am.*

Silence. Jerry runs off. His steps die away. Tempest of wind
*   and rain. It abates. They move on. Dragging steps, etc.*
*   They halt. Tempest of wind and rain.*

The play is over.

At his most accessible and Irish, Beckett, in *All That Fall*, draws on memories and characters of the Dublin of his childhood, especially the vivid and motley gang Mrs Rooney encounters on her journey. The language has the same richness of language and quirkiness as the work of Synge and O'Casey, the same humour. Though, as the play darkens the humour changes, it becomes blacker, bleaker: Beckettian. On her slow painful journey to and from the station Mrs Rooney reflects on loneliness, on loss, on decay, on marriage and death. Childlessness haunts her. There are several references to the death of the couple's daughter Minnie.

Near the end, Dan rails against "the horrors of home life, the dusting, sweeping, airing… and the brats, the happy little healthy little howling neighbours' brats".

The end of the play is famously ambiguous. What happened on the train? Is Mr Rooney responsible for the death of the child? We are never told. In rehearsal, Trevor Nunn decided to clarify this mystery. I will explain how and why a little later.

On the first day we gather around the customary tables and Trevor explains how we are going to "stage" the play. It will be very simple. There are strong unbreakable rules laid down by the Beckett estate. The setting will be a black box with nine radio mikes hanging in various positions around the stage. There will be a red studio light on one wall to indicate "recording". The actors will all sit on benches on either side of the space for the whole performance. Mrs Rooney will begin her journey stage left and while playing scenes will move slowly across the area and end up stage right at the railway station. She and Mr Rooney will then journey back to stage left where the play will end. Centre stage will be a raised wooden structure representing part of a motor car. It will have two seats and a practical car door. Trevor feels that this will be useful for comic business in the very funny scene where Mrs Rooney is offered a lift to the station and has great trouble entering and exiting the vehicle. We will all wear some small "semblance" of costume. Although in the end we wear a lot more than a semblance. In fact about ninety per cent semblance. Also, given the small budget, all the actors end up supplying their own costumes. I believe Eileen found her dress in a charity shop.

Written as a radio play, Beckett added many sound

cues. Throughout, the audience will hear a profusion of farm animals, birds, footsteps, horse-and-cart noises, some Schubert and various motor vehicles, as well as two trains, taunting children, a crying woman, rain, wind and a storm. In fact, in the hour and a quarter there are 105 sound cues brilliantly put together by Paul Groothuis.

Trevor speaks, as always, brilliantly and cogently about Beckett and his play. He is dressed, as ever, in his trademark blue denim shirt and jeans. In the last production I did with him, I became obsessed with his wardrobe. Directors who spend their days watching actors are not always aware that actors watch them. A man who is purportedly worth a few bob, and who turns up for work every day wearing the exact same denim ensemble elicits no end of serious interest in his wardrobe. It took a number of days to ascertain that he, in fact, owned more than one denim shirt. I noticed that *that* day's garment sported mother of pearl buttons. Hurrah! A further clue also presented itself. Trevor has a small but constant habit of putting one of his arms over his shoulder and scratching an exact point on his back. Standing behind him one day I noticed that this scratching had bleached the indigo dye from that spot. I then, over a number of weeks, ascertained that a similar pale patch was evidenced in all of his shirts. On one particular day, as I manoeuvred my way behind, I found that, in fact, that day's shirt had a small but distinct hole in its back.

Now, at Jermyn Street, I noticed a new phenomenon. He came to work in a pair of somewhat used trainers, which had a large either Z or N on their sides. After a few days I noticed that the right heel of one trainer was literally falling apart, in fact, coming away from the shoe. I grew concerned that his posture would suffer from this imbalance.

47

All that denim, together with his long dark hair, goatee beard and moustache give him the air of a seventies' rock guitar virtuoso. There are suggestions that Trevor dyes his hair, but I would bet my house that he doesn't. He has a very delicate way with that hair. Not for him the dramatic head lift and no-nonsense finger rake that Greg Doran employs to push *his* wavy locks away. Trevor, with gentle fingers, ushers it away from his face with a slow delicate gesture. Sadly, I myself have no significant hair gesture – perhaps because I have no significant hair to do anything with.

We have only two weeks to rehearse the play. We read it a few times, discuss various suggestions, clarify any literary references, and after two days get on our feet to stage it. A small early mystery in the text is discussed and resolved. This revolves around the little scene with Mrs Rooney and Christy, the manure seller, who meets her on the road with his cart pulled by the hinny. Mrs Rooney hears a sound:

Mrs Rooney: … (Pause) Mercy! What was that?

Christy: Never mind her, ma'am, she's a little fresh in herself today.

Trevor wonders what this little exchange is referring to and, despite there being no sound cue indicated, he has come to the conclusion that the hinny has, in fact, farted. So, a new sound cue will be inserted. A few days later the cue is produced and there is much discussion among us all as to how loud the fart should be. Trevor doesn't want it to intrude too much, so an acceptable level is eventually decided upon and used. Only in the theatre would you have nine people discussing the quality and loudness of an animal fart and its import for the production. But when two of the nine are knights of the theatre, and the third is a dame, for some reason it is even funnier. Not something that happens in the boardrooms in the City. We laughed a lot that afternoon.

It is only at the end of the play that we learn of the tragedy on the train. Trevor felt that we could help clarify this in the earlier station scenes in a number of small, visual ways. In the dialogue, Mr Barrell, the stationmaster, sends the porter Tommy to enquire of Mr Case at the signal box if he has any news of the delayed train. Tommy strolls away. A little later this normally lethargic employee is spotted running back.

*Tommy: (*Excitedly, in the distance*) She's coming. (*Pause*) She's at the level-crossing!*

In the script, there then immediately follows a number of sound effects. The upmail thunders through the station on one track, closely followed by the arrival of the very late and long expected train on the other. Here Trevor created a small dumbshow. First he delayed the trains' sound cues. Then in the silence he made Tommy gesture excitedly for me to join him. He then whispered in my ear the news of the cause of the delay – the death of a small child on the train. This he illustrated with some gestures, which I reacted to in horror. Then the train effects started.

As the passengers disembark and the train departs, Trevor directed Tommy to bring me a small knitted multicoloured ball from Mr Rooney's carriage. We exchange glances, I take it, look at it, and turn away, very upset. Mrs Rooney stands on the platform with me.

Mrs Rooney: … He isn't on it! The misery I have endured to get here, and he isn't on it! Mr Barrell! Was he not on it? (Pause) Is anything the matter? You look as if you had seen a ghost. (Pause)

Lost in the horror of the death of the child, with the ball in my hand, I am directed to ignore Mrs Rooney's speech to me. I turn, look distractedly at her and exit. These little changes, inserted halfway through the play before the long scene as the couple crawl home and the train tragedy finally unfolds, give audiences an intimation of some terrible event concerning an incident, possibly concerning a child, on the train.

Apart from the ball sequence the scene is as normal. Then at the end of the play when Jerry runs after Mr Rooney and returns something he left in the compartment he presents the ball to the inquiring Mrs Rooney.

Trevor believed that these little dumbshows, together with the introduction of the ball would make the mystery at end of the play much less ambiguous.

So we teched and opened the play and that's when the "TOILETS" sign I mentioned earlier proved interesting. There were three lavatories directly behind the stage. These were for the audience. They had to cross the stage and exit to use them. Our dressing rooms in a lower basement had no water supply. So the actors had to use the same facilities as the audience. Often before the show we would stand side by side with our public at the urinals. The stage manager, at 7:30pm, would check the lavatories were empty and then signal that we could start the performance. On occasion, as we stood waiting to enter behind a small curtain, there were scurilious comments made by a distinguished member of the cast concerning the odours emanating from the lavatories.

The production was greeted with some seriously good reviews. Queues of hopeful customers formed in the street for every performance in the hope of returns. Some waited for hours. They were overly optimistic of their chances as the auditorium only held seventy people.

In the basement there were two dressing rooms. Eileen and Catherine Cusack, the only other female in the cast, shared one and the six men shared the other. The talented Catherine is one of Cyril Cusack's four daughters who followed him into the profession.

The banter that flowed back and forth between the two rooms was sharp and funny. Michael G was as ever full of extraordinary yarns and anecdotes, some so fantastic that you had to wonder if they were totally invented. He told us he once went to meet Woody Allen in a hotel in London about a part in a film. Allen asked him what he had been working on. Michael said he had just finished a project where he played a character who slept with his daughter. We all gasped. He said Woody Allen gave him a very odd look and then handed him a scrap of paper with two lines written on it: 'Read these.' Michael read the lines. Allen said, 'Thank you.' That was the end of the interview. A couple of weeks later Michael was flown to Paris to see Allen again. He read the same two lines. He didn't get the job, he told us.

When working on Broadway he said he got to know Al Pacino who was appearing in the theatre next door. Michael asked him if he could introduce him to Robert de Niro. Pacino did and the three of them went out to dinner. The Americans were fascinated by Michael's knighthood. He told them about the Queen, the ceremony with the sword, etc. 'Yeah, but what good is it to you, what rights does it give you?'

'Well', he said, 'it gives me something called "droit de seigneur".'

'What's that?' they asked.

'It's very complicated, but basically it is an ancient law which gives me the right to have sex with any woman in England over the age of forty.'

I told Michael of an encounter I had heard between a friend of the playwright and Beckett himself. As they walked along the street on a glorious summer's day, the friend looked up at the cloudless sky and said to Beckett, 'God, Sam, isn't it a great day to be alive?'

Beckett replied, 'Well, I wouldn't go that far.'

Michael said he had seen Beckett back in the early sixties at the National. He and Tony Hopkins were climbing the stairs to the dressing rooms at the Old Vic and he noticed Beckett in front of them. But, also going upstairs and a few steps in front of Beckett, was the actress Billie Whitelaw. She would later appear in many of his plays and became his muse. 'Anyway, as we climbed,' says Michael, 'we were looking past Beckett at Billie, who was wearing a very tight skirt. Looking at her arse. Suddenly Beckett glanced back at the two of us, nodded up towards the actress, and gave us a sly thumbs-up.'

In *All That Fall,* the playing of the two leads was outstanding. Eileen created a wonderfully complex Mrs Rooney – an old woman full of frailty, bad temper, melancholy, bawdy wit, along with the great need of a little love. Her withering looks would have killed an ox at twenty paces. 'Oh to be in atoms, in atoms. ATOMS!' she roared. A very, very fine performance.

Michael brought to the smaller role that extraordinary physical presence of his. His tetchiness towards his wife was appalling, rude, and at the same time horribly funny. He hinted at the turmoil going on inside this blind man with often the most delicate gestures. Those great hands of his, with those incredibly long sensitive fingers, which would touch his forehead or his wife's sad old hat, reminded me of the badly drawn hands of some of the martyred saints in medieval religious paintings. His voice, with its range from high querulous to the dangerous low base notes of anger and despair, is an instrument of great power and expression. He confessed that he found doing the play with the book in his hand difficult and frustrating. And, though he lacked the fluidity of Eileen who had learned most of her part, when he reached the crucial moments he was mesmeric to watch. His attack on the appalling prospect of retirement and home life was unsettling and fearsome.

My favourite moment in the play is when Mr Rooney asks his wife if the preacher has announced his text for the Sunday sermon. She nods, "The Lord upholdeth all that fall and raiseth up all those that be bowed down" (*Silence.*)" Then the two actors break into wild laughter. It is raucous, irreligious, a great noise of anarchic joy. It scoffs at the gods. It is heart– thumpingly affirmative and life-enhancing. An astonishing moment. The long groan Michael gave at the end when the boy tells of the death of the child was visceral, disturbing, full of despair and worth the price of admission alone. This moment is followed by the dragging footsteps of the couple as they move inexorably towards home, followed by a loud rumbling cracking storm. This last burst of the play is Shakespearean in scale and massively moving.

The whole company was very talented. Ruairi Conaghan who appeared with me in *Philadelphia* at the Donmar, where he distinguished himself playing three roles very well, now had the luxury of playing just the one role, Christy, the manure seller.

POST-SHOW ENCOUNTERS

In the second week of the run we were informed that the theatre's patron was coming to see the performance and would like to say hello to us onstage afterwards. Fair enough. Then we were told that this person was Princess Michael of Kent, often referred to in the media as Princess Pushy. As I write this I find in today's *Mail Online* an article about her husband Prince Michael stating that despite their long separations – the ongoing rumours and the many intimate photographs of he and his wife in the company of 'close friends' – they thrive on being apart, and he dismisses rumours of marriage problems. True to form, Princess Michael is titled Princess Pushy in the headline.

As I left the dressing room to meet her I have to admit I was intrigued. This was the woman who the Queen apparently referred to as "a bit too grand for us". A woman whose father had been a member of the Nazi party, a woman who had been accused of plagiarism in her first two books and was part of a notorious couple often titled the Rent-a-Kents. When I got onstage there were four guests. She was surprisingly tall, dressed in a very stylish high-collared black wool coat. She offered her hand. I was looking into the face of a fine-looking woman, very striking in fact. She complimented me on my performance, which given the size of the role, didn't take long. She loved the show. Then she introduced me to a handsome grey-haired man standing beside her in a slightly loud jacket. *'This is Nicky'*. I instantly recognised him from the many newspaper photographs of him I'd seen over the years in celebrity night spots: Nicky Haslam. He's well known, but I do not know what for. I think, interior design. We said hello and then the princess took me over and introduced me to a very nice couple whose daughter she informed me was a very successful actress on television. I didn't recognise her name. The father protested, 'No, she's not really.' The princess ignored this and very enthusiastically mentioned a TV series the girl had appeared in. So, the former Baroness Marie Christina Anna Agnes Hedwig Ida Von Reibnitz, despite all I had heard, seemed a fairly decent human being.

Midway through the run we were informed that the Beckett estate, guardians of the flame, were coming to a matinee. Trevor sent us an email. We were told to be on our best behaviour, stifle any theatrical leanings and keep our faces in the script. Eileen who had learned ninety per cent of the part will have to lower her eyes more often.

The Beckett estate has spoken. They want some changes. The "ball" has to go. We presume it is too illustrative. Mrs Rooney only states – "It looks like a kind of ball. And yet it is not a ball". The whispered message Tommy gives me can stay, but his handing the "ball" to me as the train pulls out must be cut. The estate didn't seem to notice the inclusion of the fart.

The production rolls along. The theatre management tell us there are various West End producers interested in transferring the play to a bigger theatre. We are asked about any work offers we are contemplating. The dreaded Duchess Theatre is mentioned as a possible venue.

I meet Barry Humphries in the auditorium after a performance. He says how much he has enjoyed hearing the play. Few performers make me laugh out loud.

"When I was born my mother was lying there panting away in bed and in came the matron with a little bundle and it was a lovely child, beautifully formed with purple hair. My mother said, 'What is it? What is it?' And the nurse said, 'It's a megastar.' And that's the first known use of the word in the language." – *Dame Edna.*

There was an interesting occurence at one performance. As the play started and Eileen stood and slowly paced forward into the action, we suddenly heard some pop music playing somewhere. It continued. Eileen stopped and apologised to the audience, 'We must sort this out.' The music continued. We all moved onstage and tried to figure out its whereabouts. 'Is it coming from that fan extractor?' We listened.

'No', said Ian Conningham, who was playing Tommy, 'it's coming from under the stage.' He knelt and stuck his head under. 'No!' He then pointed to a man right in front of him sitting in the front row. 'It's you, sir!'

The man said, 'No, it's not!'

Ian listened some more and then pointed to the man's trousers – 'It is you!'

The man reached into his pocket and brought out his

mobile phone which was, in fact, playing the music. He was so flustered he couldn't remember how to turn it off. A lady sitting next to him took it and silenced the sound. There was laughter, then we all settled and started again. Despite all the pre-show announcements, I have played dozens of performances over recent years to the ringing of mobile phones. One night in Hong Kong when touring *Othello* with the National Theatre we counted sixteen phones ringing.

The amount of well-known people coming to see the play in this tiny theatre is extraordinary. The actor Greta Scacchi, the actor/comedians Jo Brand and David Walliams, writers Lady Antonia Fraser and Edna O'Brien. As I leave the theatre one night Nick Clegg, Deputy Prime Minister, and his gorgeous wife Miriam Gonzáles Durántez, are talking to Eileen and Michael in the auditorium. Being a politician he didn't miss the chance to offer his hand and commend my performance as I quietly slid past. Ian McKellen and Evgeny Lebedev, the Russian owner of the Evening Standard, turn up together. Ian is wearing a royal blue belted overcoat and a woolly cap which covers some of his face. When he comes to say hello to me in the dark auditorium, it took me a second to recognise him. It's a bit embarrassing, as I did *Coriolanus* with him at the NT and know him pretty well. He's always friendly, positive and complimentary. I like him a lot.

I'm beginning to think the Kardashians, the Emperor of Japan and Pharrell Williams will soon be attending performances.

TRANSFER ONE

With a week of the run to go we are asked to take the play to a bigger theatre in the West End. There has been a continuous clamour at the box office and after extremely good reviews, with some critics suggesting the show deserves a bigger and further showing, it makes sense to extend the run. So we are moving to the Arts Theatre near Leicester Square. It has a two-tier auditorium, which will offer five times the number of seats that Jermyn Street Theatre has. I think this is a very good move and should not affect the intimacy of the production. We will open three days after the last performance in Picadilly and play for three weeks. The publicity for the extension will need to get moving fast. The move to the Arts is historically interesting. It was at this theatre that the English-language premiere of Beckett's *Waiting For Godot* was directed by the twenty-four-year-old Peter Hall in 1955. Peter Bull, who appeared in the production, said it was greeted with "waves of hostility and a mass exodus".

We are shown the design for the poster at the Arts, with Eileen and Michael's names in large print. The names of rest of the cast are not on it. 'Don't worry,' Eileen said, 'it's going to be changed.' She and Michael have insisted that all our names be on it. Generous and typical of them both.

Gerard Horan, who plays Mr Slocum, the clerk of the racecourse, is unable to do the transfer. He has signed up to do a television job. He is very funny as Slocum and will be missed. His replacement will have to be found swiftly. On the final day at Jermyn Street we learn that Trevor Cooper is to take over from Gerard. Good news, he's a very good actor.

Thelma Holt is involved in the transfer. Seems only days

ago she was shepherding us into the Duchess with *Written On The Heart*. As ever she is full of energy, summoning support.

We move to the Arts Theatre the following Monday and tech the show. It is a slightly shabby auditorium. Given its size, central location and frontage, it could be a much more important venue if the owners would only spend some money on it. There are two big surprises. Trevor Nunn has had a haircut and has bought some brand spanking new trainers made, incidentally, by the same manufacturer as his previous ones. The first preview went very well. Surprisingly, the play works better in the bigger space. Trevor has added some small floor mikes and, along with our natural delivery, he projects our "radio" voices over them to the audience. It's a very clever stroke.

Michael Gambon as a young man trained initially as a precision engineer. He has retained an interest in the craft ever since. Over the years he has become very interested in the beauty and quality of antique guns and is now a collector as well as a respected member of a small exclusive club of antique firearms experts. He brings in a stunning late eighteenth-century pistol to show me. His excitement in showing me the exquisite engineering, the mechanism, the silver wire inlaid in swirling patterns in the highly polished walnut handle, is palpable. I am suddenly struck by the notion that I have never heard him express a comparable passion for the craft of acting.

Eileen is shortlisted for the Evening Standard Drama Awards for *All That Fall* – not bad considering she plays the part with the book in her hand. Lyndsey Turner was on the longlist for her production of *Philadelphia*, but didn't make the shortlist. A pity.

The show is bowling along to big appreciative audiences. The theatre, a world of dreams, is always a well of rumour and possibility. The latest is that some Broadway producers are coming over to see the play with an eye to moving it to New York next year. We meet with Thelma and our other young producer Richard Darbourne, who want to know if we would be interested. Everyone says yes. Will it happen? We'll believe it when the offer comes in. That said, a spell in the city so good they named it twice, would always be very welcome.

LIOLÀ

I finished *All That Fall* at the Arts on Saturday 24th November 2012 and on Monday 26th went to the NT Studio for a three-day workshop on a little known Pirandello play, newly translated by Tanya Ronder. The director is Richard Eyre. The play, *Liolà*, "a country comedy in three acts", is set in Pirandello's Sicily in 1916. It is a very different piece to the author's better-known plays *Six Characters In Search of an Author* and *The Rules of the Game*. Richard wants to explore how you do an Italian play on an English stage. What comparable, recognisable community comes nearest to the Sicilian world of Pirandello? He tells us he has been struck by the similarity of this small rural community with its harsh island landscape, its Catholic people, where most of the men have left for the mainland to look for work, with the equally harsh rural landscape and Catholic community of the west of Ireland, where emigration has always been a constant. So, he has gathered a strong group of Irish actors to explore the text, while still sticking to the Italian names and physical landscape.

Rory Keenan, a fine actor I recently worked with in *Philadelphia*, will read the part of Liolà. His talented sister Grainne is also with us. Two other fine actors, Dearbhla Molloy and Sorcha Cusack, both of whom I have worked with in the past, are also part of the group. Sorcha is half-sister to Katherine who was in *All That Fall*.

Unusually for a play, women strongly outnumber men in the cast – by nine to two.

On the first morning we watch *Kaos*, a beautiful, poetic film by the Taviani brothers set in Sicily, and based on four short stories by Pirandello. We are immediately struck by the similarities between the Sicilian and west of Ireland landscapes. Both are rocky, infertile, remote, sparsely-populated places where it is hard to scrape a living.

Liolà is a handsome Dionysian figure, with a talent for singing, who has fathered three children by three different women. He and his mother are raising all three. As the play opens we discover he has impregnated a fourth woman, Tuzza. Spurred on by her mother Croce, cousin to the old, rich and childless Simone (who I read), Tuzza conspires to pass off her unborn child as Simone's. Simone is married to the very young Mita, who he blames for not providing him with a child. He is desperate for an heir and consequently treats his wife very badly. Liolà loves Mita. Complications ensue. Much of the play deals with the women's lack of choice and power.

The play, though not long, is in three acts, with some songs.

Richard wants it to be fast and fluid. The sense of community in the piece is very strong. We experiment with having all the actors onstage as the lights go up. Each actor steps forward, introduces his/her character to the audience and retreats to sit in a shallow curve of individual wooden chairs at the back of the stage. The company/community, Richard thinks, will remain onstage for the whole production. He wants the setting to be very simple. The various locations Pirandello creates can, with a little tinkering, Richard believes, be staged without pause. The opening scene is set outdoors with a group of women shelling almonds. Here, the actors will step forward with their chairs and create the scene downstage and, when finished, return to the upstage "curve". The best place for the interval seems to be at the end of Act One. By Wednesday, Richard decides that the play would be best done without an interval. The songs that intersperse the play we improvise using old Irish tunes. The composer Orlando Gough arrives one morning, listens to the improvised songs and then teaches us a couple of tunes. Richard seems very keen to add much more music to the piece.

On the Tuesday someone in the room for some reason mentioned the comedian Des O'Connor. Richard told us that, some years before, he had received, out of the blue, a phone call from O'Connor, whom he had never met or ever had any contact with. The comedian/presenter explained that he was soon to appear as a celebrity guest on the TV gameshow *Who Wants To be a Millionaire?* He asked Richard to be his "friend", as in "phone a friend". At first Richard thought it was some colleague playing a joke. But when he realised it was in fact Des O'Connor, he agreed to take part without hesitation. When the programme was recorded Richard was "stood by" in case he was needed, but Des never resorted to phoning a friend so Richard's help was not required. To this day he has no idea why or how Des chose him. But ever since, he told us, he has had a soft spot for the comedian.

By the end of three days an enormous amount of work has been done and much achieved. Many scenes have been roughly staged, music has been experimented with and a sense of a small tight-knit community has been created. Richard has been totally focused on the project. He is open and extremely sensitive to all ideas suggested and has fostered a very creative atmosphere in the room. The play, which, in my opinion, seemed a little unwieldy on the page, has now in this short time taken on a rich vibrant life. Tanya, the writer, has been accommodating and generous to all suggestions for textual clarity and change, often taking up an idea, developing it and adding new dialogue.

As is the nature of these workshops, they are suddenly and shockingly over. Three days. Intense input, much excitement and then over. Thanks and farewells are expressed and home we go. The play is good. A production is planned for the Lyttelton Theatre next summer. I would very much like to be involved in it, but doing a workshop does not mean you will be offered the part. Nevertheless it is impossible not to treat it as an audition. I certainly did and, so I suspect, did most of the others.

THE CAPTAIN OF KÖPENICK

Ten days after the workshop I go to the National Theatre to rehearse Carl Zuckmayer's 1931 play *The Captain Of Köpenick*. Based on a true story, the play, a satire on German conformity and pre-Hitler militarism, tells the story of Wilhelm Voigt, a petty criminal of unassuming appearance who, on release from prison, finds himself unable to get proper identity papers. In comic circumstances he acquires a military uniform. Assuming the demeanour of a Prussian captain he commandeers a platoon of soldiers, fools the military and the Berlin civic authorities and steals a large amount of cash from the city treasury. He is eventually pardoned by the Kaiser and becomes a folk hero.

The play has a great showstopping central role, which will be played by Antony Sher. It will be directed by Adrian Noble in a new and very funny version by Ron Hutchinson. Coincidentally, I appeared in a 1971 production of *The Captain Of Köpenick* during the NT's early years at the Old Vic when the great Paul Scofield played the Captain.

By the opening of this production in late January 2013 the National Theatre will be celebrating its fiftieth birthday. I was lucky to appear in the company's opening season at the Old Vic in 1964 and therefore will also be celebrating fifty years work with the company.

THE BEGINNINGS

LIMERICK 1963 – DRAMA SCHOOL –
MY FIRST YEAR IN THE BUSINESS

LIMERICK 1963

In June 1963, with my brown cardboard suitcase in hand, I boarded the train at Limerick Station. I was twenty-two years old. I had my life savings, twenty-five pounds in my pocket and I was at the beginning of a long journey to the great city of London, where I had never been, where I knew not a single soul and where it was my avowed intent to become an actor.

My knowledge and experience of acting I had learned mostly from performing in amateur theatre, from going to the cinema and from listening to the radio. Television didn't arrive in Ireland until 1961. My family did not get one until four years later.

I felt that my experience over the previous four years with two amateur companies, playing locally and in festivals at small venues all over the south of Ireland, would stand me in good stead. Some of my contemporaries imputed that I joined these companies to meet girls. This is a slander! Soon I was an "experienced" player with appearances in productions of Synge, Tennessee Williams, Harold Pinter, John Mortimer and others. A few kind souls suggested that I should "go professional". After all, who saved the day at the Kilrush

Festival, when part of the set of *The Heart's A Wonder*, a musical version of *The Playboy of the Western World,* fell on me during my finest moment? As I pushed it back, as frantic hands reached out from behind to pull it upright, did I miss a note of my song? Of course not. We won Best Production. We were invited to compete at the All Ireland Drama Festival in Athlone. Surely, I was ready for better things?

In my youth, Limerick had five cinemas, their exotic names reminders of an earlier, more glorious age – The Savoy, The Grand Central, The Carlton, The Royal and The Lyric. Sadly they are all now gone, demolished, with the exception of The Royal. Its red neon piping now extinguished, its beautiful cream art deco frontage now graced with moss and stained with age and neglect. These romantic structures were where I had often journeyed, three or four times a week, to marvel at the acting of Paul Newman, Montgomery Clift, Alastair Sim, Marlon Brando, Sophia Loren, Lee J Cobb, Cary Grant, Eva Marie Saint, George C Scott, Piper Laurie, Miles Malleson and hundreds of other wonderful actors. I had watched Laurence Olivier's great performance in the film of *Richard III* three times in one week at The Carlton. The actor's effortless ability to switch from steely menace, to black humour, to sly ambition impressed me greatly. The crow-like, raffish, sexy look Olivier had created with make-up, false nose, inky wig and loping limp, along with the graceful ease with which he spoke the complex poetic language inspired me. At Sexton Street Christian Brothers' School we could barely speak three lines of Shakespeare before our brains and tongues stuttered to a halt. I thought Olivier was fantastic. I wanted to act in Shakespeare. God help us.

Professional theatre in Ireland in the fifties and early sixties was almost totally confined to Dublin. There was the Abbey, our national theatre, which had, unlike any company I subsequently worked for, a permanent acting ensemble. And it *was* permanent. All the actors were on contracts for *life.* Forty-four years later when I came to the Abbey to do Oscar Wilde's *An Ideal Husband,* I worked with the last of that contracted company, a wonderful man called Des Cave.

There was the Gaiety Theatre, which did everything from farce to pantomimes to variety shows as well as hosting visiting productions from England.

Then, there was the Gate, set up in 1929 by two giants of the Irish Theatre, Micheál Mac Liammóir and his partner and lover Hilton Edwards, who on small budgets presented both new plays and major European classics. Their work was in sharp contrast to the country-kitchen fare available at the Abbey during that period. Hearing of the success of the Gate Theatre, the great Orson Welles, then a young, unemployed and hugely inexperienced actor, came to Dublin and managed to persuade The Boys (as Mac Liammóir and Edwards were affectionately known) that he was a Broadway star. They enlisted him immediately into the company.

Hilton Edwards, a large hook-nosed imposing figure, who conformed to most people's image of Julius Caesar, was an actor/director. He would occasionally take time off from the Gate to adjudicate at some of the very popular amateur festivals around the country. At one festival he adjudicated in Limerick, I played an old and extremely heavily made-up craftsman in a long-forgotten play called *The Woodcarver.* Mr Edwards spoke well of my performance. And even now, over fifty years later my heart swells at the memory – though I suspect he was being kind to a young performer.

Micheál Mac Liammóir, despite that rich Irish name was, of course, not Irish at all. He was born in Kensal Green in London. His real name was Alfred Willmore and while touring Ireland with a play, he fell in love with the country and learned to speak and write Irish. He even changed his name. He had been a child actor in London and had worked with the young Noël Coward. At the Gate he not only starred in productions, but wrote plays, designed the sets and even wrote the music.

In 1960, he came to Limerick, to perform in our small theatre, his one-man play *The Importance Of Being Oscar*, about the life, plays and poetry of Oscar Wilde. It was a fabulous piece of work. It soon went on to tour the world to great critical acclaim. On a simple set he brought to life an astonishing array of real and dramatic characters from Wilde's life and works. Mac Liammóir was a supreme raconteur, hugely theatrical with a strong deep bass voice. He would probably now be thought of as flowery, declamatory and a little hammy, but he was truly mesmeric. In priest-ridden provincial Limerick he opened our young, raw and prejudiced eyes to the condemned, the forbidden: the never to be mentioned world of the homosexual. He was a remarkable man.

After the show, as we hung about the foyer of the little theatre, Mac Liammóir suddenly appeared, flanked by accolytes. On his head the deep, black, shiny toupee, on his face the brown make-up, and on his eyes the kohl eyeliner. Around his shoulders he wore a long black ankle-length fur coat, the buttons as big as saucers. He smiled warmly at us all as he swept out into the dark street. An "*actor*" to the life.

In the same year I saw a production of *The Rose Tattoo* by Tenessee Williams in Dublin. This production brought the wrath and full weight of the Catholic Church down upon it. It is laughable now, but the whole controversy revolved not around the play, but around the appearance on stage of a condom. In those dark and unenlightened days condoms were forbidden in holy Ireland, which led to many unplanned pregnancies and long, guilt-ridden journeys to England for secret abortions.

The Importance Of Being Oscar, *The Rose Tattoo* and a very serious production of T.S. Eliot's *Murder In The Cathedral* in a dark and echoing church in Dublin were at that time the sum total of my professional theatre-going experience.

I cannot remember now why I did not want to be an actor in Ireland. The prospects were obviously limited. There were, as far as I knew, no drama schools. Young people in Ireland at that time looked outward to England and America as the dynamic places to work and live. The Celtic Tiger was still decades away. The Church also cast a strong conservative and negative shadow over our lives. We were educated by Christian Brothers. We were beaten by them. We were never taught to dream.

Most of what I read about drama was in the "quality" English newspapers. In the theatre columns of Harold Hobson in the *Sunday Times*, and in the *Observer* by the great Kenneth Tynan. Both of these critics introduced me to the contemporary talents of a new breed of writer – John Osborne, Ann Jellicoe, John Arden, Arnold Wesker, mainly working at the Royal Court Theatre. Tynan and Hobson, who were hugely influential, also wrote of the exciting new directors who staged these plays: John Dexter, William Gaskill, George Devine, Anthony Page – most of whom I would be lucky enough to work with in the coming years.

MAKING ENDS MEET
IN LONDON

So, my journey to London took eighteen long hours. The train clattered across the green heart of Ireland to Dublin. There I found my way through the city and out to the port of Dun Laoire where I boarded a ferry and made my maiden, stomach-churning voyage to Holyhead. This ship had the black and rusted visage of a featured vessel in a Joseph Conrad novel. At Holyhead I set out on another long train journey south to London. Eventually we began what seemed like an endless approach through terraces of red-brick dwellings, vast warehouses, office blocks and towering gasometers to the heart of the city. The smelly diesel train slowly ground to a halt at Euston Station. I stepped onto the platform and was instantly bombarded by the noisy rumble of the great city. I became suddenly and frighteningly aware of what a huge step I had taken. It was a lonely moment.

'So! Who made you come? Buck up!'

Soon I was settled in a boarding house in Sussex Gardens, Paddington, which I found out later was, and may still be, a notorious haunt of prostitutes. Needless to say, during my four week residence at this salubrious address, and probably because of my Irish Catholic innocence, I failed to notice a single one of these interesting residents. My small savings very soon diminished, so a job was now urgently required to keep a roof over my head, but more importantly, to help provide savings for drama school fees. Obviously, and rightly, being an immigrant, I had no right to what most English students received in those days, a government grant. So, I went to work in the offices of the Westbourne Park Building Society and moved to a rented room in Hornton Street just off Kensington High Street. Would you find a cheap room in upmarket Kensington now? I suspect not.

My early days in London were exciting. I loved the place. I roamed over all the obvious tourist spots. The West End with all those glamorous, glowing theatres, I could rarely afford to go to. There was Hyde Park, Kensington Gardens, my discovery of the paintings of Monet and Cezanne at the National Gallery, St Paul's Cathedral, the Thames, the ferry all the way down to Greenwich, the views from Westminster Bridge. I walked the feet off myself, thrilled to be here.

After a few weeks at the Westbourne Park Building Society my employers made a monumental mistake and moved me to answering customers' telephone calls. Trying to decipher the numerous London and regional accents down the line in a noisy office proved beyond the capability of my Irish ear. I handed in my notice. Within a few days I was off on what was to me a long journey, fifteen stops by tube on the Circle and Central lines across London, to Stratford East. I was interviewed for a clerical job at the Clarnico Sweet Factory in Hackney Wick. If offered the job, the office manager asked, would I make Clarnico, my lifetime career? I

71

said I would. A bare-faced lie. A venial sin. I was offered the job. I took it.

Soon I was collecting all the information I could get on the top London drama schools. The choice in 1963 was far more limited than today. The Guildhall School of Music and Drama, then off Fleet Street by the river in Blackfriars, was one of the top three. More importantly, in financial terms, it was also one of the cheapest. In August 1963, I had accrued enough cash for one term's fees (I had originally planned to save for a year) and, aware that I was an elderly twenty-two, I applied to the Guildhall. I auditioned and was accepted. In retrospect, I suspect an Irish immigrant was an exotic choice for a 1960s drama school, given that the overwhelming intake of most schools then was decidedly English, almost totally white and middle class. I was to start classes a month later.

After getting over the thrill of my acceptance I was left with a major problem. Having handed over all my savings, how was I now going to keep a roof over my head, put food in my mouth and earn the next five terms' fees while studying for the two years?

Hey-diddle-de-de!

A friend from Limerick, Bob Clancy, arrived in London to study science and we shared a bedsit in convenient Pimlico. The rent was one pound ten shillings a week each, and I could walk to Guildhall in Blackfriars. I reckoned that four pounds a week would just cover rent and food. So at weekends, after classes at the Guildhall, I did long weekend shifts as a security guard with the firm Securicor. They provided a uniform, a cap and a truncheon, and on Friday evenings after my classes I donned these and made my way to their offices in Cheyne Walk in Chelsea. From there I was transported by van to various locations all over London that needed guarding over the weekend. Office blocks, factories, arenas and warehouses.

I would work through the night, finishing at eight the next morning, and then have to find my own way home, often from the furthermost suburbs.

At each location I had to patrol through the night at regular times, carrying a strange clock/recorder on a strap around my shoulder. At various points along the journey there were special keys fixed by short chains to small boxes on the wall, and like the Stations of the Cross, one had to pause. I would then fit the keys into the recorder which "clocked" my timed progress around the building or site. This was proof positive that one was doing one's duty. I soon learned some of the regular guards' useful tricks. For instance in one large City skyscraper – a spooky place in the dead of night – the trick was to unclip all the keys on one's first 'round', take them back to the rest room, and then spend the rest of the night dozing, interspersed with regular but measured turning of the keys in the comfort of a warm room.

I had concluded very early on that if I was ever to meet any intruders or thieves in the dead of night in any of these venues, my immediate response would be, 'Take everything, but don't hurt me.' What did they expect for four pounds a week? My truncheon I usually left at home propping open the window. To pay my way, I did this job for nearly two years.

I remember doing a twenty-four-hour shift in a cosmetic factory on Christmas Day 1963. The extra money was still shite. At one or two locations I was given very specific instructions. Going to a large paint manufacturers one night I was carefully instructed to ignore the usual procedures if a fire broke out, i.e. phone headquarters and the fire brigade. They told me to flee the premises. Immediately. I don't think I dozed much that night. We had to phone HQ regularly throughout the night and if you were late in doing so an ominous call would come, implying that you had been asleep. The idea!

On one occasion, as I was about to leave home on a Friday evening, the office rang and asked me to ensure that I wore my cap that evening. I was to guard a huge railway siding in North London. When I arrived at the gate on a cold, wet winter's night, I was greeted by a huge two-metre tall snarling Alsatian dog. The departing Securicor man informed me that the beast would savage anyone without headgear. I was then left to guard the area, with its slippery tracks, its oily sleepers, its dozens of long dark wagons on rusty wheels, all surrounded by high barbed wire fences. As I patrolled through the cold night with the creature constantly pulling on its short leash, I felt like one of the prison guards in Billy Wilder's *Stalag 17*. Of course this was as nothing compared to the waste paper wharf in Battersea where, at four in the morning, while inching my way along a narrow, dark ledge to reach a key – the Thames lapping perilously close below my feet on one side and vast mountains of paper on the other – I was assaulted by a number of screeching feral cats. At this venue I was cheerfully informed that the vast columns of compressed paper were sometimes prone to spontaneous combustion.

During the term breaks at Guildhall I took on full-time

work to raise the next term's fees. I helped a man with a truck deliver building materials. My only abiding memory of him was his ability to spit on a regular basis throughout the day at twenty-second intervals. I sold ice creams in Hyde Park. At the Fortune Theatre I sold programmes and ushered at performances by the second cast of *Beyond The Fringe* – a famously successful sketch show originally played and written by Alan Bennett, Jonathan Miller, Peter Cook and Dudley Moore. Every night I guffawed loudly through this very funny show. I can remember a very funny pastiche of a Shakespeare history play with the actors in 'chainmail', i.e. their sweaters pulled up over their heads, their faces poking through the hole.

> *"Jonathan Miller: Get thee to Gloucester, Essex. Go thee to Wessex, Exeter.*
> *Fair Albany to Somerset must eke his route,*
> *And Scroup do you to Westmoreland, where shall bold York*
> *Enrouted now for Lancaster, with forces of our Uncle Rutland*
> *Enjoin his standard with sweet Norfolk's host.*
> *Fair Sussex, get thee to Warwicksbourne..."*
> *And on it went for some time... finally he finished...*
> *"I most royally shall now to bed*
> *To sleep off all the nonsense I've just said."*

But the most interesting job I had in 1963 was at the Mecca Ballroom just off the Strand in Wellington Street. This fine cream-painted building with its impressive six-pillared portico was later restored and reconverted to its original use and title as the Lyceum Theatre. It is now, and has been for many years, home to the musical *The Lion King*.

Sir Henry Irving, the great actor-manager and first knight of the British theatre ran this building in the late nineteenth century with an Irishman, Bram Stoker (the renowned author of *Dracula*) as his manager. Irving played *Hamlet* here, as well as the famous Victorian melodrama *The Bells*. He engaged Ellen Terry as a co-star for that entire period of twenty-four years. It was closed as a theatre in 1939 and after many threats to demolish it, followed by years of neglect, it was transformed into a Mecca Ballroom in 1951. The seating in the stalls was ripped out and a big dance floor installed. Over the stage rich red velvet curtains were swagged to conceal the flytower above. Each member of the various dance bands played behind a fancy music stand with the initials or the name of the band painted on them. Each band was "fronted" by a sharp-suited band leader along with gloriously coiffed and bedizened male and female singers. The venue was enormously popular, the floor crowded every night with hundreds of smiling and swaying couples. Grand curving stairs by the proscenium arch led customers up to the "circle" where they could sit and drink and watch the dancing.

A tall, bustling, beady Irishwoman called Mrs Kelly employed me to wash glasses behind the long bar, which ran the length of what would now be the back of the stalls. Two highlights stand out from my time there.

The first was the night when the 1963 Miss World Contest was held, and filmed for television, at the Lyceum. This strange pageant later went on to become an enormously popular spectacle, watched on British television by twenty-seven million people at its peak in the seventies and eighties, and by billions round the world. Now, in these more enlightened times, it seems to have disappeared or perhaps is still staged in some less sexually-liberated foreign clime for cable TV. On that exciting evening, Mrs Kelly entrusted me with a serious responsibility. My task was to take large trays of soft drinks backstage to the thirsty competitors. I would have worked without pay to do this, though naturally I did not say so to the Catholic Mrs K. I still have a fond and sweaty remembrance of my time backstage with these gorgeous, exotic and lightly clad girls from all corners of the globe. Keeping the tray from trembling became a major problem.

It was my first experience of international glamour, if I discount the night I spent as a Securicor guard for The Beatles at Wembley Arena. I had to patrol outside the building and despite all efforts only caught a fleeting glimpse of the fab four at the back of the arena as they were hastily bundled into a van and rushed off into the night, leaving me behind to guard their equipment until eight the next morning.

The second highlight during my time at the Lyceum was a sad occasion. On Saturday 23rd November 1963 after a long shift I left the ballroom in the early morning. I remember that my feet ached and I took my shoes off as I turned into the Strand and walked down the long road towards Trafalgar Square to get my bus home to Pimlico. Passing a newsagent, the front pages of all the morning newspapers suddenly made me stop. "Kennedy shot". The *Guardian*, a large broadsheet publication in those days, had a long, black, underlined headline: "President Kennedy Assasinated". Below it, a photograph of the rear of the limousine carrying the President, showed a dark-suited FBI man on the back bumper reaching forward. In front of him Jackie Kennedy, in what we found out later was a pink suit and pill-box hat, leaned over the fatally injured President. This was obviously a tremendous shock. The Irish/Kennedy Family connection was very strong in those days. Indeed my brother Peter had shaken hands with the President's brother Robert in Limerick not long before.

GUILDHALL SCHOOL OF MUSIC AND DRAMA

'Drama school, in London, in the swinging sixties, how exciting!' people said years later. Well, apart from listening to the music, it passed me by. I was too busy trying to make ends meet. Mind you, the music was great. Obviously there were The Beatles and The Rolling Stones. There was Martha and The Vandellas, The Drifters, The Supremes, The Chiffons, Johnny Cash and The Beach Boys. And of course, we mustn't forget Rolf Harris, The Singing Nun, and from Ireland, The Bachelors. God help us.

The Guildhall School was a large impressive building in John Carpenter Street, just down the hill from Fleet Street towards the river. Built in the 1880s it had seriousness written all over it. Dozens of Ionic and Corinthian pillasters, oriole windows, stone urns, brownstone plaques decorated with musical instruments and laurel wreaths covered its surfaces. Above the theatre exits were five plaques with the names and dates of famous British composers – Tallis, Gibbons, Arne, and Sterndale Bennett. The main entrance was approached up a flight of steps between two fluted stone pillars. Carved over the doors in ornate script the words: The Guildhall School Of Music. Originally conceived as a music school, it later added departments of Speech, Voice and Acting. In 1935 it added "and Drama" to its title. Unfortunately they never altered the wording over the entrance, or compensated by installing some new plaques of famous actors. In my time there, which I really enjoyed, I felt that drama was looked on as the lesser art. It still felt and sounded like a music school. Today the Guildhall School is housed in an impressive complex at the Barbican. The old school now houses an American bank – JP Morgan. Surprisingly, the bank's name is nowhere to be seen on the outside of the building. The place looks lifeless and silent. Ominous, even.

The acting course lasted two years. Today, with the demise of most of the provincial repertory theatres, the drama schools, of which there are now many more than in my time, offer a three year course. The final year is almost exclusively devoted to staging productions. This is to replace the experience that we earlier students got in rep in the sixties. Some of the classes we attended will now sound old and fusty. Choral Speaking with Rona Laurie, Period Movement with Margaret Wildblood, Mime with Ambrose Marriott, Microphone Technique with Rowland Hill and Make-up with Margaret Leonard. In the sixties, theatre lighting was still fairly primitive, and in Miss Leonard's class we would learn to cake ourselves with long sticks of Leichner make-up. These were all numbered. The most popular "base" we put on was five and nine. Five was a creamy yellow colour, nine a rich terracotta. The blending of these two gave us, we were told, a "natural" look. On top of this base we added fine lines and shadings of brown and "lake" around the forehead, eyes and nose when we played character parts. I still do not know to this day why a stick of crimson make-up was called "lake". The sticks of Leichner were notoriously hard and difficult to spread. In winter months we applied the base in stripes and then had to slap our cheeks and foreheads to blend and give ourselves an even colour. Hence the nickname for make-up – "slap". In theatre dressing rooms the hot bulbs surrounding the actors' mirrors were often streaked with five and nine, which helped to soften the stuff. Nowadays there are no make-up classes and Leichner products seem to have disappeared. Young actors marvel or jeer at us older players who still, in certain situations, apply some make-up.

For Movement we decamped to St. Bride's Institute nearby. This was, and still is, a fine redbrick warren of rooms and halls. Our Movement teacher was called Andrew Rolla. He had long blonde hair, a permanent tan and took classes in tight T-shirts, white leather shorts and loafers. He was a tremendous show-off with famous phrases that galvanised us into action – 'Round and round and up and down and flopsy-flopsy, people!' I had never met anyone like him in Ireland. He was terrific.

Next to the Institute was the journalists' church dedicated to St Bride, or really St Bridget of Kildare, a fifth-century Irish saint. Designed by Sir Christopher Wren in 1673 this is a beautiful building whose spire is the model for the now traditional tiered wedding cake, first made by a baker on Ludgate Hill in the eighteenth century. Sometimes I took my lunch in the churchyard close to where John Milton had lived. Samuel Pepys and all his brothers and sisters were baptised here. Samuel Richardson, Izaak Walton, John Dryden, John Evelyn the great diarist, Dr. Johnson and Charles Dickens were all parishioners of St. Bride's. Just up the road past Hanging Sword Alley in the Inns of Court was Middle Temple Hall where, on the Feast of Candlemas in 1602, the first recorded performance of *Twelfth Night* was played. There's a bit of Wikipedia history for you.

Yards away was Fleet Street. In the sixties, it was the centre for newspaper and periodical publications. Here were the offices and nearby the printing presses of the *Telegraph*, *The Times* and the *Daily Mail*. On the way to and from classes we would pass these buildings and hear the loud rumbling roar of the presses inside.

The plays we performed at Guildhall were usually chosen because of their large casts. *The Provok'd Wife* by Vanbrugh, John Arden's *The Workhouse Donkey*, J.B. Priestley's 1939 play *Johnson over Jordan*, John Van Druten's 1951 piece *I Am A Camera* – an adaptation of Christopher Isherwood's novel *Goodbye to Berlin,* which eventually was made into the musical *Cabaret.* An interesting point about that production in 1964. The student Paul Greenwood was playing Christopher, who becomes friends with the delicious Sally Bowles. In rehearsal one day Paul declared that in his opinion his character was a homosexual. As one, every student in the room ridiculed the suggestion, saying that the man was blatantly in love with Sally. Our knowledge of the gay world at that time was still sadly limited.

In between the classes and productions, we had lots of parties, when you could end up in someone's flat in some far-flung suburb, drunk on Watney's Red Barrel, a truly terrible bitter. You could buy a large six-pint container of this product at no great price. People used to say, 'Don't take the piss out of Watney's – they need all the flavour they can get.' Also at that time a new and exciting tipple came to these shores. Wine. Britain was reaching for European sophistication. We were introduced to Mateus Rose, Blue Nun, Black Tower, and Neirsteiner Domtal. Our innocent tastebuds were assaulted by the cheapest and foulest plonk imported from the continent. Many hours later, slaked on the booze, the crazed dancing, the smooching, the sublime sixties' music blaring out of the large record player and with the last tube gone, one could end up sleeping in the bath. Or worse still, awake and addled at five in the morning, digging for one's coat on someone's bed and heading off cold and forlorn for the first tube of the morning. Golden days.

A new and very welcome arrival at Guildhall in 1964 was Charles Marowitz who came to teach us for a term. He was a tall, very articulate New Yorker with a dramatic black quiff, piercing eyes, a dark moustache and goatee. He looked like the Devil. Unlike all of our other teachers Charles was young. I would guess about thirty. He also came from working in the professional theatre, a rare occurrence in sixties drama schools. He had just been assistant director on Peter Brook's now legendary production of *King Lear* with the great Paul Scofield – who I would work with in the coming years. Marowitz was founder/director with Thelma Holt of the small, but highly influential Open Space Theatre in Tottenham Court Road, salubriously placed next to a couple of sex cinemas. Thelma, was then a very talented actor. Their theatre did very original and provocative work. Marowitz wrote and directed deconstructed "collage" productions of Shakespeare. He was influenced by Artaud and Grotowski. He was the first person in England to introduce what we now term "site specific" productions. His show *Exit Music* began with the audience being denied seats in the theatre, then ushered out onto a bus with darkened windows, which then travelled through parts of the city, where at specific stops pre-arranged "events" took place. Marowitz felt that theatre taken out of "playhouses" and into unexpected locations could help the art form grow exponentially. New and unique sensations could be experienced both by audiences and by actors.

He soon got us jumping. He asked us to split up, gave us five minutes each to invent a "character", then put us in couples to improvise and create conflicts, dramas, life or death situations, which we then had to talk our way out of. During these he would come and whisper contradictory instructions and on the command of, 'Change Gear!' we were expected to turn on a penny and skitter off on a new and different tack. Sometimes he would introduce a third "character" to the scene who might take it in a totally new direction. The work was wonderfully freeing, very exciting and fresh.

In an article at that time Marowitz wrote two parallel columns on the "two breeds of actors in English theatre today". It was the sixties, so he of course divided them into square and hip. Here's a small sample:

SQUARE:
Let's get it plotted
Fix inflections and "readings"

Set moves as soon as possible
Tell me what to do
My many years of professional experience convince me that…
At this moment I will play fear
HIP:
Let's get it analysed
Play for sense and let inflections take care of themselves
Move freely for as long as possible
Tell me what you want
Nothing is ever the same
At this moment I will play actions resulting in fear
"The really good actors defy all classifications, and exemplify the hip attributes even when their background has been square".

This new and inventive energy that Marowitz brought may have been a contributory factor to a stabbing in one of our productions. In a dress rehearsal of *The White Devil* two actors had to fight with rapiers. Unfortunately, one of them got emotionally carried away and in a very quick sequence of moves managed to stab his opponent three times in the chest. Bright blood appeared on the actor's ornate white shirt. Proceedings came to a sudden halt. The "dress" was cancelled, the actor, Sean Arnold, was whisked off to hospital. The perpetrator was mortified. Next evening the production's director, one of our teachers, Edward Argent, took over the role of Flamineo. With his long hair and raffish beard, and even with the "book" in his hand, he gave a very good performance. I think secretly the man would have preferred acting to teaching. Sean Arnold recovered quickly.

SIR LAURENCE OLIVIER

Sir Laurence Olivier was appointed artistic director of the new Chichester Festival Theatre in 1962 and ran it until 1965. He gathered together a company of actors, directors and designers and initiated a summer season of three plays. The plays in the first season were *Uncle Vanya* by Anton Chekhov, *The Broken Heart*, a Jacobean tragedy by John Ford, and *The Chances,* a Jacobean comedy by John Fletcher. In the next three seasons he added, among others, Shaw's *St Joan*, Shaffer's *Royal Hunt of the Sun*, Shakespeare's *Othello*, Arden's *Armstrong's Last Goodnight,* and Strindberg's *Miss Julie.*

In 1963, the Old Vic Company was dissolved and the new National Theatre Company moved into the Old Vic on the Waterloo Road. It was a momentous and long-awaited occasion. As far back as 1848 the first proposal for a National Theatre was made. It was supported by such leading figures as Charles Dickens, the poet Matthew Arnold and the actors Charles Kemble and Sir Henry Irving. In 1908 there was a strong campaign supported by Bernard Shaw, Arthur Wing Pinero, Viscount Esher and Harley Granville Barker. These efforts were swiftly followed by others in every decade right up until the sixties.

On 22nd October 1963 the National Theatre, with Sir Laurence as director, opened with his production of *Hamlet* with Peter O'Toole. This was quickly followed eight days later with *St Joan* directed by John Dexter with Joan Plowright. On 19th November, *Uncle Vanya,* directed by Olivier, opened and on 10th December Farquar's *The Recruiting Officer* followed, directed by William Gaskill. You will have noticed that some of these productions had started at Chichester.

Whilst at the Guildhall I had the good fortune to see some of these productions from the wooden benches in the Old Vic gallery, for the princely sum of three shillings (fifteen pence). I will never forget Bill Gaskill's groundbreaking, cobweb-scattering production of *The Recruiting Officer* with Maggie Smith, Robert Stephens, Colin Blakely, Lynn Redgrave, and with Sir Laurence playing Captain Brazen. At every meeting of Olivier and Stephens, the two captains kissed each other warmly on the lips. Olivier's Brazen, not the brightest of characters, had "stupid" eyes; I don't know how else to describe them, they seemed to be eternally out of focus. He was very, very funny. The scene where Maggie Smith, disguised as a raffish officer complete with jaunty moustache, has to cope with the advances of Lynn Redgrave's country wench was equally funny. This production finally put to the sword all the mannered bowing, handkerchief-flapping and general anaemic playing that had plagued Restoration comedy productions in previous decades. When characters came on, having ridden across country, their boots and coats were muddied. The farm labourers, recruiting fodder, were bone-weary after a hard day's work in the fields. The women were red-blooded, proactive and sexy. No smelling salts for them. Fabulous!

John Dexter's astonishing production of *The Royal Hunt of the Sun* was equally memorable – epic and grandiose. Set in Peru, dealing with pride, empire and the clash of civilisations it centred on the meeting of the sixteenth-century Sun God King, Atahualpa and the Spanish Conquistador Pizarro. There was a famous stage direction: "They cross the Andes". Dexter, with blazing imagination, staged this wordless scene magnificently. I remember the invading soldiers' armour growing rusty in the rich humid air. During the big massacre scene, two soldiers came to a point at the front of the stage, reached down, grabbed something and ran upstage spreading out as they went. Behind them appeared a large blood-red silk cloth, billowing and enveloping the killing scene. It was an amazing and truly theatrical moment, just one among many in that fine piece of work. Robert Stephens and Colin Blakely were unforgettable as the two protagonists. In the smaller roles – Michael Gambon, Anthony Hopkins and Derek Jacobi.

I had a piece of luck in April 1964. From drama school I was summoned to the Old Vic to meet the well-known film and theatre director Lindsay Anderson. The NT was sending out its first tour and did not have enough actors to play the small roles in one of the productions remaining at the Vic, *Andorra* by Max Frisch. A number of students were chosen from the major drama schools to meet Lindsay Anderson. He would choose a few to appear as soldiers in the play. Anderson was an imposing, sharp, flinty character. He asked me about myself. After a few sentences of my Irish accent he asked me where I came from. I was familiar with his film work, so I replied, 'Limerick – where Richard Harris comes from.' Harris was a well-known Limerick character from a little before my time. His family owned a flour mill and lived in a large house on the Ennis Road. He was locally admired for both his rugby talent and for various mad stunts and scrapes he got himself into. Now, in London, he was fast making a name for himself as a very good film actor. He was starring in Anderson's new and very successful film, *This Sporting Life,* about a rugby-playing Northern working-class tearaway. Both Anderson and Harris had a huge success with this film.

Anyway, I was chosen for the play. All I had to do was stand around in uniform holding a rifle. For many years after I would think fondly of Lindsay Anderson and how he helped contribute artistically and financially to my theatrical education.

I have two memories from that short job. Rehearsing onstage one day on the set of *Andorra,* I noticed a tall, impressive man, wearing an expensive three-piece suit and horn-rimmed glasses, stroll casually down the centre aisle of the Vic. *Golly,* I thought, *people seem to be able to just walk in off the street.* It was not until I noticed the other actors "freeze" around me that I took another look and realised that the visitor was Sir Laurence Olivier, the most famous actor in the world. He exuded a general air of beneficence, smiled at us all, had a word with Lindsay and sauntered off backstage.

The second memory was a casual invitation from the company manager a couple of weeks later. 'Would you like to come and see the dress rehearsal of *Othello* on Wednesday?' The production was to open to the press the following day, the 400th anniversary of Shakespeare's birth. *Would I like to? Would I like to be one of the first people in London to see Sir Laurence play Othello?* I'd have eaten my face for the chance.

There are interesting stories of the preparations Olivier made for this production. Orson Welles, when told of Sir Laurence's intention of playing The Moor, rumbled, 'Larry's a natural tenor and Othello is a natural baritone.' I doubt Sir Laurence needed to be reminded of this. Once the production was planned he worked for many weeks on lowering his voice. Soon it was an octave lower. He also took himself down to the Old Vic basement where the housekeeper, Harry Henderson, kept some bodybuilding equipment. Gyms were hard to find in those pre-body-conscious days of the sixties. Harry was a powerful, impressively muscled figure with grey crinkly hair and a narrow military moustache. There, Sir Laurence worked on fitness and the shaping of his body. I presume his intention was not to be a heavily-clothed Othello, with only "black" face and hands showing, which was the way many white actors (and nearly all Othello's were white in those days) played the part. I was right. This Othello showed a lot of flesh.

The first black actor to play Othello in England, in 1826, was an American, Ira Aldridge, who was unable to pursue an acting career at home. He also performed the conventional white roles of Macbeth and King Lear, for which he bizarrely "whited up". The first black actor to play Othello in Stratford after the American singer and actor Paul Robeson in 1959, was the English born Ray Fearon in 1999.

At the first day's rehearsal of a play, actors usually give a subdued reading, concentrating on making sense of the text. At the first read-through of *Othello* at the Old Vic in 1964, Olivier, bespectacled and lounge-suited, launched into a full-blooded high-octane reading of the role that stunned the room. Iago, the much larger role, is usually seen as the more interesting character in *Othello* and can dominate the production. Olivier was putting down a marker. This was going to be *his* play, the most important character in the tragedy was the man named in the title.

There is a story that Sir Laurence suggested to Maggie Smith, playing Desdemona in her first Shakespearean role, that she needed to work on her vowels, on the natural drawl of her voice.

One evening, early on in the run, Sir Laurence was being made up in his dressing room, a process that took an hour, as the dark brown make-up had to be applied to most of his body and then "polished". Miss Smith strolled in, caught his eye in the large mirror and enunciated beautifully, 'How now, brown cow?'

In the small dress rehearsal audience at the Old Vic I sat in a very good seat for John Dexter's production. Sir Laurence, Maggie Smith, Frank Finlay as Iago, Derek Jacobi as Cassio, Joyce Redman as Emilia, Robert Lang, Sheila Reid, Kenneth Mackintosh, Anthony Nicholls, Edward Hardwick – a very fine cast. Othello's first entrance was breathtaking. Olivier entered upstage, not a Moor but a dark-skinned African. His "black" skin highlighted by his costume, a long belted white cotton robe, slit at both sides to the thigh. He wore a tightly curled black wig with some grey in it. He looked magnificent. He padded downstage, barefooted, smiling shyly, sniffing and toying with a long-stemmed red rose. "Keep up your bright swords, for the dew will rust them" – delivered affably and underplayed.

In the Senate scene Othello wore a crucifix around his neck and, when rebuked by Brabantio for using witchcraft to win his daughter Olivier, crossed himself – a Christian convert. Then having taken great pride in the retelling of his adventures and their effect on Desdemona – "This only is the witchcraft I have used" – Olivier isolated the word "witchcraft" and pointedly eyed her father.

Fifty years later my memory is not so good, but I remember on "Villian, be sure thou prove my love a whore" Othello grabbed Iago by the throat and threatened him with a knife blade concealed in a thick bracelet on his arm. Later he used the same blade to slit his own throat after the death of Desdemona.

In the final scene of the tragedy Olivier went into fifth gear. The anger, the anguish, and the powerful physicality were overwhelming. Although mesmerising, I was not moved by this. Until suddenly, on the bed with Desdemona's body in his arms he spoke his final lines with great simplicity

"... I pray you, in your letters,
When you shall these unlucky deeds relate,
Speak of me as I am; nothing extenuate,
Nor set down aught in malice: then must you speak
Of one that lov'd not wisely, but too well
Of one not easily jealous, but, being wrought,
Perplex'd in the extreme..."

This I found deeply affecting.

Lying dead, with the final lines being said over him, I was aware that I had seen a "great" performance. A performance full of passion and swirling emotions with fearsome, almost frightening power. At other moments there was humour, tenderness and love; the contrasts alternated with feathery lightness and technical dexterity. A shapeshifting performance like Sir Laurence's, where the actor transforms himself and makes vocal and physical alterations to create a role, was intensely exciting to watch.

Olivier's Othello was every bit the hardened soldier, but

also with his sagging leather belts, the aging lion – "declined into the vale of years". Sir Laurence was fifty-seven that year. The age difference between Olivier and Smith was twenty-seven years. An older man with a much younger wife, in certain circumstances, would be prone to suggestions that she might be attracted to a younger man. It makes the jealousy painfully believable. Most black actors playing the role in recent years have in my opinion been a little young. Although this will change as some of them return to the part in later years.

* * *

In my second year at Guildhall, the work of drama student by day and security guard and bottle-washer by night, began to take its toll. I was constantly worried about money – mostly about how to lay my hands on some. I became physically run down and lost a fair bit of weight. Then something wonderful happened. I don't know how or who, but, I suspect one of my fellow students or perhaps one of the teachers had a word with the school and I was called to the Principal's office. His name was Eric Capon and after some enquiries about my circumstances, informed me that the school had decided to waive the final two terms' fees as a sort of scholarship. This was a tremendous relief to me. Things were looking up.

At the end of recounting my Guildhall days, I would like to pay a special tribute to four people. Three were fellow students. The first and most important was a beautiful girl, Jackie Brandon, who joined the teachers' course and soon became my girlfriend. Jackie, through her love and unstinting support, got me through the hard times in those two years. She lived in Brixton with her mother, the equally beautiful, redoubtable, Jamaican matriarch Olga. I was welcomed into their home with warmth and affection, and plied with exotic jerk chicken, with saltfish and ackee, with plaintain, breadfruit, rice and peas and fine Appleton Estate rum. They opened my eyes to a whole new life. Happy days.

The two other fellow students were Ray Hardy, sadly now no longer with us, and Sean Arnold, who I mention above. Ray and Sean held me up like scaffolding during my many hard days, befriended me, even fed me when money was short.

With the help, the love and support of these four, kind, wonderful people I sailed forward.

MY FIRST YEAR IN THE BUSINESS

At the end of the penultimate term, something seemingly small happened that was eventually to have a big impact on my life. I was interviewed by a director named Donald MacKechnie who was running a repertory company in Barrow in Furness. Yes, Barrow in Furness, in Lancashire. He offered me a year's contract. Although I would miss the final Guildhall term I immediately accepted. This turned out to be one of the most important decisions of my entire acting career.

Donald had a strong face, slightly beady eyes, a small mouth, a Karl Malden nose and a receding hairline. He was sharp as a razor. He rarely stood still. I liked him very much. He offered me a season's work as an acting ASM. This position in the theatre now no longer exists. The job comprised both acting small roles and doing other duties as an assistant stage manager, an ASM. I was to be paid eight pounds and ten shillings a week. No rent or subsistance. Eight pounds and ten shillings, full stop. Now, in the early sixties actors *had* to be a member of the union, and equity cards were rationed and difficult to get hold of. Numbers were restricted. Equity stipulated that a young actor had to join the union and do forty weeks of work in the provinces, as a form of apprenticeship, before he could become a full member. Therefore some reps had it in their gift to offer a few cards to new young actors. Having been offered a year's contract at Barrow I immediately became a provisional member of the union and the proud possessor of an equity card. This meant that at the end of my contract I would have the right to work in the West End and television. Nowadays you can appear in the West End or on television at the drop of a hat, union membership is no longer required. Be the third runner-up in a TV talent show and you might well find yourself starring in a major London musical within weeks.

The rise in popularity of television through the fifties and sixties was a huge blow to British theatre. In the fifties alone a hundred theatres closed around the country.

Barrow, until that year, 1965, had been a "weekly rep". This meant that the theatre presented a new production every week. And with the same small group of actors. So, having opened a new show on Monday night, the next play started rehearsals on Tuesday morning. Usually the season consisted of productions of post-West End hits along

94

with, if affordable, one or two more adventurous projects chosen by the director. But the standard fare was usually light comedies, usually set in a house, and usually played in a box set. A "box set" means three walls with windows, doors etc. and the proscenium arch as the "fourth" wall. The plays usually had three acts. So Tuesday morning the first act was "blocked" – the stage management marked out the outlines of the set, provided vaguely appropriate furniture and substitute props. The director then blocked Act One. He told the actors where to enter and exit, as well as dictated moves that took place within the action. Tuesday afternoon, the actors went back to their digs and learnt Act One and then in the evening did a performance of last week's play. Wednesday the same thing happened with Act Two. Thursday, Act Three. Not much time for character development or Stanislavskian discussion. Friday they ran the play. Saturday morning a little time for more work, followed by a matinee and evening show of last week's production.

All actors in those days had to sign what was called the Esher Standard Contract. This stipulated, among other things, that each actor had to provide from his own wardrobe certain items of personal clothing, which included a dinner suit, a couple of lounge suits, plus various other items of modern clothing. These would be transported in a large wicker "skip". The management were to provide any "period" clothing. Mind you, I never met a single actor who had a skip, let alone one who provided any suits. How could we? We were penniless.

So, that April, I travelled north in a train, which seemed to take all day, to reach Barrow in Furness. The *Daily*

Telegraph called it "the farthest flung rep in the British Empire". Barrow is an industrial town and seaport on the Furness Peninsula bounded by Morecambe Bay and the Irish Sea, and is 220 miles from London. Barrow Central Station featured in the railway series books *Thomas The Tank Engine* by Rev. W Awdry as the mainland terminus for the Fat Controller's North-Western Railway. Thought you'd like to know that. The town had a population then of about 75,000 souls. It had been a shipbuilding port from 1852 when it launched its first ship, the *Jane Roper*. In 1960 the UK's first nuclear submarine, the HMS *Dreadnought*, was launched there. Subsequently all of Britain's Vanguard-class submarines, which carry the Trident nuclear deterrent, were manufactured in Barrow. A bit more Wikipedia for you.

My abiding memories of the town are of the huge red sandstone town hall in the Modern Gothic style with its high clock tower; the Odeon cinema where we were given free entry on every second Sunday – that's if we weren't working; The Copper Kettle, which did a mean poached eggs on toast; and of course, the theatre designed by the great Victorian theatre architect Frank Matcham. Matcham theatres with their magical interiors, are much loved by actors. They all have proscenium arch stages and velvet curtains. The auditoria are horseshoe-shaped with most surfaces heavily and romantically decorated. The fronts of the curving circles and balconies are studded with angels, putti, garlands of flowers, masks of comedy and tragedy etc. in plasterwork. Fantastical ceilings with ornate chandeliers look down on all of this. But most importantly, for the actor, the acoustics in these theatres, produced by the curved and enveloping auditoria along with the wealth of wood and plaster, was astonishing. It brought great clarity and warm true tones to the actors' voices. Between 1890 and 1915, Matcham designed over eighty theatres. Each was unique. Many are still with us: the London Palladium, Hackney Empire, London Coliseum, Richmond Theatre in Surrey, Buxton Opera House, Theatre Royal, Newcastle.

Later, in the new brick-and-concrete theatres of the 1970s, many an actor had a strong and depressing shock when moving from the intimacy of the rehearsal room to the stage. The bare brick and concrete interiors swallowed up the voice, making it sound flat and reedy. All the warmth gone. Instant adjustment had to be made. In fact, some actors' performances really suffered when they moved into these new spaces. They certainly had to work harder. A strong diaphragm was an asset. The Olivier Theatre at the National is famously difficult and enhances the sound quality in the auditorium with discreetly placed speakers.

Her Majesty's Theatre, Barrow was, at first view, most unprepossessing. The exterior was very plain. It was situated in a side street where some of the surrounding buildings had been demolished. But the name of the road, Hope Street, warmed the heart. On entering the auditorium my spirits rose. The interior was classic Matcham: not large, but a little gem and ornamented with stunning plasterwork. There were three levels: stalls, circle and gallery. The gallery was somewhat run down and not open to the public – it was used to store the costumes. The safety curtain was handpainted with various advertisements for local businesses.

In 1965, a time of theatrical closures and cutbacks, the

Barrow theatre had managed to buck the trend and expand from weekly to fortnightly rep. This was a tremendous achievement and I was about to benefit directly. I had the luxury of joining the company for its first season of fortnightly rep. Two weeks in which to mount a play. What luxury – though a long way from the twenty-five weeks rehearsal we had for *The Oresteia* with Peter Hall at the National Theatre in 1981.

The Renaissance Theatre Company was small and run on a very tight budget. Modest grants were provided by the Arts Council and the local Barrow Council and these, along with the box-office takings, were what we had to survive on. The whole caboodle –actors, director, stage management, electrician, box office, administration, designer, set builder and cleaners – amounted to fewer than twenty souls. The "company" comprised of the director, Donald MacKechnie; the actors, whose numbers varied between eight and ten; and a designer, who was responsible for all the productions, painting the sets and running the wardrobe as well. There was a stage manager whose team was made up of two acting ASMs, myself being one. There was also a student ASM.

The acting company, though small, was extremely hierarchical and divided into rigid categories. There was Leading Man and Leading Lady, who for most of the productions played the major parts. Other categories included Character Actor and Character Actress, Juvenile Leads as well as Younger Characters. A publication called *Spotlight* published two huge glossy volumes of actors' photographs, with details of their agents (if they had one). These were purchased by theatres and casting directors. Each actor had to pay a fairly extravagant fee to have his picture included. I was in the Younger Character category.

The first show I did in Barrow was *Meet Me By Moonlight* – a play with music, which had been staged at the Aldwych Theatre in the West End in 1957. It was a Victorian comedy "with oodles of charm and some delightful songs of the period" and I played the part of a very upright and conventional butler. In those days I had thick black hair and, in an effort to look older for the role, I "aged up" with the application of make-up and some "grey" streaks on my temples. This was accomplished with a tin of Meltonian Tennis Shoe Whitener, an old toothbrush and a deal of spit. Then, in my tie and tails, I sallied forth with Osyth Devaney playing the maid, all black satin and starched linen, and together, as the velvet curtains rose on a "posh" Victorian drawing room, we sang the perky opening duet, a paean of praise to subservience. For some unknown and incomprehensible reason I can still forty-eight years later remember not only the opening couplet but the tune.

"You may think that nothing could be drearier,
Than to serve the socially superior –"

I suspect this tiny extract will give you some hint of the loyalty and love borne by working-class characters for their betters, at least in sentimental plays of the 1950s.

Obviously performing was what I most wanted to do. But I had to spend a lot of time in various productions doing stage management tasks, and these were many and varied. For *Meet Me By Moonlight* I had to compile a list of Victorian furniture needed for the production. I was then sent out to trawl all the antique and junk shops in the town, and endeavour, with "charm" and a promise to mention their establishments in the programme, to borrow said pieces for the two-week run.

The settings for most of the plays were, as I mentioned, box sets, ie. three walls of a room with various doors and windows. As the budget was miniscule, the designer, who also managed the wardrobe, had to use great ingenuity, varying these sets on a fortnightly basis. The "scene dock" was at the back of the building behind two tall wooden doors. This was run by the stage carpenter, a retired shipbuilder named Jack Pearson. There were stacks of timber, rolls of canvas, furniture, dozens of pots of paint, carpentry tools and so on. The abiding smell was of sawdust and the ever-warming bucket of "size" on a small gas burner. Size was very important. The walls of the sets were made of a number of tall narrow wooden frames called flats, approximately five metres high and one-and-a-quarter metres wide and no more than eight centimetres wide. These were then covered and tacked with a thick canvas. Then, in order to get the canvas tight, the flats were painted with the colourless and foul-smelling size, which shrank the material – ingenious. There were also door flats and window flats. All these were then, depending on the design, painted or wallpapered. We ASMs including our student ASM, Matthew Scurfield, who was paid even less than me, (four pounds a week), wielded the brushes.

Matthew had long hair and a most striking face with a large Roman nose worthy of any of the great Roman emperors. One evening, as he and I were walking in the town, we suddenly noticed five Teddy Boys approaching us. These must have been the last remnants of that 1950s subculture. Some Teds had been notorious for gang fights. This group was spread across the full width of the pavement, dressed in those long drape jackets with the curved velvet lapels, string ties, extremely narrow trousers and "brothel creepers" with thick crepe soles. The heavily Brylcreemed "duck's arse" hairstyles shone in the streetlight. They looked menacing.

Matthew slowed down and said, 'Let's cross the road.'

'Why?'I asked.

'Because,' he said, 'I've got the kind of face that people like to smash in!'

I thought this manoeuvre might show weakness in us. So, and with a suddenly dry mouth, I whispered an order: 'Sod this, we're actors. Stand tall, shoulders back – we're going right through the middle of them!'

And we did, and nothing happened. Of course they may well have been the nicest lads you could ever meet.

When the set was painted and ready, all the flats were brought onstage. Jack had attached long thin ropes to the top corner at the back of each flat and along the length had fixed at regular intervals small protruding brackets. Now, to build the walls Jack had to teach us "cleating". So, as one flat was put in place and the next one was placed tightly against it, we learned to take the rope attached to the top of one of the five-metre flats and, with a whipping motion, interlock it in a zigzag fashion on the brackets of the two flats, pulling it tight and knotting it at the bottom. As the flats conjoined and turned into a wall, we then had to steady the high structure with stage braces. These were made of two long, thin, expandable wooden struts with a steel hook at one end, which fitted into a protruding ring halfway up the back of the flat, and an iron "foot" with a hole in it at the other, which we fixed to the wooden stage floor with a long wide-handled stage screw. To get the wall to ninety degrees upright we could open the screw at the centre of the expandable brace and adjust the angle accordingly. It was hard and tricky work, especially if you had to come in on a Sunday to do it.

In that year 1965, the company produced twenty plays. I appeared in fifteen of them. My fellow actor, Lionel Guyett, appeared in all of them.

The day of the tech and dress rehearsal would go as follows: having got the set up and furnished on the Sunday, Donald, who directed nineteen of the productions, would also "do the lighting". There was no lighting designer in those days. Pre-computerised lighting equipment was very basic. Above the "prompt corner" where the stage manager ran and prompted the show, was the perch. This was a platform that one reached by climbing a rickety ladder. Confronting you when you ascended, was the rig, professionally titled "The Dimmer Bank", which looked like a long-discarded but once vital part of Dr Frankenstein's laboratory – a huge piece of machinery almost three metres long and two metres high. It had complicated metal parts and a multitude of cogs and wheels connected to thick electric cables. Along the front were five metal pipes with a number of large adjustable porcelain handles along their length. At the end of the rig was a large metal wheel. Donald lit every show, climbing up long precarious ladders on stage and adjusting each lamp separately. He would then call out the lamp numbers to the electrician, who would make a note of each one and then turn them on. So with a few minor adjustments the setting for the first scene would be lit. Then the porcelain handles, connected in a complicated way to these lamps, would be turned and locked. This then allowed the electrician to go to the end of the rig and turn a large wheel which would bring up or bring down all the lamps in that particular lighting state. For the next lighting state the same procedure had to be started again. More lamps chosen, locked on and the wheel turned again. So throughout the tech, and every performance, the electrician was locking, unlocking and adjusting about thirty lamps. Modern theatres with computerised systems can now do all this in a second with maybe two hundred lamps. If during the show there was a particularly fast or complicated change I would hare up the ladder in costume and help out, locking the hot handles. If a "fade" or "slow blackout" was required I would slowly turn the large wheel counting the five seconds silently in my head as the bulbs dimmed.

If not holding the ladder for the designer as he hung pictures on the set, I would be arranging all the off-stage props on tables in the stage right and stage left wings: trays with teacups or whisky and sodas, a gun, various documents, newspapers, bunches of flowers, an umbrella, a stack of leather-bound books, rosary beads. Characters smoked a lot in plays at that time and the theatre would be supplied with 200 free cigarettes each week. "by courtesy of John Player & Sons". Needless to say the actors took full advantage of this free gift. Sweeping and mopping the stage was also high on my long list of jobs.

If a tech took too long the dress rehearsal could suffer. On one particular play we were so late starting the dress that we had to finish Act Three with the safety curtain and tabs in, speaking very quietly as the hum of the arriving audience grew in volume. Once finished we arranged a swift curtain call and then scrambled about to reset furniture and props, do costume changes and be ready to face our public in five minutes.

The actor Edward Petherbridge topped this by telling me of a rep production he appeared in, where in a dress rehearsal, again with the audience arriving and the safety curtain deployed, they had to do Act Three of the play on the Act One set as there would have been insufficient time to do the changes required.

During a performance of the Agatha Christie play *Love From A Stranger* in which I had scene changes to help with, actors to assist with "quick changes" and tea to make for Act Two, I had to find time to play an old country gardener. This character I decided should have a rich ruddy complexion. Being only twenty-four I decided to grey my hair, as well as wear a grey moustache. A Character Actor, I. To save time I decided to wear a large tweed cap for this one-scene cameo. I could then get away with only partly-Meltonianing my hair and need only make up the lower half of my forehead. Brilliant. So, at one performance, having just completed some prop setting, I stood in the prompt corner by the door awaiting my entrance. The stage manager standing next to me whispered, 'Where's your cap?' – Bollocks! A forehead half red, half white. A head of hair half black, half white. Total panic. 'I'll get it,' she whispered and ran up the stairs to the dressing rooms.

My cue arrived. The scene necessitated my knocking on the door of the drawing room and calling, 'It's me, Hodgson.' To which Patricia Doyle, playing the lady of the house replies, 'O, come in, Mr Hodgson.' In my hand a large bunch of flowers I have brought from her lovely garden. I should now enter. Instead I call.

'I've brought the crysianthemums, Mum.' (Note the working-class mispronouncation.)

'Oh, good!' comes the voice with a more than slightly quizzical tone.

'What shall I do with them?'

'Please bring them in, Mr Hodgson'.

Suddenly I have a brilliant idea. I rattle the door handle loudly.

'O'im havin' a bit of a problem with the door,' I call.

'Let me help you,' she calls, and I listen to her steps approach. I grab the handle, just before she does. We tussle for supremacy. Then as the handle comes off in my hand two things happen. The door opens wide and from behind me the breathless stage manager plops my cap on my head and I saunter through the door.

'Here they be, Mum,' I say and am confronted with a wide–mouthed stare from the relieved Miss Doyle. After this tiny hiccup we played the scene – rather well, I thought.

Among the plays I appeared in was a Brian Rix, Whitehall farce called *One For The Pot*. In a review from the Barrow *Evening Mail* dated 18th May 1965 the headline was:

EXTRA REHEARSING TIME PAYS OFF

"Whether having plays running for two weeks is a venture destined to succeed comercially remains to be seen. But the presentation of One For The Pot *proves director Donald Mac*

105

Kechnie's point that the departure from the long-familiar weekly productions provides more rehearsal time and makes the attainment of a higher theatrical standard possible."

In the fiendishly complicated plot of this play, the actor Chris Winnera had to play a pair of identical twins. Tricky, as you can imagine. But then, a third identical brother is introduced. In the final moments of the play a *fourth* arrives unexpectedly. Four identical quadruplets, with one family name and one ambition – to inherit £10,000. There was much slapstick, sleight of hand and, most importantly, ingenious set design. For instance, in the middle of a physical tussle with another actor dressed identically as one or other of the brothers, the fighting took place around and behind a large sofa. This allowed Chris to slide out through a low unseen flap on the back wall and as the 'tussle' went on, to run around backstage, change costume, and enter through the door with much casual ease as yet another brother. I can't remember, but presume that this occurred at the end of an act.

In the same play there was an actor called Colin Kay. As a young man he was diagnosed with obsessive-compulsive disorder. Some genius of a doctor made the astonishing suggestion that he go into the theatre. Colin was excruciatingly shy. On the numerous occasions when he came to my dressing room for a chat, it would take him about five minutes from indicating he was leaving to his actual departure. Amazingly his shyness magically disappeared the second he stepped onto the stage, often to play the most ostentatious character.

In *One For The Pot* Colin played an apparently disabled man with gout. With a massive bandage on his left foot, he was doomed through some plot device to spend most of the play in a wheelchair. But when alone on stage and desperate for a strong drink he would suddenly jump out of the chair and quickly pour himself a large whisky. In the manner of farce this occurred a number of times. Now, the Barrow stage had a fairly steep rake. In one particular performance, Colin jumped up from the wheelchair for another drink. Unfortunately, he forgot to lock the brake and as he was innocently pouring the drink, was astonished to hear shrieks from the front of the stalls. Turning quickly he beheld a number of the front row audience swiftly vacating their seats. He leapt forward but was too late to prevent the chair tumbling into the auditorium. With much presence of mind he leapt into the stalls, elicited help from a burly patron and returned the wheelchair and himself to the stage, from where he whispered a swift apology to the front row, which earned him a strong round of applause.

Some fifty years previously another and more catastrophic accident was witnessed on the Barrow stage. The theatre was then home to visiting variety shows of all descriptions. One impresario in his wisdom thought it would be an astonishing and money-raising feat to bring a large elephant onstage. 'The audience would love it!' he declared. So a ramp was set up backstage to facilitate this phenonemon. Unfortunately as the pachyderm made his much heralded entrance, the floor collapsed under him and with much trumpeting and huge effort the poor frightened creature had to be rescued. A year later the impresario, assured that the Barrow stage was now equipped with a much stronger floor, returned with the elephant. The ramp was duly laid and the creature led toward it. But, despite the sweating efforts of four men, the elephant refused to appear that evening. Perhaps there is some truth in the saying an elephant never forgets. The disappointment of that Barrow audience was sadly not recorded.

Other plays in that 1965-1966 season included *Winter's Journey* by the great American socialist writer Clifford Odets, *Five Finger Exercise* by Peter Shaffer, *Dinner With The Family* by Anouilh and *The Offshore Island,* a play about nuclear warfare by Marghanita Laski. We also did adaptations of *Wuthering Heights, Pinocchio* and *David Copperfield* in which I played one of the great Dickensian eccentrics, Mr Micawber.

A third of the way through the season, one of the company left and Donald promoted me to the position of actor. No more ASM-ing, no more Sunday work, no more hunting for furniture and props around the town, no more dashing up the ladder to do lighting duties. Now I moved up to bigger parts and my wages rose to twelve pounds. I was able to save a pound a week.

My first big role was Bluntschli in Bernard Shaw's 1894 play *Arms And The Man*, a very funny piece about the futility of war and the hypocrisies of human nature. One of Shaw's first commercial successes, it revolves around the relationships between a delightful, impossibly romantic heroine, Raina; her suitor, Sergius, a handsome, swashbuckling, young aristocratic hero of equally romantic notions who is Raina's "ideal of the higher love"; and, the realist, practical Bluntschli, a professional soldier who, when chased by the enemy, unhesitatingly climbs up to a balcony and takes refuge in a girl's bedroom.

Donald brought in a very talented director for the play.

Her name was Elsa Bolam. Female directors were almost unknown in the 1960s. It would be nearly twenty years before I worked with another. Patricia Doyle, Donald's partner and a very talented and attractive young actress, with the finest cheekbones in Equity, played Raina. Lionel Guyett, who I shared an impossibly small flat with, played Sergius. He had a fine handsome face, and, now I think of it, also had exceptional cheekbones. He had all the requisite qualities for Sergius, except – and Lionel will freely admit this – he lacked a little in the height department. But he made up for that with a fine strutting performance. They were both excellent.

I, on the other hand, had no particularly striking features. But Shaw, who covers all his texts with countless descriptions and stage directions, conveniently described Bluntschli as 'of undistinguished appearance' and the possessor of 'a hopelessly prosaic nose'. Right up my street. It is a very well-written and funny part and the audiences enjoyed the character's effortless ability to deflate all the empty ideals and pomposity of Sergius and Raina and bring them back into the real world.

A small addendum. That production of *Arms And The Man* in Barrow was staged in late 1965. In 2001, thirty-six years later I was playing in Vanbrugh's *The Relapse* in the Olivier Theatre at the National. As I was leaving the theatre after a matinee, Linda, the stage door keeper, handed me a piece of paper which somebody had left for me after the performance. I thanked her and strolled out to get some air by the river. The note was on a piece of pink paper and had a message written in blue biro. It said:

Dear Mr Hayes,

I have just been to see The Relapse and couldn't believe it when I heard your voice. I lived in Barrow-in-Furness many years ago and remember you at Her Majesty's with Lionel Guyett, Donald MacKechnie, Patricia Doyle. I used to love the rep there. It really brought me out of this small industrial town. I will always remember you in Arms And The Man.

Thanks for those very good memories. Good luck in the future.

Kathleen Partington

No telephone number, no address. I didn't recognise her name.

I have the note. It means a great deal to me. To think one could, as an actor, make such a longlasting impression.

If you ever read this, Kathleen Partington, I send you my best wishes and thanks.

I have the programme of *Arms And The Man*. It cost sixpence and inside there is an advertisement offering the "unique opportunity" to buy the new Rootes car, the Singer Chamois for £581.

So, on we worked through that season. In the rare breaks, we would cross over the bridge to Walney Island for a glimpse of the sea – always a very welcome sight to me. Once I remember we managed a Sunday outing to Windermere in the Lake District. The fells and lakes were astonishing and I remember buying a couple of Alfred Wainwright's beautiful small format guidebooks with their hand-drawn illustrations and maps and vowing to return at a later date to do some fell-walking. I have yet to do so.

Before the advent of photocopiers in the late sixties, the scripts for each play we rehearsed were hired from a company called Samuel French's in London. They would send, say, ten copies of each play, small blue paperbacks referred to as *French's Acting Editions*. They consisted of:

- The text of the play.
- List of characters and their ages.
- Photographs of the sets of the West End production.
- Prop lists of that production.
- Lighting cues.
- Every single "move" made by each West End actor was listed beside their lines.

Some directors were well known for reproducing every aspect of the West End production, often copying the sets and the "moves" of the actors. Donald never did any of this and was very creative with each production, which was not easy when he was directing a new play every fortnight. It was the habit in those days for each actor to make a note in the script of all moves and positions he made and took up in each scene. Nowadays, actors cover their much larger scripts with hundreds of moves, ideas, background details of character, notes on bits of "business", costume ideas, drawings, other actors' phone numbers, squiggles and so on. But as our playscripts were on hire and would be used by other companies later, we were seriously warned not to mark the French's edition too much. Every insertion had to be done with a very light pencil, and at the end of the production we were entreated to erase all our pencilled notes with a rubber before the scripts were returned to London.

If your character called for a wig, your head measurements were sent to Wig Creations in the metropolis and a week later a wig would arrive. Obviously not specially made for you, but supplied from stock. If you were lucky, it would not only fit, but look right. If you were unlucky, your performance would be much diminished by the placing of a large dead rat on the top of your head each evening. Nowadays, if you require a wig at the National, the RSC, the West End or the better subsidised reps, one will be painstakingly made by a highly skilled wigmaker taking many, many hours and costing hundreds of pounds.

Audiences in Barrow were never large and sometimes we would cancel a matinee when only eight people turned up. In an effort to raise awareness of the theatre, Donald brought a lovely gentle actress, Betty Alberge, to Barrow for one production. She had just finished playing a much-loved character 'Florrie Lindley', who owned the corner shop in *Coronation Street*. She had appeared in 311 episodes. Alas, though her presence did raise audience figures for that fortnight, no appreciable increase in numbers followed.

Despite this, the sense of cameraderie in the company was wonderful and I was sad to leave Barrow at the end of the season in May 1966. Despite the long grinding hours, the work was excellent and I was enjoying being an actor very much. I continued to be surprised that I was being paid to do the job.

Within months of the finish of our season, Her Majesty's Theatre, Barrow in Furness closed. With the decline of audience numbers, the Arts Council withdrew the company's grant. In the following year 1967, I was deeply saddened and shocked to hear that this architectural gem with its unique theatrical history had been demolished.

Donald and Patricia left Barrow. But within a few months Donald had acquired a very good job. Later, I will write further about the exciting position he took up and how it had a large impact on my life less than two years later.

LONDON 1966

John Lennon says "The Beatles are more popular than Jesus" – President Lyndon Johnson states that the US should stay in South Vietnam until Communist aggression there is ended; soon after, troop numbers in the country increase to 250,000 – Amid death threats, Martin Luther King leads a civil march in Chicago where they are met with crowds throwing bottles and rocks – The tragedy of Aberfan in Wales, where a mountain of coal waste creates a landslide, burying a village school and killing 144 children and teachers – The Labour Party, under Harold Wilson, win the General Election – Moors murderers Ian Brady and Myra Hindley are sentenced to life for the murder of three children – Early in the year the World Cup is stolen at an exhibition, but later found by a dog called Pickles and soon after England win the trophy with a four-two victory over Germany – Barclays introduce the Barclaycard, the first British credit card – On 5ᵗʰ August, the Beatles release the Revolver album – Laurence Olivier is nominated for Best Actor for the film of Othello, but loses out to Lee Marvin for Cat Ballou –

In July 1966, while looking for acting work, I did a stint washing dishes in a small café round the corner from Matcham's Coliseum Theatre in St Martin's Lane. Two other actors also did shifts there, the talented and lovely Pamela Miles and a lad called David who seemed to have amazing connections. A week prior to the official release of the *Revolver* album, David walked in one day and handed us all a copy. A week or so later I went for an audition with the director Peter Cheeseman who was running the prestigious Victoria Theatre in Stoke on Trent. It had an extremely good reputation, was getting a lot of attention in the London press, and many actors were very keen to work there. Peter, a short, stocky and mildly pugnacious man, wearing a large home-knitted green ribbed jumper, sat throughout the interview coughing quietly, a small tin of what were then called Nigroids, small black round pellets of strong liquorice, in his hand. These were marketed as "protection for the voice, throat and chest – invaluable to singers and speakers". After a campaign following much controversy, the name of the lozenge was deemed racially offensive and changed to Vigroids. But that didn't happen until 2010.

I did my pieces. We then talked and got on well. Peter explained that twice a year the Vic did a Shakespeare production. As these needed large casts he recruited an extra four or five actors to the resident company. At the end of that production, if he liked their work, he asked two of those actors to join the permanent company. He offered me a small part in *Twelfth Night*. I accepted.

IN THE ROUND – STOKE ON TRENT

Stoke on Trent was not an attractive place in the mid-1960s. With the local abundance of coal and clay suitable for earthenware production, many of the great pottery companies had established factories there in the mid-eighteenth century. The city was studded with the distinctive tall brick bottle-kilns of the potteries of Royal Doulton, Wedgwood, Spode, Minton and many smaller companies. All of these were thriving in the sixties.

Soon after my arrival in Stoke and riding upstairs on a double-decker bus, I happened to look out the window as we passed the Twyfords factory in Etruria, manufacturers of bathroom and sanitary ware. Over the wall I was confronted by a vast, banked sea of shining white lavatories.

Stoke was the birthplace of the very successful early twentieth-century novelist, Arnold Bennett, who used Stoke as the setting for many of his books and stories. At the theatre we did dramatised versions of some of his work that season. He is one of the few celebrities to have a dish named after him. While he was staying at the Savoy, the chefs perfected an omelette incorporating smoked haddock, Parmesan cheese and cream, which Bennett insisted on being prepared for him on numerous occasions. To this day the "Omelette Arnold Bennett" has remained a standard dish at the hotel.

Peter Cheeseman was a disciple of the director Stephen Joseph. Joseph had set up a theatre-in-the-round summer season in a municipal library (The Studio Theatre) in Scarborough a few years before. When touring to Stoke in 1962 and searching for more permanent premises they came across a small derelict cinema, the Victoria in Hartshill Road, the front covered in peeling posters. It was a working-class area away from the city centre with back-to-back red-brick terrace houses and small industrial units. They decided to turn it into a theatre. Peter was appointed artistic director.

The Victoria cost £5000 to convert and became the country's first permanent theatre-in-the-round.

Though Stoke was a bleak prospect, with no theatrical tradition in the area, the thirty-year-old Cheeseman found the challenge inspiring. 'I felt I had to stay there. I don't think it's any good turning one's back on the realities of twentieth-century industrial life. You've got to live with what's there and make sense of it.' He felt in such a town there would be no prejudice about what a theatre should be or do. The area struck him as "promisingly egalitarian".

The theatre opened in October 1962 and Peter gradually built up audiences, acclimatising them to watch plays in the round and without scenery. The stage was a large square, with four steeply raked blocks of seating, five and six rows deep, surrounding the acting area. The raked seating gave the floor of the acting area great prominence. There were four entrances for the actors. Two were in adjacent corners of the rectangle and two in the centre of opposite blocks. It was a very exciting space.

Peter explored and developed a new and original theatre style. He decided to work on projects that would hold a deep interest for local audiences. Over the years he created with the company a series of highly entertaining musical drama documentaries about local subjects. The first of these was titled *The Jolly Potters* about the early history of the local potteries and was presented in 1964. Other productions included *The Staffordshire Rebels* (1965) about the English Civil War, and *The Knotty* (1966) about the foundation of the local railway in the 1840s and its history up to 1923 when it amalgamated with the London Midland and Scottish Railway.

Audiences thronged to see this new form of locally inspired theatre. In a very down-to-earth and uncondescending way it gave them a deeper knowledge of the area in which they lived; it celebrated the lives and achievements of their families over generations, and offered a great evening out, full of drama, humour, dance and music. For the acting company, it gave us a deep satisfaction in making not only good theatre but also work relevant to the community we served.

After Barrow there were new-found luxuries. I was two pounds a week better off. There was the opportunity to work on a more adventurous repertoire. Each production rehearsed for four weeks. This made a huge difference to the quality of the work a company could create. There was time to explore the text, discuss character, time to try, fail, try again, or, as Samuel Beckett put it, "try again, fail again, fail better".

Stoke had the luxury at that time of employing a resident playwright, the highly talented Peter Terson, who came to live and work with us. He had a prodigious imagination and scripts seemed to flow effortlessly from his pen. He gained national and international recognition for much of his work. His play *Zigger Zagger*, about football hooligans and their pursuit of drink, sex and trouble, was performed all over the country and in Europe.

"I've had enough, I'm for the lads at the City End who don't give a damn. Who work for the week to get to Saturday... You can get back to your telly, Les. Watch your football from there, there's no chance of you meeting anybody, not a chance of

you touching anybody... You're for the house. I'm for the City End."

Harry Philton, the leading character in Zigger Zagger.

We rehearsed *Twelfth Night* for a month and opened in early October 1966. Two of the other probationers were Mike Leigh and Ken Campbell. I remember little of the production apart from the excitement and the novelty of playing in the round. With the audience so close, performances could be more free and subtle.

During the run, Peter called me to his office and invited me to join the resident company. I was well pleased. He believed passionately in "company". Like the Russians, he wanted actors to spend years in the ensemble. It was an abiding passion of his and one I will return to later.

For the next two years I acted in twenty-one plays. Some in a straight four-week run, while others opened, played for a week and then alternated with other productions in the repertoire. The repertoire was very adventurous:

A double bill of Sophocles' *Electra* and the Roman comedy *The Pot Of Gold* by Plautus, *The Playboy of the Western World* by Synge; *Roots* by Arnold Wesker; adaptations of *Clayhanger* and *Jock On The Go* by Arnold Bennett; *Heartbreak House* by Bernard Shaw; *Romeo and Juliet, Julius Caesar* and *Henry V; Old King Cole* by Ken Campbell; *The Ballad Of The Artificial Mash* by Peter Terson; and *The Knotty*, the musical documentary I mentioned about the local railway.

The company was full of talent. Among the actors in my time there was Robert Powell, who went on to play Jesus in a famous television series; Bob Hoskins, I don't need to tell you what he went on to do; Mike Leigh, who wasn't long with the company and would probably admit that he was not the finest of actors, left and went on to make a stream of award-winning films; Ken Campbell, with that marvellous manic face, bald head and eccentric drawling voice, played a load of comic characters. At Stoke, Ken also began his writing career with his incomparable and quirky *Old King Cole*, which went on to become a Christmas staple around the British Isles. The show had a cast of wonderful characters with names like The Amazing Faz (my part) and his feeble-minded assistant Twoo, Princess Daphne, Baron Wadd, and Sporty Cyril. Years later Ken told me he judged all Fazs on my interpetation of that great role. Ron Daniels, as well as acting in the company, soon began to direct. A few years later he joined the Royal Shakespeare Company where he directed a number of well-received productions. There was Christopher Martin, Anne Raitt, Edward Clayton, Gillian Brown, Dave Hill and Jane Wood.

There was also Shane Connaughton, a fellow Irishman, who went on to do more writing than acting. He co-wrote the Oscar-nominated screenplay *My Left Foot* as well as other films. His book, *A Border Station* – a developing series of stories about a boy growing up in Co Cavan where his father is the local garda sergeant – is a vivid evocation of childhood, of poverty, violence and love. Shane organised the football kickabouts in Godden's Yard, a scruffy piece of land at the back of the theatre. He was a terrible "corpser". In a production of the actor-manager John Martin Harvey's *The Only Way*, an adaptation of Charles Dickens' *A Tale Of Two Cities,* which was first produced at The Lyceum in 1899, Shane and I played condemned aristocrats about to face the guillotine. When the executioner, Bob Hoskins, called out our alloted numbers for the chop, Shane had to burst into tears and utter the deathless line, "I'm too young to die", after which he was dragged away by Bob to his demise. With the audience so close on all four sides every performance of that particular moment was fraught with danger. It demanded very serious playing. Shane would utter that dreadful line, not in the tears that were required, but in a high-pitched hysterical fit of the giggles, his hands over his face. My only good fortune was to be called to my death immediately after. If Cheeseman had found out he'd have slaughtered us.

Clayhanger was one of Arnold Bennett's most successful novels and Peter Terson and Joyce Cheeseman, Peter's wife, adapted it for the Vic stage in 1967, the centenary of Bennett's birth. It is set in Bursley, Bennett's name for Burslem, one of the six towns that make up Stoke on Trent. The central drama of this coming-of-age story is the intense battle between the son Edwin, and his domineering father Darius. Edwin struggles to establish his right to choose his own career, and to become financially independent so that he can marry the woman he loves. Darius subjugates him. I played Darius and Christopher Martin, who was the star of the company, played Edwin. In the final scenes Darius, suffering from "a softening of the brain", becomes childlike, dependent and unpredictable and it falls on Edwin to care for him.

Peter Cheeseman handed me a letter after the production ended which had been sent him by a Derbyshire surgeon:

"We were all fascinated by James Hayes as Darius, in the final scenes his increasing cerebral softening was

perfectly realised. The shrinking and fading of old age was so natural that it is difficult to realise how one could act it... brilliant acting and a performance from which any medical student could learn far more about the effects of arteriosclerosis of the brain arteries than by any number of lectures."

Well!

THE KNOTTY

'It is very important to tell stories from within the community that would not otherwise be told.' – Peter Cheeseman

The Knotty was so successful in 1966 that Peter revived it in 1967 and I joined the cast. *The Knotty* was the nickname for the North Staffordshire Railway (its badge was the Staffordshire Knot). The company was founded in 1845 and eventually amalgamated in 1923 with the London, Midland and Scottish Railway. *The Knotty* was created by the theatre company, working from historical research by the then resident playwright Peter Terson and Peter Cheeseman. Cheeseman directed it. It was a truly exciting and groundbreaking piece of work and one of the most satisfying projects I have ever had the good fortune to appear in.

The process in creating *The Knotty*, like all the previous musical documentaries at Stoke, began with all the primary source material that could be unearthed – original documents, diaries, letters, newspaper articles. Former workers of the North Staffordshire Railway were interviewed and tape-recorded. Importantly, Peter insisted the material used on the stage must be primary source material. If there was no primary source material available on a particular topic, no scene could be made on that topic. To give an idea of this research, here is a much shortened version of the acknowledgement printed in *The Knotty* script.

> "*The authorative work The North Staffordshire Railway with its five joint authors. The book The Railway Navvies by Terry Coleman. The reminiscences and advice of over thirty men who worked for the Knotty. The librarians and staff of both local and national libraries and museums. The British Railways Archives, The House of Lords Record Office, Staffordshire County Records Office.*"

At the end of the research period the rehearsals begin. The actors assemble. This will be a group-created project so no one gets a script, just a blank notebook. The two Peters, Cheeseman and Terson, have a proposed story and a rough theatrical shape in which to tell it. It consists of a running list, detailing the subject of each scene and songs, and the order in which they will appear in the show. Small groups of actors are then alloted certain scenes and are showered with all the research material related to them. They then work as a group and begin the creative process.

Music plays a big part in each of the musical documentaries. For *The Knotty*, Jeff Parton, a local folk singer and writer, as well as the actors Gillian Brown and Anne Raitt wrote all the original music.

The first scene was set in the early 1800s. Actors created a travelling coach very simply, using stools and chairs and then climbed aboard. The driver cracked his whip and the journey began. The cast sang a traditional song during which some of the passengers called out coaching advertisements:

> *"15th December 1810. Advertisement. London, Liverpool, Birmingham, Bristol. Coaches will set off from the Shakespeare Inn, Stoke on Trent, every day at one o'clock arriving at the Saddle Inn, Liverpool at nine o'clock the same evening... Fares to Liverpool – inside coach with the gentry, sixteen shillings. Fares to Liverpool – outside coach with the weather, nine shillings."*

The actors all sway with the jolting of the coach and sing a song. Suddenly the coach crashes, chairs tumble, actors fall.

> *"Passenger: 'I was travelling by the very fast and much improved coach to Liverpool, when one of the wheels suddenly went to pieces, and had it not been for the care and attention of the coachman, many of the passengers would have been seriously injured, and some would have lost their lives without doubt. Here is proof of the typical neglect of the coach contractors."*

There is a very funny scene with a pair of highwaymen who, as they rob the passengers, offer us a witty description of their own appearances – "Note: One of the men had a quantity of pimples on his face... And the other had his right eye bloodshot and had on a black cloak!" They then exit with their spoils, roaring with laughter.

Scenes tumble along interspersed with song. There is a meeting where manufacturers, tradesmen and the great and good in the area, discuss the construction of a railway and ask Mr George Stephenson, Civil Engineer, "to make a survey and report his opinion on the amount of capital required".

The "floor cloth" on the stage had a large map of the district painted on it. Stephenson entered and surveyed the area; three actors sang to the accompaniment of a banjo:

"You've heard of Rocket's fame, Geordie Stephenson,
It was that as made his name, Geordie Stephenson."

A narrator entered wearing a black moustache and a long black cloak:

"We'll tell you a tale of days gone by,
When the rail was just beginning
How a countryman was robbed of his land
By a lawyer's crafty conniving."

There followed a scene in rhyming couplets, in the style of a Victorian melodrama, where the narrator, now a villain with a large bag of money, swindles a farmer and his wife out of their land, an area through which the proposed railway is to be built.

Soon a number of rail companies were set up to promote twenty-four different lines through North Staffordshire and wrangle for the contract to build the new railway. To stage the founding of these, to show their many meetings and to illustrate the rivalries that occurred, could prove dangerously dull and dreary. The company at the Vic came up with a brilliant and a truly theatrical solution that managed to tell this section of the tale in less than three minutes. They did it in this manner:

With musical accompaniment, four actors, each holding up a long red, white and black striped surveyor's pole, danced onstage in a high-stepping jog trot. Each poleman called out his company's name and routes. "Buxton, Macclesfield, Congleton Line" etc marking time at each corner of the stage as the next one entered. They enacted a dozen routes in their jig round the stage, the brightly coloured poles held upright before them. This scene was soon titled "The Pole Dance". Then, to a banjo tune, they began a battle for supremacy, their poles being used to bop an opponent on the head, sending them reeling away in defeat. Finally, three companies banded together on one side of the stage to drive the favourite away. To a menacing drum beat, with lowered poles as in a joust, and calling out their names, they advanced on him. He fought the three brilliantly, bopping them all and defeated them. They staggered away. Alone onstage the victor, The North Staffordshire Railway Company did a triumphant dance, twirling and circling the stage with his pole held proudly above his head, the music rising to a crescendo.

This was pure theatre. Exciting. Entertaining and done with the simplest effects. I have never forgotten it.

The show – never a play – then moved on to "The Cutting Of The First Sod", to the employment of over 2,000 navvies and the bemoaning of their conduct and manners ("Woe befall any woman with the slightest share of modesty whose ears they can assail") to the hard and dangerous work, the tunneling, the accidents ("Numerous amputations have been performed by Mr Heaton, Surgeon of Leek, with great skill and indefatigable attention to the sufferers"). There were scenes of poverty and hunger, people queued for soup and a chartist demanded representation of the people in parliament. Finally before the interval there was the "Sensational Opening Of The Railway" with a fine song by Gillian Brown called "Railway Lines".

> *"Everywhere, look around,*
> *In the air and underground*
> *We're making progress*
> *Yes, we are.*
> *Machines making angry noises*
> *Manned by men with unheard voices*
> *Where's it leading?"*

In the second half the floor cloth is changed to show the full extent of the new railway. From Crewe in the North to Colwich in the South. East and West to Derby and Market Drayton with Stoke in the centre.

The show turned to the rise of trade unions, the Great War, with the railwaymen in France, the well-known characters who became household names. From this point on, all the characters mentioned and played, were created from the reminiscences of old railwaymen who had helped with the research. In turn these railwaymen also became characters in the show played by the actors, but often their own voices narrated speeches on loudspeakers. One of the main characters the men remembered was W.D. Phillips,

General Manager. He was a strict disciplinarian, fiercely anti-union, a hard taskmaster and had the great talent for showing up in the right place at the wrong time. He was sharply-spoken and his head hung dramatically to one side. Among the roles I played was this Mr Phillips.

"APPRENTICE: Who's that man with his head on one side?

RAILWAYMAN: Watch it, that's WD Phillips, General Manager. You want to keep out of his way, specially on your first day."

Phillips spent little time in his office. He travelled incessantly on the railway and on its tracks.

"WD: Porter, what are you messing about at? You've a big head but there's not much in it!

PORTER: Aye, but at least it's set on straight."

Harry Sharratt, who worked at the theatre, recorded a lot of stories about his time on *The Knotty* and spoke on the tannoy about 'knocking up'.

"LOUDSPEAKER: If you were cleaning on the night shift, at about three am they would give you written instructions to go and knock up four or five drivers and firemen, all at different times. Often, there would be about half an hour between calls and, in the event of rain, we would take shelter in someone's doorway. In the event of the driver not answering to the knock, you would have to repeat it louder and possibly shout.

LAD (shouts): Wake up driver! Time you were up! Can't you hear me?

A driver enters with a tea can and crosses the stage.

DRIVER: All right, I've got neighbours, you know. Don't have to wake up the whole street."

There was a wonderful "shunting sequence". This was done very simply with an actor holding a shunting pole in one hand, a lantern with a red and a green light in the other and a whistle in his mouth. The stage was very dark, the man stood in a tight shaft of light and with shouts, whistles and wavings of the lantern stage managed the movement of vast black engines and carriages. All this done on an empty stage, but with loud steam hissings, the sound of huge rumbling wheels, the screeching of brakes and the crash as carriages coupled. It was helped along with an amount of steam and smoke. Thrilling.

In the company's research with the Knotty veterans, the First World War was revealed as a watershed in the history of the railway. So it was decided to follow one of the railwaymen to France and dramatise his time there. Harry Sharratt initially fought in France as an infantryman.

"SHARRATT: Then I got hit by a piece of shell, which smashed me rifle on me back and put me in hospital till after Christmas.

SOLDIER: You're a railwayman, aren't you?

129

SHARRATT: Yes I am, aye.

SOLDIER: You ought to join the R.O.D's mate.

SHARRETT: R.O.D's, what are they?

SOLDIER: Oh, the Railway Operating Division."

So he applied and within a week he was back on the footplate. There then followed a sequence of short scenes on the movement by train of troops or munitions up to the front line, and the return journeys with the maimed combatants. There were verbatim accounts of these men's misfortunes. The tragedy, suffering and upset of this episode was also not without some mitigating humour.

Then in 1923 amalgamation came. In this final scene, the actors came on in their railway jackets and caps and spoke the transcribed speeches of the old men who had remembered their feelings at the time. Peter wanted no characterisation in this scene, just plain statements by the actors as they faced the audience on all four sides, speaking as they removed their jackets and caps with the Knotty badge and placed them on the floor in front of them.

> *"There was a lot of old drivers used to have their own engine you see. They was very proud of them, Old North Staffs drivers… and everything had to be absolutely, just to perfection. When they were cleaned they used to shine of course, there was no doubt about that, and they looked a picture.'*
>
> *Charles Edward Dawson – Driver.*

'The efficiency of the men on the Knotty was proved by the fact – I think we can boast – that we never had a major disaster.'

Frank Oakes – Traffic.

SONG: Goodbye to days of Knotty fame,
Engine bearing driver's name,
The loss for some was hard to take,
Golden sovereigns hard to make
Farewell to the world of WD
Of tip your hat for courtesy
The personal touch on the personal line
The NSR. was lost to time..."

This was a very moving and eloquent ending to this extraordinary show. Even now, over forty-five years later, I have vivid memories of it. There was nothing of this originality, theatricality, community-serving entertainment going on anywhere else in the country. It was an important work. I count it as a highlight in my life.

THE TOAD INCIDENT

A fond memory of my Stoke sojourn is the "Toad of Toad Hall Incident". In 1966 Peter Cheeseman brought into the company a new actor. Let us call him Richard. Richard had worked at the Old Vic in London in the 1950s but had given up the profession and in 1966 was training to become a Church of England vicar in Birmingham. During his training he had a fierce row with one of the clerics who was instructing him. Blows may have been exchanged. Anyway,

Richard was suspended for a time. I presume to cool down or perhaps rethink his vocation. He wrote to Peter asking for work and soon joined the company. He was a very good actor.

Some weeks later the company mounted a production of *Toad of Toad Hall* and Richard was cast as the eponymous hero. His portly body and chubby face made him ideal for the role. Now, imagine if you will, the theatre-in-the-round stage with the set for Mr Grahame's classic. To one side a low doorway leading into Badger's den, a small cosy room with comfortable chairs, ancient rugs and a small table with a soft lamp glowing. Assembled onstage are Ratty, Mole, and Badger – played by myself in a wine-coloured smoking jacket and an embroidered tasselled Turkish skull cap. My black hair and beard were striped with bands of badger-like white. This was accomplished with the use of my trusty tennis shoe whitener, applied liberally, with an old spit-soaked toothbrush.

It is a bright afternoon in Stoke. The four sides of the auditorium are packed with 300 restless children. Cheeseman's decision to give the production a Chekhovian subtlety – admittedly an ambitious choice – is going way over the heads of our young audience. We reach a climactic scene: Toad's arrival, in great haste and huge distress, having been chased through the woods by the stoats and the weasels.

> *"Everyday the stoats and weasels*
> *Hope that he will get the measles–"*

Suddenly the door is thrown open. Toad bursts in. Richard is on fine form, eyes wide open, gasping for breath. We have been playing the piece for over two weeks. We are relaxed, on top of it all. Richard is magnificent in a bright green-checked suit with voluminous plus-fours, yellow stockings and brown brogues, a green checked shirt with a flowery yellow cravat. His face is made up frog green, topped by a leather driving cap with earflaps, crowned with a large pair of driving goggles.

Ratty, Moley and I relax. Apart from enquiring, 'What's the matter, Toad?' we don't have to speak until Toad has rattled through a hugely self-regarding and highly questionable account of his encounter with the vagabonds of the wild wood. Richard stares, his breath coming and going in big chest-expanding bursts. He doesn't reply to the question. We three wait. A tremendous, if unexpected, pause. So dramatic. We wait. Nothing. We wait. 'What's the matter, Toad?' is repeated. Nothing. I look at the others. Apprehension now beginning to show in their eyes.

The children begin to get restless.

Ratty: 'Were you perhaps chased by the stoats and the weasels?'

Richard doesn't speak. He starts to sway.

Badger: 'Did they *perhaps* try to grab you and throw you to the ground?'

Richard walks forward and puts a large hand on my shoulder. He brings his fraught face close to mine. An abject plea in his eyes.

Moley: 'Were there about *fifty* of them?'

Richard now walks over to Moley and Ratty, puts his hands on their shoulders and looks deeply into their eyes.

No words are forthcoming. The children smell blood. Too many pauses, too little said. They begin to rumble. It sounds like the tanks on D-Day. Together, we three, delving through our shaky memories, begin to improvise the whole of Toad's speech. Mr Grahame would have been horrified at the lack of shape, language and structure we brought to his masterpiece. Richard just stands and moans quietly. We begin to improve. We might get away with this.

But then, Richard, after a slow, sweeping, fifty-mile stare around the stage, suddenly turns heel and exits through the up-centre gangway. We hear him go through the door that will take him out past the box office and around to the dressing rooms. At this point I remembered that Ratty and Mole had a duologue a little later in the scene. Anyway I saw this as an opportunity to move the tottering production forward. So I looked at the others and uttered the deathless line: 'I think I'd better go and see if Toad is alright.'

Ratty and Moley glared at me. Ratty mouthed a foul swearword. But I was now on my way up the gangway after Toad. As I came around past the box office I noticed the sunlight flashing on the street doors. The fiercely *swinging* street doors. Odd. Suspicious. I ran to the doors and outside a strange sight assaulted my eyes. To the right up the sunny Hartshill Road, bemused shoppers and passersby opened their collective mouths, twisted their necks and gawped, as the greenfaced, green-check besuited and bedizened Mr Toad strode purposefully past them. His digs, his destination, three roads further up on the right.

Behind me the rich London tones of Bob Hoskins reached my ears. 'What the fuck is goin' on, Jim?'

I pointed up the road. I said, 'Richard's gone a bit funny. Quick, Bob, go and get him. I'll go back and rescue the lads.'

Bob, a complete pro, hared up the road in pursuit of Richard. Now, Bob was playing The Judge, a character he had based on an owl. So imagine the scene. Bob dressed in a judge's robe and wig, with long feathers sticking out of it. To give him an owl-like mien he was wearing huge round black spectacles, and, for some reason I now forget, a pair of richly striped and odd football socks. I viewed this spectacle for a few, never to be forgotten seconds, an owl chasing a toad, and then hurried back onstage. My colleagues greeted me like a long awaited rescue ship. The children were in uproar. I shouted, vainly trying to be heard over the noise, 'Quickly, Toad needs our help,' and led the drained pair offstage. A heavy nod from me to the lighting box alerted the stage manager that we were taking a somewhat early interval and they immediately brought the houselights up to a tremendous cheer from our raucous public.

Meanwhile in Hartshill Road, Bob had jumped on Richard's back, halting his onward rush and with soothing words and a little muscle led him back to the relative sanity of the dressing room. There, with further honeyed words and a very sweet cup of tea, we slowly convinced him that the incident was as nothing. Actors in situations like this are very supportive, perhaps thinking, *There, but for the grace of God...*

It is worth pointing out that Richard then went back onstage after the interval and played a very fine second act. We knew nothing of what was going on in his private life.

We probably didn't want to know. But, given the state he was in, it was a truly brave thing he did to continue.

That was Richard. He had a wife and children. He stayed for a production of Bernard Shaw's *Heartbreak House* and left the company some weeks later. Over the years, on a number of visits to Birmingham to work at The Rep, I often thought of Richard and wondered what became of him.

* * *

In 1966 a much-publicised quarrel between Stephen Joseph and Peter Cheeseman regarding the future of the Victoria Theatre developed. In January 1967 Peter was sacked, we were told, over a difference of opinion with Studio Theatre Ltd. There was widespread local outrage at this announcement. The final production of the season *Julius Caesar,* in which I played Cassius, was staged by an outsider, Iain Cuthbertson, a well-known television actor brought in over Peter's head. The final performance was on 1st April. The theatre closed down. The next day I got married in the small Staffordshire village of Swynnerton.

In 1963 a young woman called Jackie Brandon made the journey from the City of London School for Girls to study drama at The Guildhall School of Music and Drama – a journey of precisely forty metres. Both schools were in fact then in the same block in Blackfriars. There, Jackie became my girlfriend. I discovered during the writing of this book that it had been she who had approached the Principal of Guildhall back in 1965, made him aware of my dire financial circumstances and persuaded him to

waive my final two terms' fees. It was Jackie I married in
Swynnerton in 1967 and who became the mother of my
children, Abigail and Séamus, mentioned in this book.

We, the acting company decided to support Cheeseman and to show the strength of our feelings we stayed in Stoke. Our appearance at the local Labour Exchange was greeted with much perplexity. How long we could continue in our support of Peter was debatable. We had little money and no sure prospect of a return to the Vic. Two things happened that supported us in the conflict. Within a few weeks we, the company, were contracted to do two television productions. Both were adaptations of Arnold Bennett stories. The first, *Jock On The Go,* which we had played in repertoire from the previous November to February, was adapted for television and we went to London and recorded it for BBC Television. Then we rehearsed *The Heroism Of Thomas Chadwick* in Burslem Town Hall in Stoke and moved to Thames Television Studios in Teddington to record it for ABC Television. Both productions were written by the Vic's resident writer Peter Terson. The money from these shows enabled us to continue our support for Peter and our work towards his reinstatement.

By July 1967, a new theatre trust was set up, Peter was re-appointed and we returned to the Vic in August. A picture of the company walking back into the theatre appeared in the local *Sentinel* titled "Victoria Theatre Company Return". We then started rehearsals of a new play by Peter Terson, its title *The Ballad Of The Artificial Mash.* As the title suggests, this play, was an attack in words and music on the evils of modern food production.

Norman Dodd, the hero of the piece, who I played, is a travelling salesman in artificial mash. He visits farmers, selling them hormone-laden animal feed, and, given half a chance, bedding their wives. But his constant proximity to the product has a disastrous effect on his health and sex life, and he ends an emasculated victim of the fattening hormones, like the poor beasts he supplies. Terson wrote the piece with great feeling but also with a wonderful comic touch. He had some firsthand knowledge, for he had once worked in animal foodstuffs himself. He was years ahead of his time in tackling this subject.

Peter wrote dozens of fine plays for the stage, for television and radio. His plays at the Vic, his work on the musical documentaries, his involvement in all the creative work at the theatre, as well as his huge life-enhancing spirit and energy contributed to what made Stoke such an exciting theatre. As I write this there has just been a retrospective of some of his television plays – *Peter Terson: The Artisan Playwright* – at the British Film Institute at the South Bank in London. A revisiting of some of his theatre plays might prove very fruitful for some new young directors.

On we went, happy to be back at the Vic. Play followed play. The work was always exciting and fulfilling. But in early 1968, having spent eighteen months at the theatre, I began to fancy a change. This was where my decision in 1965 to go to Barrow suddenly paid off in a very big way. As I wrote earlier, going to Barrow "was one of the most important decisions of my entire career as an actor". In the summer of 1968 Donald Mac Kechnie contacted me. He was now working with Olivier at the National Theatre at the Old Vic.

He invited me to go to London to audition for the company. So began a process that went on for some weeks.

I decided to give my notice to Peter Cheeseman. Now, I was well aware that Peter did not like actors leaving the company. A year previously a bunch of us had borrowed a car and driven over to Liverpool to see the work of the very talented and much lauded Everyman Theatre Company. Peter heard of our visit. We were made aware that he was not pleased. He apparently decided that we were scouting for work. He was absolutely right. But now as I mounted the stairs to his office I felt a certain self-satisfaction. Had I not spent over a year and a half with the company? Did I not stay in Stoke and go on the dole for some weeks in protest at his dismissal and in support of his reappointment as artistic director? Peter's door had two lights outside. Green, to indicate that he could be interrupted. Red signalled that you should return at a later hour. The light was green, so I knocked and went in. We chatted for a while and then I told him I felt it was time for me to move on. In my innocence I at least expected a gracious acceptance of my decision, perhaps an appreciation of my work with the company and a sincere thank you for my support in helping him regain his position. Instead, as my news sank in, he took a pause, leant back in his chair, and looked somewhat coldly at me. 'Yes,' he said, 'I always thought you had your eye on the West End.' I was shocked and saddened.

I don't remember anything else of the interview. I remember leaving the office and saying to myself, 'Fuck you, Peter, I deserved better than that!'

Peter Cheeseman, who sadly died a few months before my writing this, was one of the most talented and innovative theatre directors of the twentieth century. From nothing, he created a theatre and a theatre company in the industrial sprawl of the potteries and made it into something very special. He continued to work at Stoke until his retirement in 1998. He was appointed a CBE and continued his involvement with the new theatre as well as working on other projects. He ran the company for thirty-six years during which he directed more than 140 productions. In 1986 he masterminded the move to the 600-seat New Vic in Newcastle-under-Lyme, Europe's first purpose-built theatre-in-the-round. Peter Cheeseman had tremendous vision. He created a theatre that was accessible, inclusive, political. He developed a huge raft of talent in the acting, writing, designing and directing field. His achievements will live on. I believe I left the company a much better actor because of all I had learnt from Peter.

FROM THE NEW VIC TO THE OLD VIC

AUDITIONING FOR SIR LAURENCE OLIVIER

During my final production at Stoke I travelled to London for two auditions for the National Theatre. The first was for Robert Stephens, a leading actor with the company, whose work I had seen in *Royal Hunt of the Sun*, *The Recruiting Officer* etc. By now he was married to Maggie Smith and was, from my humble position, theatrical royalty. The Old Vic, where the National was in its fifth year, had a rehearsal room at the top of the building overlooking the Waterloo Road. It was here I did my pieces for him. I was extremely nervous, but I must have done all right. A week later I was asked to return to meet one of the the the associate directors, Frank Dunlop, a short, round, bearded man with eyes as black as liquorice. The audition went well.

I then returned to Stoke and a few days later packed my bags and bade a sad farewell to a company and theatre where I had spent a very happy and creative time.

A couple of weeks later, on a Sunday evening, and now living in a flat in Brixton I received one of the most terrifying telephone calls of my life. I picked up the receiver. It was Donald MacKechnie in full dry-humoured vein.

'Where have you been all weekend? I've been trying to get in touch with you.'

'Well, you know, I've been in and out. Went to Greenwich, saw a great film, *Rosemary's Baby* – why?'

'Oh, nothing, just that you are seeing Sir Laurence, in the morning. Old Vic rehearsal room, ten o'clock, OK?'

'What?'

'Come in early, the rehearsal room will be empty, give you a chance to prepare. Right? See you then.'

It is worth pointing out the circumstances for this bombshell. In 1968 we had no answering machines, no fax machines, no mobile phones. My brain went into shock. *Act in front of Laurence Olivier! My God, one of my audition pieces is Richard III – one of Olivier's most famous roles. I'll have to drop that sharpish! What can I do?*

I remembered my Cassius from *Julius Caesar* at Stoke the previous year. I rushed to look at my tattered old copy of the *Complete Works*. This had been given by an aunt of mine to some member of her family as a Christmas present in 1935. It sat on my shelf tired and spineless – a little like I felt. I picked one of Cassius' speeches, the longest and most dramatic. I still have the copy. The pages are thin, like Rizlas, and, despite the fact that each page has two columns of small printed text, the volume extends to 1312 pages. They even manage to get six sonnets on each page. My God, the talent and output of the man!

The speech is on page 862 and begins:

> *"I know that virtue to be in you, Brutus,*
> *As well as I do know your outward favour.*
> *Well, honour is the subject of my story –*
> *I cannot tell what you and other men*
> *Think of this life; but for my single self,*

I had as lief not be, as live to be
In awe of such a thing as I myself.
I was born free as Caesar; so were you..."

I can still remember the readings and stresses I gave to these lines all those years ago. It is a speech deeply critical of Caesar, and as Cassius launches further and further into this fierce attack it builds in imagery and intensity. A great audition speech, and – if you cut Brutus' three-line interjection – you can continue the tirade into Cassius' following speech seamlessly.

This will do. For the remainder of the evening I familiarise myself with it and then work on both audition pieces.

At eight the next morning I walk to nearby Brockwell Park. Thankfully there is only the odd dog walker and fleeting cyclist about. I do some loud vocal warm ups, I run around waving my arms furiously. To any onlooker I must look a complete nutter. I don't care. I AM ABOUT TO AUDITION FOR LAURENCE OLIVIER. THIS IS THE MOST IMPORTANT DAY OF MY CAREER. I WILL BE READY. I WILL BE RELAXED. By 9:40am I am climbing the concrete stairs to the Old Vic rehearsal room. It is a long high-ceilinged oblong room with a large half-moon-shaped window at one end overlooking the Waterloo Road. Placed menacingly in front of the window is a long table with some straight-backed chairs facing the room. I am alone. I go quietly through the speeches while windmilling my arms and shaking my legs out. I start to relax. I am halfway down the room when suddenly the door opens and four or five people enter. Donald is first. Suddenly Sir Laurence, in a very smart suit and black rimmed glasses, is walking with that familiar gait towards me. My mouth suddenly feels as dry as a camel's ear. My knees feel weak. He is smiling broadly.

'James, how are you?

'Very well, Sir Laurence,' I hear a voice say – in no way like my own.

He puts his arm casually round my shoulder and walks me away down the room. I am vaguely aware of the others taking seats at the table.

'What, are you going to do for us?' he asks, licking his lower lip, a small habit I recognise from some of his performances.

I tell him Cassius and a speech from the American Edward Albee's short play *Zoo Story*. This latter intrigues him and we continue round the room as he tells me of a Birmingham accent he had to do some years before for a play called *Semi-Detached*. This is fascinating. I relax. We walk on.

Suddenly his arm leaves my shoulder and he moves away towards the table and the others.

'Let's hear the Albee first,' he says, over his shoulder.

Jesus Christ! They all sit looking and smiling at me.

Zoo Story is a two-hander set in Central Park in New York on a Sunday afternoon in summer. The two characters are Peter who is sitting on a bench reading. He is tweedy, pipe-smoking, bookish. Jerry is younger, carelessly dressed and is in possession of a flick-knife. He has, Albee tells us, "a great weariness". They don't know each other. Jerry is spiky, provocative, changeable. He continually goads Peter over the possession of the bench and eventually the knife appears. They tussle, Peter stabs and kills Jerry. Jerry thanks him. "Thank you, Peter. I mean that, now – thank you very much".

Early on, Jerry launches into a long story about his relationship with a vicious dog who continually attacks him in the hallway of his rooming house, and where he eventually decides "First I'll kill the dog with kindness, and if that doesn't work – I'll just kill him". This extraordinary speech he titles "The Story of Jerry and the Dog". There is a long cat-and-mouse game with the beast: there are many hamburgers lavished on it – bringing no diminution in the attacks – then the rat poison mixed with the meat – "And it came to pass that the beast was deathly ill". The dog survives, the attacks stop, and lo, there is an understanding, a truce, between man and dog. The speech is over six pages long. Yes, over six pages long. I loved this speech and I had learned a large chunk of it.

So now I prepared, faced the table and launched into "The Story of Jerry and the Dog". I was well into the story when a ringing voice called out—

'Thank you!' It was Sir Laurence.

He stopped my audition! HE HATES ME.

'Let's have your Cassius.'

My mind was in flitters. But on I went. I delivered the Shakespeare. I got through it. I didn't dry.

'Thank you, James.' He whispered something to Donald, rose and came towards me. He was smiling broadly. He banged me gently on the shoulder. 'Well done, *very* good.' He looked me in the eye. 'I look forward to working with you, baby,' and strode away out of the room, followed by the others. Donald came over.

'There, you see, a piece of cake. I thought the Albee was a tidge long,' he remarked drily. 'Talk to you later.'

And he departed. I was alone suddenly in this very large and extremely quiet room.

I'm in. I'm going to be a member of the National Theatre Company. The rest of that day went by in a blur. I was unbelievably happy.

Audition pieces are usually around two to three minutes long. Later I timed the Jerry speech. I think Sir Laurence stopped me when I was about five minutes into it. I felt a right idiot.

THE NATIONAL THEATRE AT THE OLD VIC

The National Theatre in 1968 consisted of three separate buildings. There was the Old Vic, the Annexe, and the offices and Rehearsal Room in Aquinas St.

The Vic in '68 was a little different from its current state. The stage door was on the other side of the building in Waterloo Road – conveniently located next to it was a pub called The Victoria, a haven for actors and crew. In the basement of the theatre was a tiny canteen. Under the stone title on the front of the theatre that proclaimed The Old Vic was a long painted canopy, which, in large black letters, said "The National Theatre Company".

On The Cut, next to the theatre, was an airy, handsome modern concrete, brick and glass structure which we called The Annexe. It is now the NT Studio, which currently houses rehearsal spaces for writers, directors and actors to workshop new writing. It also houses a new and fast expanding Archive of all NT work from the inception of the company to the present day. But here in 1968, in various rooms, dwelt the costume department run by a small, brilliant, beaky-nosed acid-voiced man. His name was Ivan Alderman, and in all the years I had contact with him he was never without a nifty little trilby hat perched on his uplifted head. There was also the wig department and along one side of the building and running the height of the four floors was the paint frame, where huge backdrops could be draped and painted. This contraption is still there today.

Situated halfway between the Vic and the South Bank was Aquinas Street, where we spent nearly all of our daytime. On a bombsite behind a small street of redbrick terraced houses was the heart of the organisation: a long row of interconnecting prefabricated wooden huts with tarred felt roofs housed the administrative offices. At one end of this was a structure, which consisted of four of these huts adapted to make one large, interior space, was the rehearsal room. This interior had, of necessity, a number of hardboard-covered pillars that held up the roof. The floor was stained in various places from the leaks that occurred during heavy rainfall. There was a small "yard" outside where we would sometimes play football, until a stage manager would bustle out and tell us to keep the noise down as Sir Laurence couldn't hear his cues.

There was also a small "canteen" attached to the rehearsal room. Here under the low wooden roof the food was dispensed by two unforgettable women. In charge was Rose who, on hot summer lunchtimes with her red perspiring face, hair bristling out of her white cap, worked fiercely at the counter filling our plates. Always up for a laugh, a human dynamo, constantly on the move. Behind her, and in total contrast, was Nellie, a small, thin, pale, creature. Her hair was pulled tightly back behind her small ears. She would slowly approach the counter with fresh supplies. She was a woman of one pace: slow. She never spoke, never made eye contact, very shy. The two worked seamlessly together and we all loved them.

One day in the queue for lunch the actor Ronnie Pickup remarked to Maggie Smith, 'God, isn't Rose marvellous?' Miss Smith looked at the two women slaving away, paused, and then said in that droll way of hers, 'Yeees – but Nellie's the better part!'

I have always thought this a brilliant observation. The showiest character in a play is not always the best part. On stage Rose's ebullience could tire the watcher. What you saw was what you got. While Nellie's quiet, contained quality would slowly mesmerise the observer and inexorably draw them in to want to know more about her.

My first day at the National was a re-rehearsal of a production of Brecht's *Edward II*. Some actors had left the cast and a few of us new boys were replacing them. I was taking over a small part and was somewhat nervous at becoming a member of this august company. Two small incidents relaxed me completely. The first was when Derek Jacobi, playing the Bishop of Coventry, had his ornate crozier kicked from his hand by some villains. As it fell to the floor he said in a very camp voice, 'Oohh! I lose all my croziers that way.' There was much laughter from the other actors.

Minutes later Edward Petherbridge, playing Spencer, had the line, *"Honi soit qui mal y pense'* – *or as we say in*

English 'Evil on him who thinks evil'". Instead Edward said, *'Honi soit qui mal y pense'* – or as we say in English, *"There's no business like show business".'* Again much laughter.

Now these gags were not particularly funny, but when a production has been running a number of months and the cast are understandably getting a bit tired of it, it takes very little to get them going. Actors are always up for a laugh on these occasions. Re-rehearsals are invariably boring. These two interjections I still remember, simply, because they took the curse off my first day with the National Theatre Company.

Over the next ten days I also joined the casts of two remarkable productions. One of these was Tom Stoppard's *Rosencrantz and Guildenstern Are Dead,* which was a massive success at the Vic with two unforgettable performances in the leading roles – John Stride as Rosencrantz and Edward Petherbridge as Guildenstern. As is well known, the play expands upon the lives of two minor characters from Shakespeare's *Hamlet.* The action takes place mostly "in the wings" of that play with brief appearances of the major characters who enact fragments of the original scenes. Unlike the audience, our two hapless heroes have no idea of the onstage events that govern their lives and lead to their deaths. I had seen the play months before and had loved it. Although I was joining to play a tiny part, one of the strolling players, I was excited to become a part of this production.

I recently found tucked in one of my books a small brown envelope. Printed on the front were the words: "Post Office Telegram" and my address. Inside, on a form dated 19th December 1969 and turned sepia with age, were several thin strips of paper stuck to the form. Typed on these was the message:

"ROSENCRANTZ CALL 3:30PM ON STAGE –
STAGE MANAGER"

The third production I took over in was Clifford Williams' all-male *As You Like It*. Twenty-first-century audiences take all-male or all-female productions of Shakespeare in their stride, but in 1968 this was seen as an extraordinary and risky venture. But audiences thronged to it and the press acclaimed it. The setting and costumes had a very modern sixties look. "A cross between a Pierre Cardin shop window and HG Wells' *The Shape of Things to Come*" said the *Sunday Telegraph*. The designer was Ralph Koltai. The stage floor was shining white onto which, in the forest scenes, brightly coloured lighting patterns were projected. All around hung transparent plastic tubes (trees) with giant jagged plastic honeycombed fragments (foliage) hanging above and behind. The furniture was made of perspex cubes. The costumes were predominantly white and silver with large fur capes and cloaks in the forest scenes. It was a beautiful production.

The performers included Ronnie Pickup as a tall, willowy barefooted Rosalind, who in disguise wore a white suit with a long silk scarf knotted around his neck and a white peaked John Lennon cap. Jeremy Brett was an absurdly handsome and romantic Orlando. Charlie Kay in a mini dress, large outsize glasses and big hair was a terrific Celia, and bore a strong resemblance to the famous newspaper columnist Marjorie Proops. Derek Jacobi played the court jester Touchstone, with both a physical and vocal resemblance to

Frankie Howerd. This worked brilliantly in the character's final speech where the many "Ifs" and "Lies" took on the strangled elongated tones of that great comedian. Robert Stephens was a fastidious, and lonely Jaques. Richard Kay in a short silver dress and Veronica Lake wig turned Phoebe into a very sexy, husky-voiced, rustic charmer. John Stride's Audrey was a rough lump of a girl. He had taken over the role from Tony Hopkins. I took over the part of Amiens and with my guitar and accompanying band sang most of the songs in the show. These, like the production, were very modern. So, "Under The Greenwood Tree", "Blow, Blow, Thou Winter Wind" and "What Shall He Have That Killed The Deer" had strong sixties pop and Bossa Nova influences.

With the play's gender-twisting plot it was still a bold decision at that time to ask audiences to entertain questions of gender construction, when representations of homosexuality were still banned from the English stage. The Lord Chamberlain's censorship of plays only ended with the passage of The Theatres Act a year or so later.

So, within a short few weeks I was established in the company.

In those days you signed a one-year contract. The wage structure for the actors was unusual. We were paid a weekly wage, plus a "performance fee" for each performance we played. My contract was for seventeen pounds a week and thirty bob (£1.50) a performance. Now, many decades later, the National continues to use this method of payment for actors. It is the only theatre company in Britain that does so. In my first twelve months at the Vic, the National presented thirteen productions, some new, some old. I appeared in seven of them. That year's repertoire, along with the productions

I have mentioned, included plays by Somerset Maugham, Feydeau, Congreve, Chekhov, Shaw, as well as a new play by Charles Wood, titled *H*, about the Indian Mutiny and others by John Spurling, Maureen Duffy and Natalia Ginzburg.

Along with these, there was August Strindberg's *Dance Of Death* directed by Glen Byam Shaw. Sir Laurence played Edgar, a brutal hard-drinking captain of an artillery detachment, based on a small island off the coast of Sweden in 1900. Geraldine McEwan played his wife Alice, a former actress, and Robert Stephens played Kurt, Alice's cousin who is on a visit. The garrison tower the couple live in is a former prison. It is a spectacularly bleak play, concerning a twenty-five year marriage gone very wrong. That said, it is not without some humour. "Our twenty-five years of misery", Alice calls it. The couple, over the course of the play, tear each other apart. Alice uses her sexuality to seduce her cousin in a calculated act of revenge on her husband. Edward Albee was obviously indebted to it when he wrote *Who's Afraid of Virginia Woolf.*

"Once more I returned, to be rewarded with open contempt... I could see plainly now that I had been in the power of a vampire. I only wanted to live long enough to cleanse my name from the filth with which she had sullied it. I wanted to live long enough to revenge myself but first of all I must have proof of her infidelity. I hated her now with a hatred more fatal than indifference because it is the antithesis of love. I hated her because I loved her."

– Strindberg, writing about his first wife, the actress Siri von Essen.

I appeared in the production for about six performances, playing one of the three non-speaking sentries, a role Tony Hopkins had played a few months earlier. I basically had to patrol – upstage and cruelly underlit – outside the Captain's house. As he exited I had to come to attention and give a sharp salute. Sir Laurence would stop for a moment and improvise a little chat with me. For the short few days I was involved in the production I was lucky enough to watch a lot of the play from the wings.

A few things I remember:

Sir Laurence's pronunciation of Copenhagen – which he did as "Shopenhaben", preceded by that trademark lick of the lips. How much humour he found in the early scenes. His ornate cheating at cards and his "comic" annoyance at being found out. His physical playfulness. All this eased the audience into thinking that, contrary to their preconceptions about Nordic gloom, not to mention the play's title, the piece was very funny. We were actually laughing at a Strindberg play. And *then* the bitterness and savagery were introduced, which soon took the smile off our faces. It was clever not to go for the jugular from the beginning.

Sir Laurence insisted on having a "practical" morse code machine for contact with the outside world. So, typically, he learned to do it properly. This necessitated some poor ASM having to learn it as well, so he/she could tap out orders and replies to his messages from the wings. And there was no cheating.

There is a great photograph of Sir Laurence doing a dance in his dark navy uniform, with its bright brass buttons and three gold stars on each side of his stiff upright collar. His uniform trousers had two broad yellow stripes down the sides. These are tucked into a pair of knee-high beautifully polished riding boots with sharp brass spurs. His right hand is elegantly placed behind his head. The wrist of his left hand is on his waist with the hand resting behind on his hip. What struck me when watching him was how little make-up he was wearing for this role. An unusual occurence. His hair, short back and sides, was slicked down with a little Brylcreme. He had grown a short stubby military moustache. His bearing was bullish, upright, military. He moved with a certain swagger. But it was the least "characterised" performance I ever saw Sir Laurence give. It seemed to come from some dark place inside him. He was sly. He was funny. He was breathtaking in his cruelty. It was for me the best performance I had ever seen him give. Magnetic. Mesmerising. Unforgettable.

Geraldine Mc Ewan who, in Feydeau's *A Flea In Her Ear* gave one of the great comic performances, here gave Alice a combative low-voiced spitting intensity. She matched Sir Laurence toe-to-toe, giving as good as she got.

Sadly, my few days as the sentry was the only time I ever appeared with Sir Laurence onstage.

* * *

An Aquinas Street yarn. Michael Gambon, who I have worked with on many productions, told me of his audition for Sir Laurence, a few years before mine. He had chosen the speech of Richard III after he had seduced Lady Anne:

"Was ever woman in this humour woo'd?
Was ever woman in this humour won?"

'I was shitting myself with nerves,' he told me. As he was about to start he noticed the plywood-covered pillars in the room and decided to grab one and swing out from behind it to give a dynamic and dramatic start to the speech.

This he did, but after about four lines he heard Sir Laurence call out loudly, 'Stop! Stop!'

Jesus Christ, thought Michael, *I must be terrible.*

Rising and coming towards him, Sir Laurence said, 'Your hand! Your hand!'

Michael looked down to see his hand pouring blood. Sir Laurence, as ever immaculately dressed reached into the breast pocket of his jacket, pulled out a handkerchief and helped him wrap it round his bleeding finger.

'I was so terrified of him I didn't notice I had gashed my finger on a nail sticking out of the pillar!'

'So, did you do the piece for him again?

'Naw. But he offered me the season!'

* * *

There was a little canteen in the basement of the Old Vic where there was always the danger you might end up at a table on your own with Sir Laurence. He often popped in. We were all in awe of him and, invariably and pathetically, dried up and couldn't think of anything to say to him. It happened to me once when the others at the table went off and left me alone with him. Luckily, after a short stab at conversation, a young actress rescued me by asking my help to take some cups of tea up to the dressing room.

This happened to Michael G, when like me, he was a very

minor member of the company. Lost for words he glanced down at the table and in front of Sir Laurence he noticed a really nice leather wallet with the word "Norge" embossed on it. With great relief he said to Sir Laurence, 'Norge!'

'What?' said Sir Laurence.

'Norge!' said Michael, pointing at the wallet.

'What?' said Sir Laurence.

'I suppose they gave you that when you played Hamlet?'

'*What?*' said Sir Laurence.

'You know, when you played Hamlet. At Elsinore – Elsinore Castle?'

'Elsinore?' said Sir Laurence.

'You know, Hamlet – did they give you that when you played Hamlet in Norway?'

There followed a short pause, then, 'Elsinore,' said Sir Laurence rising from the table, 'is in Denmark! And anyway, that isn't my fucking wallet!' and walked off.

* * *

So, my first year went on. Despite the long hours the work at the Vic was enormously exciting. We were The National Theatre. This was a very big deal. We played in repertoire. At the time this was incredibly new. I often appeared in three different plays in a week. We toured productions round the country, playing in large provincial theatres in Sunderland, Newcastle, Liverpool, Bristol, Bath, Manchester and Leeds to huge, appreciative audiences. I was offered another season. I was about to start a family. I happily accepted.

THE SEVENTIES

I stayed with the company for five more seasons. In all that time I appeared in about twenty-five plays. Here's a mishmash of memories from 1970.

In 1970 the National took two productions on tour to Los Angeles. Chekhov's *Three Sisters,* directed by Sir Laurence, and Farquhar's *The Beaux' Stratagem,* directed by Bill Gaskill. This production reunited Gaskill with Maggie Smith and Robert Stephens with whom he had done that famous and groundbreaking *The Recruiting Officer.* During the National's visit to Los Angeles, Maggie Smith was nominated for Best Actress in that year's Oscars for her performance in *The Prime Of Miss Jean Brodie.* Appearing in two classy NT productions in Hollywood while the Oscar deliberations were going on must have been a very happy and opportune coincidence for her.

I was in neither production for that tour, but soon after they returned to the National the management decided to set up a short season at the Cambridge Theatre in the West End. The plays chosen were *The Beaux' Stratagem* and *Cyrano De Bergerac* with Edward Woodward, in which I was already playing at the Vic. I was asked to take over the role of Foigard in *The Beaux' Stratagem* from Derek Jacobi. He had not enjoyed playing the role and I suspect felt miscast.

Foigard is a very funny part. He purports to be a French parson serving in the French Army, and is involved in a subplot to wed the French Count Bellair to Mrs Sullen (Maggie Smith). In fact he is a rogue and speaks throughout the play with a strong, undisguised Irish accent. Aimwell, one of the two heroes in the play, threatens him with exposure and death:"You're a subject of England and a traitor against the Government".

Foigard's stage-Irish dialogue can be delivered in a less insulting manner than the way it was written on the page.

> "Foigard: Upon my soul, noble friend, dis is strange news you tell me; Fader Foigard a subject of England! The son of a burgomaster of Brussels a subject of England!
>
> Aimwell: The son of a bog-trotter of Ireland, sir. Your tongue will condemn you before any bench in the kingdom."

I remember being "off" one night in a mercifully short scene, where with a servant called Scrub, played by Bernard Gallagher, I had to enter Mrs Sullen's bedroom and drag out a burglar. I had three lines to say. I was sitting in my fifth-floor dressing room when on the tannoy I suddenly heard my cue. *INDESCRIBABLE PANIC*. I fled towards the stage, tearing down the dozens of concrete stairs as my name was being called on the tannoy. By the time I arrived in the wings the scene was over. Bernard had entered and covered for me. I expressed my thanks to him, aware how much stick I might get later from Miss Smith. She was a big star, and a formidable character with a sharp tongue. After the curtain call I knocked on her door and although I knew she liked me I didn't know what to expect. I entered and abjectly apologised. She couldn't have been nicer. 'But don't let it happen again.' Bet your life! This, by the way, was not the first or last time I was "off". More later.

Maggie Smith, of course, won the Oscar in 1970. But she was performing with the National Theatre in London, so couldn't attend the ceremony. In 1994, when Nigel Hawthorne was nominated for an Oscar, he was performing in a play in the West End. But the world had changed and the producers of his film were allowed to buy out three performances of the play and fly him out to Los Angeles for the ceremony.

One evening, after a performance, we were all invited up to the rehearsal room at the top of the Vic to watch Miss Smith being presented with her Oscar by Sir Laurence. This event would be broadcast live on BBC TV's *Late Night Line Up*. Sir Laurence duly and wittily presented the Oscar. Maggie was then interviewed by the presenter and was very funny about the whole thing. When asked in what hallowed spot in her home she would exhibit the statuette, she replied as a doorstop in her lavatory. During the interview, and in shot, Sir Laurence walked back and forth behind the two women shamelessly mugging, pulling focus and making them laugh.

Earlier that year, at a press night at the Cambridge Theatre, I had seen Maggie Smith play Hedda Gabler in a production by the great Swedish director Ingmar Bergman. With her hair combed up and back from her face and wearing a high-collared black dress, she moved with icy languor around the blood-red set. She was magnificent, predatory. A strange and abiding memory of that night was the loud laughter emanating from the stage-right box. When the lights came up at the end of the performance I looked up and was surprised to see the playwright Tennessee Williams rising from his seat. He had for some reason found the play very amusing.

Also in 1970, I appeared in a Simon Grey adaptation of

Dostoevsky's *The Idiot* with Derek Jacobi and Diane Cilento, directed by Anthony Quayle. I have only two memories of that production. For some reason the set design encompassed a diagonal raised "track" across the floor on which some sets trucked on and off. The track was about ten centimetres high. In one scene (in a ballroom?) we all appeared in evening dress and spent the whole scene nonchanantly stepping over this barrier as if it wasn't there. Surreal.

The second memory was when Sir Laurence invited the company to a party at his London flat. It was in a tall skyscraper called Stag Place in Victoria. Diane Cilento was a big star at that time, having appeared in films like *The Wicker Man*, the western *Hombre,* playing opposite Paul Newman, and *Tom Jones* with Albert Finney, for which she was nominated for Best Supporting Actress at the Oscars in 1964. This, by the way, was the film where, for the first time, three actresses from the same film were nominated in that category. The other two were Dame Edith Evans and Joyce Redman – all unsuccessful. The winner was Margaret Rutherford for *The VIPs*. Anyway, it was a very swish party. Diane was accompanied by her then husband Sean Connery. I'd never been to anything so glamorous in my life. But the abiding memory was of one small incident in the evening. One of the ASMs lost one of her contact lenses. At the time these were really expensive and the wearer usually had only one pair. I can still see Sir Laurence, Joan Plowright, Diane Cilento and Sean Connery down on all fours with the rest of the company scouring the lush carpet for the missing lens. I can't recall if we found it.

THREE PRODUCTIONS WITH ANTHONY HOPKINS

WELL, TWO AS IT TURNED OUT

HOW HE FURTHERED MY CAREER

NUMBER ONE.

In early 1971 the National was producing Shakespeare's *Coriolanus*. The eponymous role was to be played by the Hollywood film actor and star of *The Sound Of Music* Christopher Plummer. The play was to be staged by two directors from the Berliner Ensemble, Manfred Wekwerth and Joachim Tenschert, who had mounted a famous production a few years earlier in Berlin of Brecht's version of the play. Given a choice of directors, Plummer chose the men from the Berliner. They arrived with a number of very large photograph albums. These held dozens and dozens of huge images, documenting the staging of each move and scene from their Berliner production. They were going to stage the Shakespeare play *exactly* the same way as they had staged the Brecht version, even down to the use of a large white curtain that swept across the stage after each scene, though without the "title" of the upcoming scene printed on them – a favourite Brechtian alienation device. The purpose of this was to bring a cold full stop to each scene, to alienate the audience from being swept along by the narrative, or from getting too emotionally involved and thus, importantly, sacrificing their critical/political faculties.

Plummer, who arrived at rehearsal in a white Rolls Royce, only rehearsed for three days before he left the production. I don't know all the reasons for his departure but I was one of a few actors who did the first three days' rehearsal with him. From the beginning he seemed very unhappy. We subsequently learned that he was demanding the restoration of twenty substantial cuts. Most of these he justified and the directors agreed to their return. But he was also unhappy with the directors' interpretation, refusing to take direction and demanding new costumes. Comically, the confrontation of actor versus directors mirrored Coriolanus versus the people's tribunes in the play.

Manfred and Joachim, whose English was not good, used a translator. They were extremely insistent on the way the language was spoken, and when they wanted a pause, they wanted a *pause*. On the third day they asked Christopher for a pause. He told them he had left a pause. No, no, a big pause. Christopher turned to the translator and said very angrily, 'Tell them I left a fucking pause big enough to drive a fucking horse and cart through.' The translator looked appalled. 'Tell them!' said Mr Plummer. The translator did so. There then followed an extremely long pause. Christopher, in front of us actors, made some joke about the directors and very soon they stood up and walked out. Much embarrassment all round. Rehearsals were suspended. Negotiations by intermediaries followed for the next twenty-four hours. The company were then called to a meeting with Sir Laurence. He told us there was an impasse. We were asked and offered the choice of who we wanted to continue working with: Christopher or the two directors. The company opted for the directors and very quickly Tony Hopkins, who was already appearing with the company in two other productions – *A Woman Killed with Kindness* by Thomas Heywood and *The Architect And The Emperor Of Assyria* by Fernando Arrabel – was swiftly drafted in to play Coriolanus. The production was not well received.

NUMBER TWO.

On the 9*th* November 1972 we opened Michael Blakemore's production of *Macbeth*. Tony Hopkins and Diana Rigg were the Macbeths. I was playing the small role of Second Murderer. Now, it is well documented that at that time Tony liked to drink. I knew nothing of his private life, but it was obvious that he was troubled. He didn't enjoy playing Macbeth. I don't think he hit it off with Michael Blakemore. His Macbeth, like his Coriolanus, was exciting. He played with fast, passionate energy and was always very emotionally involved in the character. There was never a false moment in his work. But I noticed how changeable he could be during each performance, often brilliant in playing, say Scenes Two, Four, Six, Eight etc. And yet, on the following night he would walk through these scenes while other scenes suddenly took on a new excitement.

The production was not successful and Tony suffered from some poor reviews. London at that time had two evening papers and Felix Barker writing in the *Evening News* was particularly unpleasant. Tony obviously took the reviews to heart and shortly after the press night left the production.

John Shrapnel the understudy stepped in, took over the role and did well. But Sir Laurence called Denis Quilley, who was playing Banquo, to his office. 'Tony's fucked off,' he told Denis, and asked if he would take over the role within a week. Denis said he would but asked Sir Laurence if he should phone Tony to ask if could hang on until he was ready to play it. Sir Laurence leapt into a rage. I can easily imagine the scene, those high, crisp clear notes bouncing off the walls. 'Don't go near the fucking phone. I never want to see the little bastard in this building *ever again*!'

With Denis taking over, we all moved up the pecking order. I moved from Second Murderer to the very good part of Ross, a character who, throughout all the murderous political machinations, cleverly manages to survive unscathed. I remember Sir Laurence complimenting me on my performance.

NUMBER THREE.

– Let me now jump on some months from Tony's exit from *Macbeth*. The great director John Dexter was about to start rehearsals for Molière's *The Misanthrope* in a new version by the poet Tony Harrison, which moved the action of the play forward 300 years from 1666 to the Paris of General de Gaulle. Tony Hopkins was cast as Oronte. Apparently he had never properly read the play and, just before rehearsals were to begin, discovered that Oronte was not the leading role. He once again walked away, refusing to appear in the production. John Dexter (who I will write a lot about), was a fiery character and on hearing the news said, 'That'll teach him not to read the play. Shifty, spineless Welsh c**t.'

That was two productions at the National Theatre Tony had departed from in a few months. I remember thinking at the time that this actor was heading into career suicide. And of course I was right…

Parts once again had to be rejigged and John asked me to join the cast to play Dubois, the hero's valet. Another step up. Thanks, Tony.

That fine poet Tony Harrison (who uncannily resembles the actor Albert Dieudonne who played the title role in Abel Gance's great masterpiece of silent cinema *Napoleon*) had written a superlative verse translation of the Molière. Funny and elegant, his rhyming couplets made the language modern and colloquial and provided a wealth of audacious parallels.

The designs by Tanya Moiseiwitsch were very beautiful. Diana Rigg was a very funny, sharp and sexy Celimene, with long curly red hair, bare arms and a very simple, very beautiful long floor-length red silk dress, cut brilliantly by Stephen Skaptason in the NT Wardrobe. Even now I get palpitations thinking about her. The conflict in the play lies within Alceste (Alec McCowen), and the battle is fought between his mind and his heart. He has a puritan's allegiance to truth and honour, yet cannot help loving Celimene who embodies with irrestible attraction all that he detests. Unimpeded by wigs, ruffs and period mannerisms the play took on a new vibrant life.

The rehearsals were very exciting and from the beginning one sensed that this could be a big hit. I remember a morning when Alec McCowen and I were rehearsing a scene, which had been going very well. John Dexter liked it and it got lots of laughs from the other actors. We were a bit complacent, a bit lazy I suspect, and "corpsed" a couple of times during the rehearsal. Fatally, we had forgotten the volatile side of our director. We finished the scene, expecting some good reaction from him. He looked at us, unblinking and took a pause.

'I suppose you think that scene is funny?' A pause. 'That scene is about as funny as a child's open grave. Do it again!'

The production opened in February 1973 and was one of the National's biggest successes at that time. Dexter, Rigg, McCowen and Harrison got rave reviews and the rest of us also fared very well.

***

On first nights in London it is not unusual for a number of actors to receive a "Good Luck" postcard from their fellow actor Vernon Dobtcheff. The man is legendary in the business. Vernon is Franco-British of Russian descent and is reputed to speak many languages. Very successful, he has appeared in countless European and foreign films, comfortable in all the languages. His cards are often sent from some foreign city. Tony Hopkins, talking of high unemployment in our profession, said to me in 1971, 'Things are so bad in the business at the moment, Vernon Dobtcheff is out of work on three continents.'

JOHN DEXTER

John Dexter took an interest in me and cast me in a number of his productions over the years. I remember opening the *Guardian* one day in 1989 and, flicking through the pages, coming across a half-page obituary of John with a large photograph of him in the middle. I took it in but continued turning the pages. It was at least three seconds later that I realised what I had seen. I turned back to the obituary. I was absolutely shocked and saddened at the news but realised that my mind had just done an extended double take. John was such a larger-than-life character and such a powerful presence in the minds of all of us who had worked with him that it was hard to believe he had actually died.

If you look at some of the most iconic plays of the mid-twentieth century you will find that John created brilliant productions of a number of them. He staged the premieres of the great "kitchen-sink trilogy" by Arnold Wesker, first at the Belgrade Theatre, Coventry, then at the Royal Court. Later he directed Wesker's *Chips With Everything* about young Air Force conscripts doing National Service. The play creates a world where individuality must be suppressed, but where class still dominates. The actors were drilled by a professional soldier. Dexter staged an outstanding production. There was a great silent scene, set outdoors in a military camp in the middle of the night. Sentries patrolled around a high wire-fenced enclosure, which protected army supplies, while a few of the men with crucial timing and breathtaking precision surmounted this obstacle and stole some bags of coal.

He also directed Wesker's *The Kitchen*, a play set in the kitchen of a large restaurant where thirty chefs, waitresses and kitchen porters prepare meals. Kenneth Tynan wrote of the production in the *Observer*: "It achieves something that

few playwrights have ever attempted; it dramatises work...
rising at the end of the first half to a climactic lunch-hour
frenzy that is the fullest theatrical expression I have ever seen
of the laws of supply and demand".

At the National, John directed Sir Laurence in the hugely
successful *Othello* and of course, being a product of the Royal
Court, did things democratically. After the first runthrough
of the play he gave the company notes. Afterwards he was
taken aside by Sir Laurence – 'John, baby, don't give me
notes in front of the company!'

As a director, John was brilliant, fiery, lucid, inventive,
bursting with energy and very dangerous. For a period he
came to rehearsals in a blue boiler-suit. I never understood
that fashion statement. With his black hair and blacker eyes
he demanded complete concentration from everyone in the
room. No sitting at the side reading a newspaper. He did
his homework and expected the actors to do the same. You
had to be sharp and accurate on the lines and remember the
moves from the previous rehearsal. He knew exactly what
he wanted and if a scene he was staging wasn't working he
would apologise to the company and state that he would
have it sorted by the next rehearsal. John, famously, had
"whipping boys" – usually a good-looking and often
inexperienced young actor. Woe betide that poor bastard if
he did something to upset him. John was a workaholic, an
obsessive and could be monstrous. When in a bad mood he
would pick on people, and sometimes, although very rarely,
sack them.

Next to the Vic stage door was the pub where actors
often retreated for a drink at lunchtime. During a Dexter
rehearsal period, the talk invariably turned to John with

much moaning and complaining about him, his methods and his rudeness. One day, as the usual, complaints went on and on, an actor raised his arm and frustratingly stated, 'Look, I am sick of this. John Dexter! Every lunchtime! The next person to mention John Dexter buys the next round, OK?'

There followed a long pause and then an actor blurted, 'I'll buy the round, do you know what that fucker said to me this morning?'

John had started in the business as an actor and had, for a short time, appeared in the radio series *The Archers*. Years later, when directing Albert Finney and giving him some notes, the actor would quietly whistle *The Archers* theme tune straight back at him.

John was a great director, but a troubled soul. He once rather plaintively wrote in his diary:

"Why does bringing out the best in others always bring out the worst in me?"

In a production of Oliver Goldsmith's little-performed play *The Good Natured Man* John gave me a great lesson on comic business that I have never forgotten. I was playing Timothy Twitch, a bailiff who turns up at the house of our hero, Mr Honeywood, to confiscate all his furniture due to the bad debts he had accrued. Soon after my arrival, Honeywood's bespectacled, blue-stocking fiancée, Miss Richland (a stylish and very funny Maureen Lipman) and other guests, are announced. In a panic, Honeywood (the very good-natured Desmond McNamara) pleads with me to postpone the removal of his belongings and begs me to "pretend" to be a friend of his until the lady departs. I reluctantly agree. Soon the room is filled with some very sophisticated characters. Timothy Twitch is feeling like the proverbial duck out of water. Suddenly "tea" arrives. Timothy is quickly laden with a dainty cup and saucer – two fine, delicate objects he has clearly never handled in his life. As he ponders this dilemma, a small plate is put in his other hand and shortly after a cake is placed on this. Total panic sets in. How does he handle the food and drink surrounded by the fashions of the town? As we work on the scene I try sipping tea from the cup and saucer with one hand and then lift the plate to my mouth with the other and quickly and surreptitiously take bites out of the cake. John liked this. And this is where his direction then kicked in. Although these little moments would only be a few small grace notes in a crowded scene with much dialogue, he then began to focus the audience's attention on Timothy's problem. John had the wonderful ability of telling the audience where they should be looking at any point in his productions. So for the moments when I sipped tea from the cup and saucer or bit into the cake on the plate he drilled the company into stillness for those seconds. It worked a treat, it got the laughs. But God help any actor who moved during those moments.

This is a small and inconsequential detail of John's methods. Many directors nowadays are not interested in little moments. The actor's inventiveness is often surplus to requirements in the director's "concept". I remember two "pieces of business" Charlie Kay had in Jonathan Miller's Victorian production of *The Merchant Of Venice* with Sir Laurence as Shylock. Charlie played Arragon, one of the three suitors for Portia's hand. For some reason, and very funny it was, he played him as an extremely doddery old man. The three caskets were displayed on a mahogany pedestal that swivelled. When offered the choice of caskets he reached out for the lead casket which would have won him the very wealthy lady, but Joan Plowright, playing Portia, swivelled the pedestal and his hand fell on the silver one.

During the same scene he was offered a cup of tea while a maid in a long black dress and white apron stood beside him with a bowl of sugar lumps and some tongs. Slowly, Charlie carefully dropped about five sugar lumps in his tea and stirred it. He then tapped the spoon on the side of the cup before replacing it on the saucer. Then, tasting the heavily sweetened tea he made a sour face, which got a good laugh from the audience. He paused, reached for the tongs and dropped another two lumps in the cup. Bigger laugh. Brilliant.

I remember a bit of business Sir Laurence did in Congreve's 1695 play *Love For Love*. He wore a frock coat, knee breeches and long stockings. In the middle of a scene, we the audience realised he had padded his "inadequate" calves, for while doing some complicated dance steps his "calves" suddenly swivelled round and appeared on the front of his legs.

Yes, I know all this can be seen as cheap laughs, but audiences love these small inventive moments.

John Dexter was a great director and, very importantly, especially for young actors, a great teacher. Not many directors have this extra talent.

When I rejoined the NT on the South Bank in 1980, John was the first director I worked with. I will write more about him later and about his outstanding production of Brecht's *The Life Of Galileo* with Michael Gambon.

MICHAEL BLAKEMORE

In 1972 Michael Blakemore directed *The Front Page* by Ben Hecht and Charles MacArthur, one of the greatest American comedies of the twentieth century. The play is set in the press room of the Criminal Courts Building in Chicago in 1928. In the adjoining jail a man named Earl Williams is to be executed for murder. While waiting for this event, a group of cynical tabloid reporters play poker and trade wisecracks. At the end of Act One Williams escapes. Panic ensues.

The main story revolves around one of the star reporters, Hildy Johnson, who arrives to tell his fellow scribblers that he has chucked in his job, is getting married and is about to leave for New York. Now, you may have seen one of the three *Front Page* films so I'll keep it short. Hildy is alone in the room when Earl dramatically crashes through the window. He hides the escapee in a roll-top desk and then manoeuvres to get Earl out of the building under the noses of his fellow reporters to interview him and to achieve a fantastic scoop. Much revolves around the rival reporters, Hildy's editor – the Machiavellian Walter Burns – Hildy's fiancée and her mother, a tart called Molly Molloy, a gangster called Diamond Louie, not to mention the Mayor, the Sheriff and a character called Woodenshoes Eichhorn.

I played Murphy, one of the reporters. The rehearsals in Aquinas Street were great fun. The play had been cast from the permanent company. Denis Quilley played Hildy with raffish charm and high energy. He was terrific. But the surprise was the performance of the actor Alan MacNaughtan as Walter Burns. Alan, a quiet, reflective, pipe-smoking and very Scottish actor, was not one's idea of the fast-talking aggressive and cynical American editor. And this is where casting from within a company can be so exciting. There is a leap of faith, a chance is taken, an actor is challenged and stretched and the result is a performance of unexpected brilliance. Our production was seen by a Hollywood producer and led directly to the Billy Wilder film of the play. You may have seen Jack Lemmon and Walter Matthau in it. They were both excellent, and Matthau, who I bow to no one in my admiration for, played the editor Burns in the film, but, his performance was not, in my opinion, a patch on Alan MacNaughtan's.

A diversion. Years later, while working together on another film, Matthau collapsed very ill on the set. People ran for help, a pillow was put under his head and a concerned Lemmon knelt down and asked his friend –
    'Walter, are you comfortable?'
Matthau replied in that wry tone of his –
    'I make a living.'

Apart from the whore Molly Molloy – very well played by Maureen Lipman, alternating toughness with vulnerability – *The Front Page* is stuffed with hard-talking, hard-boiled, cynical, and corrupt characters. Great parts for actors and we got to do American accents. Blakemore, a tall Australian with a dry sense of humour, directed the play at a furious pace, urging us to think fast, talk fast, even at times to overlap our lines. At one rehearsal, unusually for him, he got very angry at the lack of pace in a scene. Next morning he arrived with a small hand bell and rang it loudly if any actor failed to come in exactly on cue. We had never done a play like this before. The humour was sensational. Rehearsals were a joy. Blakemore let nothing slow the rapid-fire delivery of the dialogue. Most actors doing comedy are protective of every laugh they get, small or large. Michael, had been an actor himself and insisted on our playing through the smaller laughs, not pausing for the reaction. The play, he stated, is so full of humour that we could drive on, make the audience bottle their reactions and then, on the really big laughs, let them rip. Michael, who loved the movies, managed the escape of Earl Williams with cinematic elan. Through the large window in the shabby press room, searchlights raked the buildings and the sky, a fusillade of bullets riddled the wall of the room and plaster flew. We all dived for cover, soon fleeing the room. A pause. Distant shouting. Then in that very quiet moment the window shattered and glass flew as Williams (Clive Merrison) crashed into the room. Sensational. By the way, upstage left in a small toilet unseen by the audience, the scene painters had created the most disgusting lavatory bowl it has ever been my experience to behold.

The only script I have kept from those Old Vic years is *The Front Page*. I've dug it out. Inside the well-worn orange cover I've written the names of the actors opposite the reporters we played. John Shrapnel, David Bradley, Ben Whitrow, Gawn Grainger, Allan Mitchell, Richard Howard and David Ryall.

Sadly David Ryall died recently. Over the decades we appeared together in sixteen productions. He was a wonderful, funny man, a terrific actor and a very good friend to me. Whenever David and I met we invariably traded lines from *The Front Page*.

Inside the *Front Page* script I found a brown envelope with

"Props" written on it. Inside, a small well-worn reporter's pad with a crude sketch of a man hanging on a gallows on the cover. There is a pencilled list of people I mention in a phone call – 'Herman Walstein, Abe Lefkowitz, Henry Koo…' I also find a homemade eyeshade I had made with shiny green cardboard, gaffer tape and black elastic. I had seen people wear these while they typed in old movies. Michael had urged us reporters to create highly individual characters. These props were small tangible reminders of my efforts to do so. I believe I kept this script and props for two reasons. One, because it is one of the funniest plays ever written. Two, because they served to remind me of what a great production I was lucky enough to have appeared in. The cast, the direction, the design were truly wonderful and the show was an enormous success. Morecambe and Wise came to see it. Every day during rehearsals the Watergate scandal was unfolding in Washington, and this became a great topic of conversation throughout the weeks.

In 1973, I was offered a hard choice: to either go to Australia with *The Front Page* or to Broadway with *The Misanthrope*. I chose Australia and for years to come was to be admonished by John Dexter over my choice.

'Of course, *you* wouldn't come to Broadway with me. *You* chose to go to Australia with *Michael Blackmore!*' he would sneer.

PAUL SCOFIELD

In 1971 I had the great good fortune to appear in two plays with Paul Scofield; Carl Zuckmayer's *The Captain of Köpenick* and Luigi Pirandello's *The Rules Of The Game*. He gave a superb performance in each. *The Captain of Köpenick* is a very funny satire on German militarism, set just prior to the First World War. Wilhelm Voigt, the main character, a shoemaker who has spent most of his life in prison, is released, and in a Catch-22 situation, is denied a permit of residence, which then precludes him from getting a job. In frustration he acquires a second-hand Prussian military uniform and, masquerading as an officer, commandeers a platoon of soldiers and marches on the Köpenick Town Hall, where he arrests the Mayor and treasurer and takes possession of 4,000 marks from the town treasury. He then disappears with the money, eventually surrendering and offering up the cash in exchange for a passport, a proof of his identity. He is sent back to prison. But the Kaiser, on hearing his story, grants him an imperial pardon and subsequently Voigt makes a living touring Europe as the legendary Captain of Köpenick. Based on a true story, the event became famous as a symbol of the blind obedience of German soldiers and officials to authority.

Voigt is a terrific part. In the early prison scenes Paul played this petty criminal with a defeated hangdog demeanour. He had a tight crew cut and a straggly excuse for a moustache. His voice had a wheedling shifty whine. He was the kind of man that officials instantly recognise and dismiss. Then with the assumption of the uniform, he straightened his back and seemed to grow six inches. His voice now bristled with authority and rasped with command.

In the Pirandello tragicomedy he played the elegant and upper class Leone, married to Silia, who is having an affair with a man called Guido. Rather than allow himself to feel betrayed and angry, Leone empties himself of all emotion. He believes that life is a game played by arbitrary rules. He manipulates Guido into taking his place in a duel, in which Guido dies. His subtlety in showing us the fire beneath the seemingly complaisant husband as he plotted his revenge was masterful. I played Paul's servant, Filippo, and in one scene I had to teach him to make a soufflé. Because of his inability to whisk the eggs properly I had to roundly ridicule him. It was a very funny scene and Mr Scofield would endeavour to "corpse" me occasionally. Two very different plays. Two utterly different and brilliant portrayals.

In 1963, when at drama school, I saw Paul's great King Lear at the Aldwych Theatre, the then London home of the RSC. Kenneth Tynan wrote of his king, "You will never see such another". Even though I was very young, inexperienced and new to English theatre, Peter Brook's bleak, brilliant production with Paul's towering, lowering king at its centre made a deep impression on me. With that craggy noble face, imperial manner and deep mesmeric voice I instinctively knew I was watching a great actor. There was no showiness, no flashy arias. There was truth, simplicity, real emotion. I was watching the first great modern actor.

Three years later Paul won the Oscar for Best Actor for his Thomas More in *A Man For All Seasons*. He brought unflinching faith, a deep humanity and an enormous dignity to the character. His end was unshowy, hence unbearably moving. A very private man, he did not turn up to collect the Oscar. It was posted to him from Hollywood and got broken in transit, which apparantly didn't worry him in the slightest. Honours seemed to mean little to him. He declined the offer of a knighthood on three occasions. He wanted to remain "plain mister". After finishing a play, I was told, he often refused further offers of work and chose instead to take himself off with his family for prolonged holidays on a small Scottish island.

In a rare interview he said, 'As an actor I don't admit to any limitations. In rehearsal one comes up against apparantly insuperable barriers, but if you can imaginatively get past them, overreach one's natural reach, it is astonishing how elastic one can become. I've got to go not so far as I can, but as far as is needed. It's up to somebody else to say if I've made a fool of myself.'

Sometime in 1972 a group of us Old Vic actors were taken to the South bank of the Thames by Waterloo Bridge and shown a large muddy derelict site filled with *Daily Mail* delivery vans and told that this was to be the site for the building of a theatre that was first proposed in 1848. The National Theatre.

Nine years after my first two plays with Paul Scofield, I was lucky enough to work with him again in that new building on the South Bank, in Peter Hall's production of Peter Shaffer's play *Amadeus*.

GALLIVANTING

After returning from the tour to Australia in 1974 with *The Front Page*, I was offered more work at the National, but decided it was time to move on. For the next six years I did a lot of television and radio work, as well as theatre all over the country.

The repertory system was still alive, if not flourishing.

Hugh Goldie, Director at the Theatre Royal, Windsor, contacted me in an emergency. They were in the middle of a run of Agatha Christie's *The Spider's Web*. An actor had fallen ill, left the cast, and, to keep the production running, Hugh himself had quickly stepped in and read the part. He needed someone to come and take over at short notice. 'How short?' I asked.

'Could you come down and watch tomorrow's matinee, rehearse the following day and play that night? The character is only in Act One. I can get a script to you right away.'

I said yes. Next day I went to see the matinee, watched the first act, then rushed home and frantically started knocking lines into my head. Funnily, the lines proved the least of my problems. The character I was to play was the butler and a lot of my time onstage was timing entrances to announce guests, then returning on various occasions with large trays of tea things or drinks, which I then had to serve. In the rush you concentrate on the lines more than on the cues. I can tell you my trembling hand was on the door handle very early for each entrance. Like all of Christie's plays, this was a murder mystery; I knew it wasn't the butler who did it, but in the panic of going on I had not had time to read the rest of the play. I only discovered who the villain was, as I stood listening in the wings preparing for the curtain call. Needless to say I had guessed the wrong man.

I returned a year later in less stressful circumstances to do *Arsenic And Old Lace*. It will sound extraordinary now but, in the mid-seventies, the Theatre Royal, Windsor served trays of tea and biscuits to theatregoers in their seats during the intervals at matinee performances. Throughout the second half of these performances the actors' dialogue would be interspersed with tinkling, as cups and saucers were kicked over by the patrons whose trays had not been collected by the end of the interval.

Chester had a very good rep run by Chris Honer and his choice of repertoire was adventurous. I did four plays there between 1976 and 1979. A fine production of David Rudkin's *Ashes,* as well as Pinter's *Old Times,* Neil Simon's *The Odd Couple* and Christopher Marlowe's *Doctor Faustus.* Chris directed *Ashes,* a discomforting study of a childless couple's efforts to reproduce and their subsequent disappointments at the hands of the adoption agencies. I played the husband. My first morning's rehearsal was very embarrassing. Having been introduced, the company did a swift reading of the play. I then had to begin rehearsals of the first page of the first scene. This entailed lying on top of the actor Annie Tyson, whom I had never met before that morning, and pretend to have vigorous sex with her. The play is a raw and powerful human drama – tragic and shocking. On the first night about twenty members of the audience walked out. "Emotional impact too much for some" a local headline proclaimed. "See it quick before local 'porn-on-the-rate' spotters do". Nevertheless the production was very successful.

Annie Tyson, a terrific actor, played the wife who fails to conceive. Throughout rehearsals she seemed to eat nothing but lettuce and cottage cheese but often complained of putting on weight. Some weeks after the end of the run she gave birth to a son. She had had no idea or indication that she was pregnant. An ironic but very happy coda to the production.

David Thacker, who later went on to run the Young Vic and stage successful revivals of many Arthur Miller plays there, directed *Doctor Faustus*. The plot is based on the Faust legend in which a man, to acquire power and knowledge, sells his soul to the Devil. David wanted to stage the production in the refectory of Chester Cathedral but his request was turned down. So he chose the Chester Arts Centre, a small venue near the rep. We rehearsed onstage there for a couple of weeks. One afternoon as an exercise, David suggested we turn all the lights out, sit in a circle on the floor, hold hands and in total darkness conjure up the Devil. This we did. I was playing Faustus and given my Irish Catholic upbringing found the experience very spooky. The next day we turned up for rehearsal to find that the Arts Centre had burned down. Very, very spooky. The production was suddenly without a home. Luckily the Cathedral authorities took pity on us and gave permission for the play to be performed in the refectory. So Marlowe's great play would be staged in a religious space that had been in existence for over three hundred years before he wrote the work. The architectural style of the refectory was Perpendicular Gothic. Below a magnificent hammerbeam ceiling and at the east end of the refectory where we had a raised stage, was a large high window with many stained glass segments set in the delicate stone tracery. The performances began with bright colour-filled daylight streaming on the stage, but as the darkness of evening crept in, it was matched by the darkness of the developing drama. The large window suddenly became a black hole. David staged the play very simply. With no scenery, no props, a small company dressed in modern black clothes doubling and trebling roles, the version lasted two hours without an interval and was very well received.

On one evening during the run the refectory was

unavailable due to some pre-booked religious event and David suggested we perform the play in the rehearsal room back at the rep. This seemed a very unappealing prospect. The room was modest in size. It had a low ceiling, no atmosphere and was lit with bare neon strip lighting. We all agreed. Two rows of chairs were put round the walls. Nothing was added in the way of lighting and we just did the play. Given this highly inappropriate setting, for some inexplicable, though magical reason, the performance soared and the company felt afterwards that this had been our best show. I was very proud of this production. Faustus is a big and challenging role and David and I had worked hard on the character. I believed that Faustus was the best performance of my career up till then.

Fringe theatre was still fairly new in the seventies and many actors at that time were very politically committed. In 1976 I met the director Pam Brighton, who asked me to do a play marking the fiftieth anniversary of the General Strike of 1926. The venue was the Half Moon Theatre, a converted synagogue in Alie Street in Aldgate. The play showed how the strike affected a gathering of idealists who came together to form the Stepney Council of Action in May 1926, when there were troops in Victoria Park, armoured cars in Commercial Road and police baton-charges in Poplar. The play, as yet untitled, was being written by Phil Woods, but a week into rehearsals Pam dispensed with his services and suggested we improvise it. Improvise a two-hour play? Sure, why not? We decided communally on the eventual title *Out For Nine* – the number of days the strike lasted. The company of eight actors threw themselves into the improvisations and fine work was done. But inevitably, although actors love the invention

Playing Razor, the impudent valet, in Vanbrugh's The Provoked Wife, *at Guildhall in 1964*

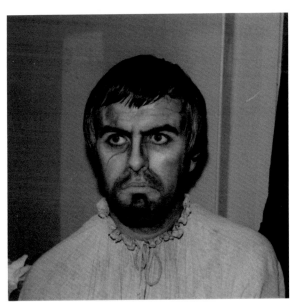

Tremendous use of the Leichner greasepaint sticks – No. 5, 9, 7 and 'Lake' in Webster's The White Devil

Spotlight mugshot 1966.

As the gardener, Hodgson in Agatha Christie's Love From A Stranger, *Barrow in Furness – a personal triumph!*

With Jane Wood in Tony Perrin's Get Out In The Green Fields
– Stoke on Trent 1967

As Darius Clayhanger in Arnold Bennett's Clayhanger adapted
by Peter Terson and Joyce Cheeseman – Stoke 1967.

The huts at Aquinas Street – NT Old Vic Headquarters 1963-75.
(Photo by Chris Arthur)

Rose and Nellie in the kitchen at Aquinas Street 1968.
(Photo by John Haynes)

Sir Laurence Olivier in Strindberg's The Dance of Death, *NT Old Vic 1967. (Photo Zoe Dominic)*

The second cast of The Front Page *NT Old Vic 1973. (See List of Illustrations for the actors' names)*

With Desmond McNamara in The Front Page *in Australia*

Michael Gambon and John Dexter at the first rehearsal of Brecht's The Life of Galileo, *with Michael Beint behind. NT 1980.*
(Photo by Zoe Dominic)

Michael Gambon in foreground with John Dexter, Simon Callow, Michael Thomas and myself. Rehearsing Galileo. *(Photo by Zoe Dominic)*

Playing a Celtic Envoy in The Romans *in Britain. NT 1980.*

The Great Paul Scofield
(Photo by John Haynes)

The Oresteia *cast and Peter Hall in Epidavros 1982.*
(Photo by Nobby Clark)(See List of Illustrations for the names)

A Horde of Unemployed Ventriloquists *my one-man-show at the NT Cottesloe Theatre 1982*

Ian McKellen Coriolanus *in Athens.*
(Photo by John Haynes)

Peter Hall rehearsing in Athens 1985

Alan Ayckbourn's Company at the NT 1986.
(Photo John Haynes)(See List of Illustrations for the names)

Adrian Rawlins and Michael Gambon in A View From The Bridge,
NT Cottesloe Theatre 1987.(Photo Nobby Clark)

As Autolycus in Michael Bogdanov's production of The Winter's Tale *for the English Shakespeare Company 1990. (Photo Laurence Burns)*

With Jenny Quayle in Brendan Behan's The Hostage *at the RSC Barbican Theatre 1994. Can't beat a comb-over. (Photo by Laurence Burns)*

NT Othello *group on the Great Wall of China 1998.
(photo by Michael Owen, Evening Standard)
(See List of Illustrations for some of the names)*

*Finbar Lynch, Ariyon Bakare, Rob Carroll, me as Julius Caesar,
John Light and Keith Osborn in Julius Caesar at the RSC in
Stratford 2006. (Photo Tristram Kenton)*

Messin' with Donald Sutherland in Budapest

The company of David Edgar's Written on The Heart *onstage in the Swan Theatre RSC 2011. (See List of Illustrations for the names)*

The company of All That Fall *at the Jermyn Street Theatre 2012.*
(See List of Illustrations for the Names)

Myself, Rory Keenan and Paul Reid in Friel's
Philadelphia Here I Come *at the Donmar 2012. (Photo Johan Persson)*

Carla Langley, Rory Keenan and myself in Liola,
NT Lyttelton Theatre 2013. (Photo Catherine Ashmore)

Messin' with Michael Gambon in New York.

and the freedom, we also need some sense of security to sustain us in front of an audience. The ability to remember and reproduce our work, however roughly, for a number of performances is also paramount. Pam had no idea of this actors' dilemma. Whenever she felt we were "improvising" a scene in much the same manner as in a previous rehearsal she would yawn, turn to the actor Arbel Jones and drawl, 'Christ, this is so boring. Arbel, roll us a joint.'

We were flying by the seat of our pants. Each day was brilliant, then disappointing, then promising, then unpromising. We had a long way to go. The first night on May Day was ten days away when Pam called us together and announced that there was a trade union conference in King's Cross in two days' time. 'Why don't we take the show over and play it for them?' Blimey! We did. It went well. We opened to the press a week later.

For eight months in 1977 I joined a company at St George's Theatre to appear in four productions in repertoire of Shakespeare's *Hamlet, Measure For Measure, The Merchant Of Venice* and *The Merry Wives Of Windsor*. I played Horatio in the first, the Provost in the second, Gratiano in the third and Nym in the fourth. St George's, alas now no longer with us, was a converted Victorian church in North London's Tufnell Park and had the ebullient Falstaffian George Murcell as its artistic director. George's plan was to perform Shakespeare's plays in a space similar to those for which they were written. Looking at the photographs in the lavish programme today, I am struck by how very like it was in configuration to Shakespeare's Globe on the South Bank. With its circular interior it had the same thrust stage, the same two-level pillared structure behind, with curtained recesses for entrances. Productions also made a feature of the Victorian pillars on either side of the stage. It seated 450. Like at the Globe, George was also very keen on simple settings and authentic costuming.

The company for the four plays was full of good actors – George himself, Joseph O'Conor, Anna Carteret, David Horovitch, Alan Dobie, Ronnie Stevens, Elvi Hale. The productions were very solid, traditional. We, as a company, had a great time, but audiences were not large and the venture floundered a few years later.

Within a twenty-mile radius in Surrey in the 1970s there were three repertory theatres. The Yvonne Arnaud in Guildford, The Redgrave in Farnham and The Thorndike in Leatherhead. Only The Yvonne Arnaud is currently functioning professionally. In 1968–1969 I did four productions at the Thorndike, which was then run by the redoubtable Hazel Vincent Wallace. The first play was Tom Stoppard's *Travesties* in which I played James Joyce and was reunited with two of my old Barrow colleagues, the director Donald MacKechnie and Lionel Guyett, who was playing Tristan Tzara. The play focuses on the fictional meeting of three important revolutionary figures who all happened to be living in Zurich in 1917 – the Russian revolutionary Lenin, the Dadaist poet Tristan Tzara and the novelist James Joyce. A character called Henry Carr tells of the trio's interactions through his very unreliable memory. It is a very funny play full of Stoppardian ingenuity which explores art, revolution and war. Donald did a very good production. Not sure that Leatherhead was ready for it though.

I did Shaw's *Saint Joan* there, directed by the scholarly Joseph O'Conor. Shaw had written the play for the actress

Sybil Thorndike, after whom the Leatherhead theatre was named. The very beautiful Ciaran Madden played Joan. I saw Joan as a rough, pugnacious country girl, fierce with religious passion. However, I thought Ciaran captured Joan's courage, passion and good sense and gave a very good performance. I played that terrific role Peter Cauchon, Bishop of Beauvais, a man loyal to the principles of the Church, who refuses to compromise his fundamental beliefs for the sake of politics: "You great lords are too prone to treat the Church as a mere political convenience". Murray Melvin, who I remembered from the 1961 Shelagh Delaney play and film *A Taste Of Honey*, was a wonderfully elegant and devious Dauphin. Also in the cast, playing the Archbishop of Rheims – a part which I was later to play in Marianne Elliott's production at the NT in 2007 – was Frank Gatliff. Frank was cool. He had the most soft, enticing voice and every piece of clothing he wore was black. I never saw him in any other colour. He was wonderful in one of my favourite films of the sixties, *The Ipcress File,* playing the urbane kidnapper Grantby.

My final play at Leatherhead was another Stoppard – *Jumpers* – in which I played the funny Inspector Bones opposite that fine comic actor Frank Thornton. Two Stoppards in one year was a little too much for some of the patrons. On a number of evenings our dialogue was interrupted by the banging of seats as irate theatregoers left the theatre with loud mutters (can you have loud mutters?) of, 'Rubbish!'

I did my first commercial theatre job in 1980, in what was then called a Number One Tour. A "Number One Tour" was a tour to the biggest and best commercial theatres in the major cities. This invariably followed a successful West

End run of a play and usually starred the original cast, or a completely new cast with a big star or two leading the company. The play was Brian Clark's hugely successful *Whose Life Is It Anyway?* which had starred Tom Conti in the West End, and now toured with Simon Ward playing a man paralysed from the neck down, but still possessing a very lively and active mind who demands to have the final say in terminating his own life. I played his psychiatrist. Simon Ward was very good to work with and the tour did very good business. I learned something new on that tour. The audience numbers and an account of box-office takings for each performance, were presented to the star each evening. Obviously the star got a much larger paypacket than the rest of the cast, but I discovered he/she would also be "on a percentage" i.e. extra payment depending on the week's takings. Nice work if you can get it. By the way there were also Number Two and Number Three tours which played the less salubrious venues.

1980

THE LIFE OF GALILEO
THE ROMANS IN BRITAIN
AMADEUS

In June 1980, John Dexter, who was now director of productions at the Metropolitan Opera in New York, asked me to return to the National to be in his production of Brecht's *The Life Of Galileo*. The part was Federzoni, one of the astronomer's disciples. Galileo was to be played by Michael Gambon.

Four months later at the NT I was playing in two hugely successful productions, as well as in the most scandalous theatrical event for many decades – *The Romans In Britain*.

On my first day in the "new" National I was overawed by the size of the place. I had loved the Old Vic. But this was another kettle of fish. Most stage doors are poky, with the keeper in a cramped little cubicle. The impressive NT stage door had a staff of three. Rehearsal Room One was almost the same size as the Old Vic auditorium. I entered to be confronted by a mass of faces. I guessed there were nearly seventy people in the room. We all milled about getting coffee, looking desperately for a familiar face, someone to say hello to. There was lovely old Harry Lomax, who had been in *The Front Page*; Kenneth Mackintosh, another actor from the Vic; now the staff director on this production; the gorgeous Sandra Fehr, who I had been at drama school with. John Dexter came and said hello. Then a tall and slightly dishevelled figure lumbered over and offered his hand. 'Hello, Michael Gambon, we worked together on TV a couple of years back, right?' We had. I was very touched that in such a large group he'd made the effort to come and introduce himself.

This was going to be a very big production for the Olivier stage. There were forty-seven actors in the cast. There was no formal meet-and-greet. We went straight into a strenuous physical warm-up. After that the voice teacher asked us to lie on the floor to do some breathing exercises saying, 'You deserve a rest now.'

'*Wrong!*' chimed Dexter, who then patrolled amongst the prostrate actors. 'This is where I like my actors,' said the director, 'at my feet.'

Jim Hiley (who penned a terrific book about the production – see Acknowledgements) wrote:

"Gathering them round the model of the set, Dexter talked briskly and fluently about the play and his ideas for the production – 'My approach might be heretical, but if it's heretical like Tyrone Guthrie's Henry VIII, I won't mind and neither will the Brecht estate.' There would be a vocal warm-up every day. He wanted vocal precision, intensity and a positively Shakespearean relish of the text in Howard Brenton's adaptation. 'I want everybody to act honestly and without decoration.'"

John then announced that we would not sit and "read" the play. He wanted us on our feet. He was going to roughly block the first four scenes – over an hour of playing time – by the end of the day. 'Coffee break!' he shouted.

Along one wall of the rehearsal room John had the carpenters build a temporary two-metre-high, five-metre-long, narrow platform. When not directing and moving the actors about on the floor, he would climb up to this eyrie, to study how his blocking of the play was working. John easily got through those four scenes by teatime. He knew what he wanted in each scene and worked hard. If some staging didn't work he was quick to change it. Howard Brenton's version was a pleasure to speak.

We ploughed on through those early days, with John giving the odd succinct note to the actors. To an actor playing one of Galileo's adversaries – 'Don't "comment" on your character and don't play him from Galileo's point of view.' An actor playing the Fat Monk was told not to act fat. John urged another actor playing a fanatical priest not to shout. He stated that the character's centuries-old beliefs give him the confidence to never raise his voice.

At the end of that first week we were ready to do a rough run of the play. It was like being back in Barrow in Furness. John wanted to see if all the pieces fitted together and wanted Michael Gambon to get some sense of the character's journey through the piece. He said nobody would be watching the acting and that we should just try to get the moves right and be clear. We started. John prowled the high platform. It was a rollercoaster ride. At the end John seemed very pleased. 'Thank you. Very well done. It'll never be as bad as that again, and some of it will never be as good, unfortunately.' He then talked of changes he would make – "improvements". He was going to drop one small scene and change where he had placed the interval.

Jocelyn Herbert was the designer. She and Dexter had worked together on many projects and were much exercised on how to use the Olivier to its full potential. They decided that the stage should be a raised circular playing area cantilevered to look as if it was floating. A large square platform (a "truck" in stage terms) about twenty-five centimetres high would be winched on from the back for domestic scenes, or ones which demanded a more intimate playing space. At the back of the platform as it stopped, a large plain white screen would be lowered, onto which various slides would be projected – a skyscape with a huge moon, a townscape with the title "FLORENCE 1624" etc. The juxtaposition of circle and square was important to John and Jocelyn. It had an astronomical connotation. At the back of the Olivier stage are three vast black walls. In fact they are panels which can be raised to reveal a large space behind, usually used for storage of sets and furniture for other plays in the Olivier's repertoire. John and Jocelyn decided that the production should use the stage's great depth, even deciding that the central panel would be raised and the opening scene of the play begin in the scene dock, fifteen metres from the front row of the stalls. I will return to this brilliant idea later.

Jocelyn, a tall, graceful woman, was one of the twentieth century's greatest theatre designers. On *Galileo* she pared things back to essentials. The set, especially in the airy Olivier, created, with little show, a sense of the universe. She took infinite care over every small detail of set, props, costuming and was always open to the actors' concerns and ideas.

John Dexter could stage large epic scenes better than any director I have worked with and *Galileo* was full of them. One particular scene is still vivid in my memory all these years later. The setting was the Pope's bedchamber, a scene where Stephen Moore, playing the Cardinal Inquisitor, debates with Basil Henson's newly installed Pope Urban VIII. The only setting was a small two-tiered rostrum. The Cardinal was in full crimson garb, the Pope on the rostrum wore a cotton vest and a pair of knee-length underpants. The two men debate the use of torture and threats to force Galileo to renounce the Copernican ideas set out in his *Dialogue Concerning The Two Chief World Systems*. Throughout this delicate political scene the Pope gets dressed. By getting dressed I mean that eight actors in long monks' robes enter and exit carrying various Papal vestments and proceed to clothe the Pontiff. They bring on the fanon, the faldo, the stole, the alb, the chasuble, the pallium – the lot. They fit red slippers on his feet, they place the zuchetto on his head and finally top it with the three-tiered crown. At the end His Holiness is in full pomp, brimming with Papal authority. Then, and only then, does he assent to the threat of torture.

Now, for the scene to work, all this physical activity must be carried out with seamless smoothness and ease, and must not, in any circumstances, pull focus from the playing of the two protagonists. John drilled the eight actors relentlessly. Because of the complexity of the choreography, the tension in rehearsal was palpable. Woe betide the poor actor who, in slightly mistiming his task, threw the whole sequence into disarray. The Dexter wrath would descend upon him.

While Galileo is being questioned by the Roman Inquisition there is a scene where his disciples, Michael Thomas, Simon Callow and I, are told that a bell will ring at five o'clock to signal his recantation. We wait, watch the time slowly pass five and realise that he has not recanted. We begin a celebration, cheering, hugging, charging around the room. Suddenly a loud bell chimes out. He *has* recanted. Despair all round. John's staging of the emotional graph of the scene was masterly.

Hiley wrote, "Before the final runthrough of the play Dexter announced with a grin that he 'intended to enjoy the afternoon's run and he defied any of us to stop him'".

Afterwards he praised Gambon and then announced: 'The rest of you – soggy!' He then told us we would be onstage in the Olivier on Monday. 'We'll see if that knocks some of the sogginess out of you. And if that doesn't, I will. Some of you are playing small parts as if they were small parts. If that's your attitude you'll stay playing them for the rest of your life.'

He told one actor that his character needed much more fanaticism. 'Do you know what a fanatic is? You're looking at one, dear. Give me a performance, and I'll give you a note.' Earlier he had taken a part away from an actor and given it to another. Apart from the humiliation, the actor found this hard to bear as it was his only speaking part in the play.

John could show warmth but his social skills were minimal. I had to ask for a morning off during rehearsals because my son was ill. In those days getting any time off was frowned on. A day or two later John came up and enquired about my boy – an astonishing show of interest – 'He's much better, John. Thank you fo—'

'Good!' said Dexter and strode off.

The Olivier Theatre is a hard space to work in. The vast open space above the actors' and audience's heads makes intimacy extremely difficult. John arrived for the tech dressed in a navy sailor's smock and espadrilles. Through the morning he moved around and sat in different parts of the auditorium observing the action. He urged us to do the same so as to get a sense of the vocal energy and clarity required. He said we didn't need excessive volume, but that each syllable should be energised and we must play to the furthest seat in the circle. He then told a couple of actors to stop smoking and asked a casual visitor to go away. During the Pope's dressing scene Stephen Moore came on dressed in his usual red cardinal's hat, gloves and shoes, but in place of his ecclesiastical robes he wore a green running vest with three big numbers on it and a pair of white running shorts, one of his costumes from *Sisterly Feelings* an Ayckbourn play also in the repertoire. We all fell about, of course. Dexter walked silently onstage at the end of the scene, pulled back Stephen's shorts, looked at his backside and then called 'Blackout!' Later he rehearsed the curtain call. He asked Michael Gambon to step forward. 'One solo bow,' he called to the leading actor. 'Two, when you've got some notices.'

The press night arrived. At lunchtime John laid on a champagne buffet. Usually an event like this would be for cast and stage management only. John invited all the stage crew as well.

The opening scene. In the "preset", hanging downstage over the bare circular floor was a huge armillary sphere – a framework of brass rings representing the principle circles of the heavens. Behind this, darkness, a black hole. Upstage in the distant scene dock, and as yet unseen by the audience, was the "truck" – a wheeled platform. On this was Galileo's workroom with tables laden with scientific instruments. At the front of this platform on a three-legged structure was a large copper washbasin and behind this stood Galileo naked to the waist. Hanns Eisler's opening music began to play, the houselight began to dim, the sphere began to fly out. Michael Gambon about to play this huge role, a performance that would make him a star, prepared to wash himself. The lighting on the platform came up. The truck was winched downstage. The performance began.

On the press night, standing in front of the washbasin waiting for his cue, Michael told me later that he was very nervous. 'I stood half naked in the semi-darkness, trying to pull my stomach in, trying to stay calm. I had just been given the standby when I heard a loud whisper.

"Oi, Mike!" I looked left. It was Big Roger on the winch.
"What?"

"You look a right c**t!"– and the truck moved forward.'

* * *

One morning back in the early sixties when playing a tiny role in a Dexter production, Michael told me, he was twenty minutes late for rehearsal. John laid into him. Next morning for some unexplained reason he was again late. Half an hour late. He came into the rehearsal room, sweating, having run all the way from the station. He knew he was in big trouble. John ripped into him, called him unprofessional, threatened him with the sack – 'What possible excuse could you have?'

Michael looked John straight in the eye. 'I'm terribly

sorry. You see... ah... my mother died last night, and I didn't get much sleep and...'

John dissolved, apologised, and later gave Michael time off for the funeral.

We now move forward sixteen years. One day during the previews for *Galileo* John says to Michael, 'God, Michael, do you remember that awful day when I shouted at you, the day your poor mother died?'

'Yes, John, I remember it very well. I was very upset.'

Michael told me this story, explaining that his mother was still alive and well and living in Streatham and couldn't come to see him in the play until John left for New York.

Galileo was greeted with universally good notices. Irving Wardle wrote in *The Times*:

> *"John Dexter's production is by far the best version I have seen... during the recantation scene the disciples change from wild jubilation... to dumbstruck despair, recall[ing] the moment of the Indians' masked despair in Dexter's production of The Royal Hunt Of The Sun..."*

Michael Billington wrote in The *Guardian*:

> *"John Dexter's production, is something to which any thinking theatregoer should hasten... with a soaring performance by Michael Gambon... gives us an impatient slave to passion, a man who guzzles ideas as greedily as he does food. And he is quite splendid in the final scenes when, tuft-haired, stray-bearded, short-sighted, he combines Galileo's self-disgust with*

his fervent cry that 'the only aim of science is to relieve the toil of human existence'."

But the greatest enthusiast was the poet James Fenton, then the drama critic of The *Sunday Times*:

"GALILEO: A NEW STAR IS DISCOVERED

I do not know when it was, exactly, that this production established itself in my mind as a great work of art. I was not expecting to be so terribly moved – I have an intense dislike for the majority of Brecht's plays... this production is by far the best thing now showing in London... the design by Jocelyn Herbert gets to grips architecturally with the whole of the space available, a space unparallelled in our theatres, but one which has proved very difficult to manage... Mr Dexter's production has splendour of scale, economy or lavishness of means where appropriate... But of course this is the great triumph of Michael Gambon who plays Galileo."

Fenton returned four months later to revisit the play:

"This production remains for me the most exciting theatrical event of 1980 – and does so by virtue of one central performance. I had previously very much admired Michael Gambon as a comic actor of a mournful disposition... in the eyes of all who have seen his Galileo, he has taken such a decisive step forward in the direction of great tragedy.

So I returned to the National in the hopes of working out just what it is that he does in order to establish that devastating transformation we witness in the play. I had imagined it as something that must take place back-stage in the interval – but in fact it happens in full view of the audience. He turns his back on us during a scene shift, and keeps it turned for a while. When his features become visible again, they are ravaged by the combined effects of disease, indulgence and intellectual disgrace. It is not a question of make-up. It is something he has done to his brain. It is quite useless to return to the play in the hope of working out what the trick is. What the trick is must be great acting".

Throughout rehearsals I had watched Michael build this performance. Actors are always highly critical of obvious technique and surface tricks. But the change in his performance into the ravaged old man, his ability to add depth, despair, a new harshness in his voice, impressed me. I was lucky to watch a great performance evolve. It was thrilling to observe and it epitomised all that every actor strives and wishes for. Never showy, always modest, often taking the piss out of himself, he was the envy and the hero of every actor in the cast.

The NT dressing rooms are built on the four floors of a quadrangle with big windows looking out into the square. We can all see each other. There is often much banter and chat criss-crossing the space. We returned to those rooms after the press night high on the event, aware that we were part of a great production, but particularly aware that we had witnessed a great performance. A rare event. Someone shouted, 'Well done, Gambon!' Others joined in: 'Well done, Mike'. He came to the window. Suddenly we were all at the windows calling and applauding Michael Gambon. The cheering grew. Michael was embarrassed, clearly moved. Actors began to bang their hands on the windows, a thunderous noise in the enclosed space. Nothing like this had happened before. Eventually Michael shouted at us to, 'Shut your row,' and the ovation died down.

John Dexter never appeared backstage after press nights. He just melted away. Although his abrasiveness, his cruelty and rudeness, were unforgivable, I, along with many actors, felt he was a great director and deep – way down deep – a kind man. He was someone who strove hard to do great work, a director who never settled for less, from himself or from others. He instilled those high standards in all who worked with him. I still think about him.

THE ROMANS IN BRITAIN

While rehearsing *Galileo* the director Michael Bogdanov offered me two parts in a new play by the translator of *Galileo*, Howard Brenton. It was titled *The Romans In Britain*. The play had a broad historical sweep, beginning in 54BC with the invasion of the Romans, followed by a long scene set in a field in Northern Ireland in 1980, and finally another scene set in a field in Britain in AD515. Peter Hall was very keen that the Olivier Theatre should not only stage classic plays but should also be a home for new and large-scale work by young modern writers. So Howard Brenton was commissioned to write one. *The Romans in Britain* was epic in scale, with a cast of over thirty actors doubling and sometimes trebling roles.

In the first half I played a Celtic envoy. Naked to the waist, with a rough cloak over one shoulder, I wore tight leather breeches, high boots, a large gold earring, a drooping moustache and topping all this a long brown, high, spiky wig which I thought gave me an uncanny resemblance to Rod Stewart. In the second half I played an IRA leader who interrogates a disguised British officer in a field in Northern Ireland.

The play dealt with imperialism and the historical parallels between British intervention in Ireland and the Roman occupation of Britain. It was not well received by the critics. In fact it was deeply disliked. Thirty-three years later it is mostly remembered for one very violent scene, in which a Roman soldier attempts to rape a young Celtic warrior. The actors were naked and the scene was staged graphically and in full view.

"NATIONAL CLANGER" trumpeted the Evening Standard.
"ROMAN SCANDAL" – the Sunday Telegraph.
"NAUSEATING RUBBISH" blared the Sunday Times.

There was worse, much worse to come.

In rehearsal we had no inkling of the coming storm. The language of the play was strong, to put it mildly. There was male nudity. We presumed the production would be controversial. It was a hugely ambitious project. The rape scene was rehearsed in private with only the actors involved allowed into the rehearsal room. Later as the production came together we all obviously watched it. It was violent and very explicit. I remember a debate on whether the line "It's like fucking a fistful of *marbles*" should remain in. It was hard to relate the strong language of the play with the sweet and gentle character of Howard Brenton. In the rape scene, the two actors were naked. Peter Sproule improvised a very effective piece of business. For the attempted rape he placed his fist around his penis, protuding his thumb to give the impression of an erection. He then used this as he straddled Greg Hicks.

For the Irish country scene the full Olivier stage was covered with yellow stooks of corn. Here the disguised British Officer (Stephen Moore) is waiting to meet with and assassinate the IRA leader O'Rourke, the part I played. I entered with two accomplices. Michael Bogdanov made a very good suggestion. Instead of looking like a cliché IRA man he suggested that I enter in a business suit and tie as if I had popped out of the office for an hour. I thought this was a brilliant idea. Howard had written O'Rourke as a strong, intelligent, laidback character with a wry sense of humour, not your usual heavy. O'Rourke, with great good manners, questions the officer. At the end the man is shot and the IRA men stroll casually away. I laboured for a while over how to play O'Rourke. I wanted to do menace, but with grace, with a smile. Actors acting tough onstage often come across as tossers. I thought hard about the truly strong characters I had watched in Hollywood movies. Clint Eastwood, I thought. That's it. Clint's the man. Clint with an Irish accent. And that's how I played him. Harold Pinter paid me a compliment which featured the word "menace", so it must have worked.

The press night arrived. Next day, Friday October 17th 1980 all hell broke loose. The story filled the front pages of both the Evening Standard and the Evening News. The headlines in bold black five centimetre-high letters.

The *Evening News*:-
"DISGRACE TO THE STAGE
G L C Chief threatens to stop grant over National's new play"

The *Evening Standard*:-
"FURY OVER NUDE PLAY SHOCKER

Milton Shulman's review
'Remove it as soon as possible'"

The Standard had a picture of Sir Horace Cutler, the Greater London Council leader, on one side with the strapline:… "No artistic merit" and on the other a picture of the recently ennobled and smiling Sir Peter Hall with the strap:… "remarkable writing".

Sir Horace told a journalist that his wife had been forced to "cover her head" during the sodomy scene.

Two days later the *Daily Telegraph* wrote an editorial:

"Is it quite impossible for the director of the National Theatre to find good new avant garde plays, by young authors, which do not include scenes of revolting sexual violence and themes of ludicrously obtuse political propaganda? According to Sir Peter Hall, the alternative to putting on The Romans In Britain would be to turn the National Theatre into a museum. Another alternative might be a new director.

> *Public patronage – the tax-payers' money – does make a difference. Where the private patron has only his own taste to consider, the public patron cannot be so self-indulgent. When a play is judged artistically worthless by the critics and morally offensive by the audience, is there not a strong case for the director to take it off? This would not be bowing to censorship, merely common sense."*

Threats of withdrawal of the NT grant and suggestions that Sir Peter should consider his position, were taken up by other papers. But these were merely a prelude to a darker, nastier campaign that was about to explode on to the scene.

Mary Whitehouse, the morality campaigner and president of the National Viewers and Listeners Association, was about to take to the national stage. She refused to see the play, stating that she was too frightened it would lead to the "corruption of her soul". She requested that the Metropolitan Police examine whether the play was an offence against the Theatres Act of 1968. She suggested that men after seeing the rape scene would be "so stimulated" they would "commit attacks on young boys". The police attended some performances. Eventually the Attorney General Lord Havers, father of the actor Nigel Havers, decided there was no case to answer. Relief all round.

But Mrs Whitehouse wasn't finished. She had discovered a legal loophole. One evening at the NT Bogdanov was called to the stage door. He was greeted by a small smiling man who asked him if he was Michael Bogdanov. He replied he was. Still smiling the man handed him a letter and departed.

Michael thought it was a fan letter. It turned out to be a writ accusing him of "having procured an act of gross indecency by Peter Sproule and Greg Hicks on the stage of the Olivier Theatre". The man in fact was Mrs Whitehouse's solicitor Graham Ross-Cornes. Mrs Whitehouse was bringing a private prosecution.

Over the coming weeks Michael had to put up with threatening phonecalls, excrement pushed through his letterbox, and the bullying of his children at school. At the committal hearings at Horseferry Road Magistrate's Court, Michael was sent for trial at the Old Bailey. He was facing a possible three years in jail. The lawyers had to fight hard to get bail. The judge wanted to keep him in the cells.

Sproule and Hicks were called to interviews by the defence counsel and discussed their possible cross-examination. Greg was asked whether he became sexually aroused during the scene and whether he found it necessary to masturbate afterwards in the wings.

At the trial the prosecution called only one witness, the solicitor Mr Ross-Cornes. He had attended the play and insisted he had seen the tip of Sproule's penis. Geoffrey Robertson QC, then a junior defence counsel to Lord Hutchinson, on a hunch brought a copy of the Olivier theatre seating plan to the court. He thought it might be crucial to know where Mr Ross-Cornes had been seated during the performance. Mr Ross-Cornes was asked to put a mark on the plan showing where he had sat. He put a cross on a back-row stalls seat. Sir Peter Hall slipped a note to the lawyer stating that that seat was ninety feet from the stage. Asked if he was sure he had seen the actor's penis Ross-

203

Cornes replied, 'Well, what else could it be?' Mistake. Lord Hutchinson then showed how Sproule had used his fist and thumb.

With the witness discredited there was no case to answer and it was soon dismissed.

Michael Bogdanov, born in Wales to a Jewish father and Welsh mother, is commonly and fondly called "Bodger" in the business. He is a short, fresh-faced, good humoured man who I have worked with over many years. Throughout what must have been a prolonged nighmare he remained positive, equable, in fact his usual jolly self. I have great admiration for him.

Sir Peter Hall during the whole *Romans* period did what a good leader of any organisation should do. He backed the play, he backed Howard, he backed Michael, he backed the whole company. No weasel words, no backing out of the limelight. He was one hundred per cent there for the show, a tremendous and supportive leader.

Throughout the run, the papers continued to have a field day. Howard Brenton's phone was ex-directory, which was unfortunate for another H. Brenton who was in the phonebook and lived in the same area. This man's wife interviewed by The *Sunday Times* said "We've had about twenty phone calls already. We'll probably have Mrs Whitehouse on our doorstep next". At the head of the article was a cartoon showing naked actors being chased across a stage by a policeman with a dog, watched by an irate audience gesticulating from the stalls. The article headline was – "Psst... wanna see a show?" Another paper carried a cartoon showing two actors looking on to a stage. One of them says to the other, "I'll be buggered if I go on there". Entering or leaving the stage door especially in the early performances we had to run the gauntlet of press photographers. Audience numbers neither increased or decreased, but some of the cast noticed what can only be described as members of the "dirty mac brigade" seated suspiciously near the front during some performances.

Greg Hicks received a letter from a brigadier in Shropshire inviting him to dinner 'which will be served by my African manservant'. Others followed from a retired Army officer who admired his performance and invited him to lunch at the Garrick Club. Later it was revealed that these homoerotic missives were a practical joke emanating from the NT. I know the culprits but deem it wise not to reveal their names.

Twenty-five years later, Howard's first new play for the NT since *The Romans In Britain* opened. It was a drama about the life of St Paul. Even before its first performance Artistic Director Nicholas Hytner received hundreds of letters from Christians protesting at its staging, some warning him that he would go to hell.

AMADEUS

Within a couple of weeks of the opening of *Romans* Peter Hall asked me to join the cast of his hugely successful production of Peter Shaffer's play *Amadeus*. It was already into its run in the Olivier and starred Paul Scofield as Salieri, Simon Callow as Mozart and Felicity Kendal as the composer's wife Constanze. Two actors were leaving the cast and Greg Hicks and I were to take over their roles. The story of *Amadeus* is well-known by now, but I'll quickly give a short precis. Set in Vienna at the Court of the Emperor Joseph II in the late eighteenth century, the successful composer Antonio Salieri has been hugely impressed by the music of the young Mozart. But when he meets the young man he is horrified by his childish and graceless behaviour. He is disgusted to hear Mozart engage in sexual banter with his future wife Constanze. A devout Catholic, he cannot believe that God would bestow genius on such a creature. Bitterly jealous of the young composer's talent, Salieri renounces God and sets out to destroy W Amadeus Mozart (Amadeus, of course, "loved by God") as a way of getting back at his Creator. At the end Salieri attempts suicide, leaving a false confession saying he has poisoned Mozart. He survives. The confession is disbelieved. He is left to wallow in his mediocrity, having outlived his fame.

Replacing actors in a play is a huge inconvenience for all the cast. They have been playing it for weeks, months even, and are very settled and comfortable in the production. They don't want anything to change. Also, they will have to *rehearse*. The replacements will get as little time as is necessary to slot them in. They will have to turn up with the lines learnt, having hopefully watched a few performances, and then be expected to faithfully copy the moves of the departing actors. This leaves little room and time for new ideas from the incomers.

Greg and I had our work cut out for us. We were taking over the parts of two paid gossips called the Venticelli – little winds. We were Salieri's creatures and throughout the play we swept on stage bringing news of Mozart's triumphs and disasters. These characters spoke in short sharp sentences and at great speed, overlapping and finishing each others' lines. Announcing Mozart as a new rival:

"1: They say he wrote his first symphony at five—
2: I hear his first concerto at four—
1: A full opera at fourteen—
Salieri: How old is he?
2: Twenty five—
Salieri: And how long is he staying?
1: He is not departing—
2: He is here to stay—"

Rehearsing was reasonably straightforward. Our problems were offstage. The Venticelli made many entrances and exits throughout the play. We were on and off all night and used all available entrances, even coming on from the auditorium. The backstage area of the Olivier Theatre is massive and we often had to run between these entrances. In the early performances after each exit we consulted numbered index cards telling us where to go for our next entrance.

Paul Scofield had a big success playing Salieri. As the wheelchair-bound minor composer in old age, full of despair and jealousy or as the younger infinitely dangerous, elegant and scheming courtier he was mesmerising. His voice, a great instrument, sweet in the quiet passages then rumbling like thunder when in full flow. Now and again it also had a surprisingly camp quality. There was a wonderful scene when the brash and brilliant Mozart – which Simon Callow, using his high energy, distinctive giggle and bright intelligence played brilliantly – sits at the piano talking to Salieri. He suddenly begins to play from memory Salieri's rather pedestrian *March of Welcome* and in a fit of exuberance improvises with the tune and suddenly turns it into a piece of Mozartian brilliance. Paul's face throughout this recital went through anger, despair and jealousy. Subtle, understated, wonderful.

Over the years I had watched his principled Thomas More, his towering, unforgettable Lear and been reduced to quiet sobs by his last scene in *Uncle Vanya*. I consider it a great privilege and honour to have been lucky enough to work with him on three plays. A great actor. But one always had to be on the lookout. Now and again he took on a twinkle and could very easily corpse you.

One evening during the run of *Amadeus* we were told that Margaret Thatcher, the Prime Minister, was in the audience. To put it mildly I was not an admirer of hers. At the curtain call I spotted her, surrounded by men in dark suits. She didn't look as if she had enjoyed the play. Her hands barely touched each other during the applause, her eyes turned heavenwards.

Peter Hall spoke to her afterwards and related, 'She was not pleased. In her best headmistress style she gave me a severe wigging for putting on a play that depicted Mozart as a scatological imp with a love of four-letter words. It was inconceivable, she said, that a man who wrote such elegant and sublime music could be so foul-mouthed.' Peter told her Mozart's letters proved just that. He said the composer had a scatological and childish sense of humour. 'I don't think you heard what I said,' she replied. 'He couldn't have been like that!' Later Peter sent her a copy of Mozart's letters to Number Ten. She did not reply. Of course she didn't believe in the subsidised theatre and would refer to the NT Director as "that awful Peter Hall".

A letter from Mozart to his cousin Maria Anna in verse:

"Well I wish you good night
But first shit into your bed
Sleep soundly my love
Into your mouth your arse you'll shove."

Many months later the play was tranferred to the West End. Most of the NT cast didn't want to go with it, including Greg and I. A new company was formed and would rehearse and open in the Olivier and then move across town. Peter Hall asked Greg and I to stay with the production for the first dozen performances. The Salieri/ Venticelli scenes were fast and intricate and Peter wanted us to ease the new Salieri (Frank Finlay) into the play. Fair enough. But the West End production was going to use the new and much shorter version of the play that had opened on Broadway with Ian McKellen as Salieri. So, during the rehearsal days Greg and I had to clear the old NT version from our minds. We had to cope with cuts, rearranged scenes, new entrances and exits and learn all these changes. Now this is where it got complicated. The original production was still playing in the Olivier. So Greg and I would finish rehearsing Version Two at 5:30pm, have our tea-break and at 7:30pm would go on stage and play Version One with Paul Scofield. It addled the brain but was a really exciting few weeks.

A short digression. *Amadeus* was a big hit on Broadway and in a long run went through many cast changes. One of the last actors to play Mozart there was Mark Hamill. I like the image of Luke Skywalker ditching his spacesuit for the wig and breeches of Wolfgang Amadeus Mozart.

THE ORESTEIA

One Monday morning in early June 1981 sixteen actors entered Rehearsal Room One at the NT and after twenty-five weeks rehearsal stepped onto the Olivier stage to perform an extraordinary piece of theatre. Yes, twenty-five weeks rehearsal – probably the longest rehearsal period in the history of the British Theatre.

The production was Aeschylus' great trilogy, *The Oresteia,* directed by Peter Hall. The plays would run for over five hours. The curtain would rise at five pm and there would be a forty-minute interval for audiences to get a bite to eat. The actors would all be male, would play a chorus of old men, of Trojan women and of vengeful Furies, as well as all the principal parts – and would wear masks.

Aeschylus was the founder of European drama, and his plays enable us to follow the development from chorus drama to actor drama. When he was born, drama was mostly lyrical with little development of plot and character. Dialogue was confined to one actor and a chorus. Aeschylus was responsible for the introduction of the second actor and later the third actor, which enabled the dialogue to develop far more freely. He also reduced the chorus from an unwieldy fifty to twelve.

The Oresteia was first performed in 458 BC and it deals with guilt, atonement and absolution. In the first play, "Agamemnon", Queen Clytemnestra, kills the Greek king

Agamemnon, because he sacrificed their daughter in the war against Troy. In the second play, "Choephori", his son Orestes takes revenge by murdering his mother and her lover. In the third play, "Eumenides", Orestes is pursued by the Furies, ancient goddesses who condemn his matricide. In the end he is absolved by the intervention of the younger gods.

The version of the trilogy was by the poet Tony Harrison, whose version of *The Misanthrope* was a work of art in its own right. He said: "The whole of Greek society speaks through the consciousness of Aeschylus. To find an equivalent I had to go back to our own Heroic age and filter my modern sensibility through the rhythms of our earliest English literature. So the Anglo-Saxon rhythms I have chosen, with their heavy emphasis on consonants, are intended to convey the particular weight of the original Greek without losing narrative momentum".

With Harrison's use of the rhythms and alliterations of Old English verse, one could easily think that *Beowolf* and *The Oresteia* trilogy might have been written by the same author. Here's a short extract from the opening chorus of the Old Men:

"So Agamemnon first clanchief of Argos
found no fault in the clanseer's foretelling
and went where the winds of his life-lot were listing
the Achaian armada still anchored off Aulis.

Wind-force and wave-spell   keep the ships shorebound
Men sapped of spirit   supplies running short
Foodpots and grain jars   crapping their contents

211

ship planks gape open   frayed cables and rigging
time dragging   each day seeming two days
the flower of Argos   bedraggled and drooping."

The music for the plays was by the distinguished classical composer Harrison Birtwistle. The sets, costumes and masks were designed by Jocelyn Herbert.

The initial rehearsals started with work on the chorus' speeches. We split into groups and experimented, saying some of the lines together, then one or two actors saying half a line, or one line, or two lines on their own etc. Tony's language, with all those compound phrases and alliteration was meaty, chewy and needed much vocal energy and articulation. Challenging but exciting. In performance the many long speeches of the chorus were eventually split up, with sometimes the full chorus speaking, but often couplets and single lines spoken by pairs and individuals. Through repetition we learned all the speeches and became like a well-drilled team. We covered each other, and if someone didn't come in on the beat, someone else would say it for him.

We also began to do some mask work. Various full masks were produced. The actors donned them and then studied their faces and bodies for some time in long full-length mirrors. Pieces of cloth would be added round the head and bodies. All reaction proceeded from the mask. The work was fascinating. A huge emotional and physical freedom was achieved. Heads, bodies, perceptively altered, became plastic. The actor Peter Dawson made a mask from a photograph of a beautiful model on a cover of Vogue magazine. He cut out the eyes and stood in front of the mirror. He experimented with long pieces of material. In a little while he had transformed into a beautiful young woman. It was astonishing. For the chorus of Trojan women I remember working with a female mask. I spent time in front of the mirrors draped in a long dark robe. These women were captives, torn away from their children and families and taken into exile. Wearing the mask helped me become one of them. Then in an improvisation someone approached me and holding up an urn told me that it contained the ashes of my children. I was so immersed in what the mask had released in me, in the character I had created, that I began to weep and couldn't stop. I had to take the mask off and go and sit down out of the scene. Now, I know this kind of thing can sound so "theatrical", but that is what the power of a good mask can do to an actor. In fact, this emotional breakdown was useless for the purposes of a masked production. The *mask* does not weep. You must channel everything *through* the mask. The moment was only useful for emotional memory.

Over the weeks we played around with all kinds of masks while Jocelyn observed. The vengeful Furies in the final play proved the hardest to achieve. We tried masks with gouts of blood on the mouths, which were initally very dramatic and shocking but in the end were counterproductive. We finally settled for a paler more neutral look with bright red lips. This together with long flowing hair made of dyed red and black twine was very effective and made us look like a coven of fiery witches. We wore robes of a net material to just below the knee. These moved and slithered around us and it became necessary for us to wear flesh-coloured Marks and Spencer women's knickers. Marvellous.

So, on the weeks and months went. Harry Birtwistle's music was scored for six musicians using percussion, woodwind and harp. The music punctuated and accompanied the action. Percussion was provided by the drumming on long hollow wooden boxes. Much of the chorus lines and speeches were spoken to a pulse played on these. But rhythmic speaking can easily become dull and predictable, so the actors learned to "ride" the pulse, using syncopation and rubato. In the end with much practice we developed a free, Sinatra-like delivery that was very exciting.

Twenty-five weeks in a rehearsal room with an all-male cast is a long time. There were days and weeks of hard exciting and innovative work, and inevitably these were punctured with moments of anarchy and humour. I remember an afternoon when rehearsing the Trojan women's speeches. By this stage we were using masks and rehearsal costumes all the time. Peter Hall tended to direct from his chair, in front of which was a music stand that held his script, which he often consulted. We came on delivering the lines in various vocal configurations. David Roper had noticed that Peter's head had dipped and in fact he was having a bit of a doze – which sometimes occurred. David entered backwards. He had put his mask on the back of his head and twisted his arms so his hands faced front. He stood amongst us and spoke all his lines to the back wall. It was one of those afternoons. We all thought it was hysterical. Peter, obviously, didn't notice.

There were other afternoons when we would all get a bit tired of rehearsing. Jim Carter and I began a little competition. He would sidle up to me and quietly ask, 'Have you looked?' I'd reply, 'No.' A while later I would approach him and ask the same question. 'No!' he would doggedly reply.

This would go on for some time until one of us would given in.

'Have you looked?'

'Yes.'

'What is it?'

'Twenty past three!'

'Jesus!'

We were hoping that it would be at least 4:45pm.

Eventually we got to the stage. The tech went on for days. Everyone got very tired and tensions became evident. One evening on about the fifth day of the tech I was on stage playing in the Trojan women chorus. The scene is set before the palace of Clytemnestra. Upstage centre, a flight of steps led up to a pair of huge five-metre-high steel doors During the scene I had to quietly exit into the wings and then change into Orestes' old Nurse for my next scene. In my mask and costume a reviewer later said that my "Nurse was irrestibly reminiscent both in voice and appearance, of Sybil Thorndike in the role of Peer Gynt's mother way back in 1944". Meanwhile onstage, Orestes, disguised as a messenger, is telling his mother Clytemnestra that Orestes has died in Phocis. They then enter the palace where he will murder her and her lover Aegisthus. The great doors close. The scene is one of the most dramatic in world drama. Birtwistle's music builds to a climax, the drumming is thunderous, the chorus wail:

Loyal supporters of the true bloodkin
When can we let our pent feelings out,
When snatch out the galling gag of grief
And give Orestes the victory shout.

The stage is empty except for the chorus. The audience wait breathless expecting Orestes to return with the slaughtered bodies.

Shakespeare learned from the Greeks. In *Macbeth* there is the great scene where Macbeth and Lady Macbeth, steeped in blood after the murder of Duncan, are interrupted by the knocking at the gate. They retire to their chamber to wash the blood from their hands. The writer pauses the onward rush of the drama and ratchets up the tension by inserting a comic scene with the drunken Porter. Aeschylus did the same thing 2,000 years before.

The palace doors are closed. Then one of the doors slowly opens and Orestes' old Nurse comes out. She has heard of the "death" of Orestes, is saddened by the news and tells the audience in a long funny speech what a dance he led her when he was a baby.

"Trouble! That lad gave me trouble in tonloads!"

So, I'm waiting in the wings for my cue. It's a tech, so I know I'll probably have to do the entrance half a dozen times. The lighting will have to be altered etc. etc.

As I waited my eye was caught by two objects on a prop table. A moment of devilment took over. I couldn't resist it. I crossed and picked them up and then returned to behind the doors. I stood there waiting for my cue light. The chorus' wail halted, my cue light came on, I slowly opened the door and stepped out. I didn't speak, but leant down, placed the two objects on the step and went back in, closing the door.

Onstage and in the auditorium laughter exploded. *My God*, I thought, *I hope Peter finds this funny!*

The objects I had placed on the step were two empty milk bottles.

For many years after when working at the NT I would be approached by people who had witnessed this event and still laughed about it.

The trilogy opened and became a big success with audiences. The critics were divided, admiring Peter's production and the ambition of the project but critical of the masks. Some felt the masks enabled audiences to come closer to the manner in which the plays were originally given. Others felt they hid all human feeling and expressiveness and made the actors' voices difficult to hear. Michael Billington writing in the *Guardian*:

> *"Only in the third play, Eumenides do the masks become something more than an obstacle... the most chilling moment in the whole evening is the assembly, one by one, of the Furies, white-masked, gory-locked and to a sound like the murmer of innumerable bees. Their transformation into kindly beings and their final exit through a silent, standing, astonished Olivier audience is also a moving piece of theatre."*

Months later we had the incredibly exciting chance to take the trilogy to Greece, to play in the ancient 15,000-seat open-air arena at Epidaurus. We were all very excited to perform in this hallowed place. One of the cast, Tim Davies, had made the journey from Balham to Greece on his powerful motorbike and got a huge cheer when he arrived. We were only doing two performances. There is a strange magic about Epidaurus. The stepped arena is cut into a hillside and fringed behind with a wood of dense green trees. The audience look down onto a circular sandy arena behind which other hills and woods fill the horizon. The acoustics are perfect. The audiences arrived like a football crowd, tumbling out of dozens of coaches clutching cushions and rugs.

The first performance began in front of 8,000 souls. It was June and still daylight. Slowly the natural light faded and soon the moon appeared above our heads. The audience were rapt. The drama surged on. Suddenly we actors were overtaken by a new and exciting realisation. This is what we had worked all those months for. Here in this vast sacred arena, in front of this huge audience, the use of the masks made sense. They were necessary for the communication of this great drama. There was no need to justify them any more. The excitement and satisfaction was almost tangible. We felt we had the right to be here. At the end there was wild enthusiastic applause. Peter Hall and Tony Harrison took a bow. We were all drunk with excitement. An astonishing evening. The second performance was equally well received. Tony Harrison commented, "I feel overwhelmed. I felt as if we were also playing to 2,000 years of ghosts – ghosts who created the culture we are so excited by. I'm not normally given to these kind of spooky experiences but tonight I really felt like Aeschylus. I felt possessed by him. It is as though the language I had written had come home". That night he laid on a party for us all at a local taverna. The owner had slaughtered a sheep for us. We ate and drank into the night. Many toasts were offered and drunk as dawn approached, but the one that produced the loudest cheers and applause was when Tony lifted his glass and very simply said, 'To Aeschylus.'

Once when travelling in Ireland, Tony met an old woman on a train who asked him what he did. 'I'm a poet,' he told her and she nodded in approval. 'That's a good line of work,' she said. 'That's a good thing for a man to be.'

THE MIGHTY BODGER

During '82 and '83, I did five productions at the NT with Michael Bogdanov. The first was Thomas Kyd's 1589 play *The Spanish Tragedy* which embodies all the ingredients of the revenge play conventions – madness, feigned and real, a play-within-a-play, a ghost, various melodramatic incidents and a number of violent deaths. It is possible that we would not have had *Hamlet* without *The Spanish Tragedy*. The production was simply and excitingly staged in the Cottesloe Theatre. Michael Bryant played the old avenger Hieronimo whose son is murdered. In revenge he puts on a play in which he kills four people. In the end while being tortured, rather than talk he bites out his own tongue. A fabulous play and a terrific performance by Michael.

Bogdanov also had a production of Calderon's *The Mayor of Zalamea* running at the NT at that time. It first opened in the Cottesloe, where during the tech Michael decided that the set didn't work and just got rid of it. This was a typical example of Bodger's fearlessness. The production was then played with a backdrop of simple "blacks" ie. high, thick woollen curtains, usually used to darken out the backstage areas. It starred Daniel Massey and Michael Bryant. It was a success and moved up to the Olivier Theatre. Later the production was invited to an international festival in Denver, Colorado. The actor Nick Selby, playing Phillip II, King of Spain, decided not to tour and Michael asked me to take over the role. I was very happy to do so. I didn't get cast as kings very often. You get very dazzling costumes and also get to stand centre stage *all the time.* We had a fine time in Denver, the show was well received and on our time off we trekked in the Rockies. One Sunday evening we went and watched an aerialist walk a very high wire between two of the tallest buildings in the city. No safety net. It was Phillippe Petit, the Frenchman who had previously walked between the twin towers of the World Trade Center in New York. You may have seen the films *Man on Wire* or *The Walk,* which celebrated that feat. To watch him live was astonishing.

Back at the Olivier I then did Michael's production of Alfred de Musset's nineteenth-century play *Lorenzaccio* about the goings-on in the Medici family in sixteenth-century Florence. It was newly translated and adapted by the distinguished novelist John Fowles. I have absolutely no memory of the play or production apart from a giant headless statue of Michaelangelo's *David* and a very dramatic scene where eight similarly dressed actors in bright red costumes appeared as the Council of Eight. I was one of them. Early on in rehearsals of this fateful scene we became hysterical one day when a priest addressed us from a pulpit during which he mentioned "the Pope's fiat". Of course you know that a Fiat is a car. But on the off-chance that you don't know, dear reader, a fiat, in religious terms is an authoritative decree, a formal document. Naturally, while rehearsing any serious scene, actors are very prone to seeing anything funny therein. The Pope's fiat set us off. Thereafter every performance of that scene was prone to a serious outbreak of corpsing. We were eventually fiercely admonished by the stage manager – 'This is the National Theatre etc. etc.' – but we couldn't stop.

In 1982, I did two workshop productions with Michael. His idea was simple and fresh. He gathered together eight actors to do a small-scale production of Brecht's *The Caucasian Circle.* The play was on many school syllabuses and Michael's plan was to do what he called an unashamedly modest production that we would tour to schools, colleges and small arts centres around the country. The production would have no sets, no lighting, no props, no costumes. He wanted a style of presentation that would be imaginative, contemporary, clear and unpretentious. We would use whatever we could find in the way of props and furniture at each venue. To leave the NT, where we were coddled and cosseted, where every production was painstakingly and expensively staged and set out on the road with nothing, was a daunting prospect. But as presented by Michael it was a fresh and exciting idea and we were all up for it.

The first problem we addressed in rehearsal was how we could use "found objects" to represent something else. We stood in a circle around the room and one of the actors picked up a kitchen chair and turned it into a prison door, staring through the "bars", another strummed it and it became a harp, another sat on it and drove it as a motor car. Since drama school we had all done this kind of exercise. Now, given the limitations we would soon encounter, these exercises took on a new and necessary urgency. How, when chased by the soldiers, could the girl Grusha, with a baby in her arms, cross a bridge over a swollen river? Where would we find a "baby"? Where would we find a "bridge" in a school hall in Milton Keynes? We worked on all the scenes with much improvisation, inventing a wide range of physical circumstances. Very little was set. We would be playing in small and large spaces, traditional pros arch, in-the-round etc. We became very adept at instant invention. Anything in the rehearsal room could be put to use. There was a tremendous excitement and satisfaction in the connection between creativity and spontaneity. With no time to agonise over a decision we could act instantaneously and instinctively.

We travelled to and from the venues in a small coach. We had one hour to get to know the space we would play in, to plan entrances and exits, to scour the building for anything that might be useful for the show. Though we wore no costumes, we tended to wear something from our own home wardrobe that might be helpful for the characters we were playing. We mixed with the audiences as they arrived and talked about the play and how we were going to do it.

Given the physical circumstances, each performance was different from the last. For instance Grusha's "baby" was easy, a couple of tea towels or a scarf borrowed from an audience member. But how to do her escape with the baby over the rickety bridge with the rapids bubbling below was trickier. Sometimes we used four chairs placed side by side, sometimes a "found" ladder placed flat on the floor, sometimes a plank between two boxes. On one occasion in a small theatre in the Cotswolds, Emily Morgan, playing Grusha, bravely walked round on the curved balustrade of the circle above the heads of those in the stalls – a hair-raising but very effective moment. Pre-health and safety days, of course.

Months later and with two more actors we did the same kind of staging with *Macbeth*. I played the First Witch, Macduff and various other parts. Three men played the witches. How could we make these effective and disturbing to a modern young audience. How to get away from the cliché representation. Shakespeare was writing for an audience that believed in witches and black magic. We tried various ideas and finally decided to *start* with the cliché.

Opening the play and without any atmospheric lighting to help us we entered draped in old bits of cloth and black plastic bin bags like three old "bag ladies" and lit a small fire in a "pot". One of us had a bottle that we drank from. Soon we began to do "witch" acting with lots of "oogly-boogly" noises and clichéd witch fingertwisting gestures. We cackled. We were taking the piss out of ourselves. The audience found this funny, comfortable. Then one of us wet his finger and began to move it around the rim of a large wine glass. That high, clear unsettling single sound filled the space. The audience went quiet. We "witches" went quiet. Then we played the scene very simply. Now, the audience saw the real witches. It worked. At one venue someone found a *Daily Mail* with a large front page headline. It said something like "The Witch Women of Northampton – Exposed!" We used it in the show that afternoon. We sat round and read it. We thought it was hysterical. We cackled at it. We showed the audience. They laughed. Then the glass screech started and we got serious.

Of course some of our decisions didn't work. The one that I remember most vividly was when, in the scouring of a school for ideas, an actor found two bright plastic children's telephones in a cupboard. In the scene where the four thanes meet on the way to Birnam Wood – reduced in our slimmed down production to two, Menteth and Lennox – the two actors decided to do the scene from either side of the acting area as a dramatic telephone conversation. Now all the actors when not in a scene sat in a semi-circle at the back of the stage. The scene arrived, the two actors hadn't had time to rehearse it earlier. They paused. They stood by their red and yellow phones. The rest of us had no notion of what was coming. Then one of the actors uttered that great Shakespearean line – 'Brrring brrring! Brrring brrring!' They picked up the phones and spoke. Don't ask me how the scene went. The rest of us sat heads down. Suppressed hysterics is how I would describe our reaction.

I remember we found three black folding screens, which we used not only as screens, but, when banged by fists, they became thunder-sheets and drums. We fought with broom handles. We found a strong four-wheeled canteen trolley which became a stretcher, a bier, a platform for Malcolm to harangue his troops from. We never got bored. Each performance presented new challenges and we grabbed them with both fists. During the run of these two productions we would often return to the NT to perform in our other plays in the repertoire. No matter how fine they were they lacked the danger, the immediacy and the excitement of our small-scale work.

* * *

In the mid-eighties I did nine plays at the NT. In the Cottesloe for Michael Bogdanov I did *Strider –The Story of a Horse* written by Mark Rozovsky, from a story by Tolstoy. Using a blend of mime, music, dance and story-telling Michael's production, which again delighted in a very simple staging, told the story of a horse, Strider, a piebald, given away to a groom because it was the wrong colour. It was then sold to a prince who used it to draw his elaborate sleigh and who also raced it. Finally the horse ends up back where it was born, worn-out, slaughtered and flayed, its remains devoured by wolves. Paralleling Strider's decline is that of the prince, his fortune dissipated, his health ruined by drink. Michael Pennington gave a remarkable performance as Strider, first as a gawky foal, then a proud winner and finally a broken hack.

At this time Peter Gill was running the NT Studio. This was, and still is, a workshop for the NT company. It is based in what was, back in the sixties the Old Vic Annexe. For Peter, in 1983–84, I did two productions in the Cottesloe. *Antigone* with Jane Lapotaire in the title role, and Peter's own adaptation of William Faulkner's novel *As I Lay Dying* about a poor Southern family attending to the burial of their mother in Yoknapatawpha County, Mississipi in 1930. This production in its acting, design and intention brought to mind the work of the photographers who documented the Farm Security Administration's Historical Unit during the Depression, the great Walker Evans and Dorothea Lange, who with unflinching eyes captured the lives of the poor sharecroppers and their families. The Bundren family travel by wagon pulled by two mules across the worn landscape taking their mother to be buried in Jefferson. Anse, the father, the sons, Cash, Darl, Jewel, Vardaman and their pregnant sister Dewey Dell. In the novel, Faulkner uses stream of consciousness and multiple narrators. Peter stuck with this technique and it worked very well theatrically. I played a very conservative pharmacist, Moseley, who refuses to sell Dewey Dell (Joanne Whalley) a drug to abort her unwanted pregnancy. A memorable production.

Also in the Cottesloe in 1983 Giles Block did a fast and inventive production of John Marston's rarely seen 1604 comedy *The Fawn.* As ever, the plot takes some recounting. Suffice it to say that Marston's play is a sly and cynical exposure of the sexual vanities of Elizabethan high society. I remember this production for a particular reason. In fact for several reasons, the very good reviews I received.

"There is James Hayes, cringing and strutting to great effect as a pathologically jealous husband who revels in the supposed infidelities of his innocent wife" – Milton Shulman, *Evening Standard.*

"Only one episode (much the best in the play) touches on the dark side of human nature; and this is in the tormenting of a jealous husband who is led to believe his wife has been adulterously impregnated. James Hayes plays him with a spade-bearded frenzy that puts you in mind momentarily of Ford in The Merry Wives of Windsor, and at that point Marston acquires a genuinely cruel perceptiveness" – Michael Billington, *Guardian.*

"The most spectacular of the gulls is James Hayes as a pathologically jealous nobleman; he has a great scene hanging from a wall by his fingers, agog to observe his wife's infidelities" – Robert Cushman, *Observer.*

Sorry, couldn't resist that!

CORIOLANUS II

In 1959 the Latin master took a group of boys from Bolton School to Stratford upon Avon for a week's camping in bell tents. He later recounted the day when one of the boys queued to stand through a matinee performance of Laurence Olivier's *Coriolanus*. The boy tore back to camp for tea and then charged off again to stand through the evening performance. The boy was Ian McKellen, the director of the production was Peter Hall.

Twenty-five years later, in the Olivier Theatre, Ian played *Coriolanus*, with Peter again directing the play. I played Junius Brutus, one of the two Tribunes of the People opposed to Coriolanus. In the Old Vic production of the play, which I had done with the Berliner directors, the hero was called Coriol*ah*nus –very harsh, very German. In this new production Peter insisted that the hero be called Cor*eye*olanus. He insisted that the military victory achieved by Caius Martius over the city of Cor*ioli* led to his being given the new title Cor*eye*olanus.

The production was very successful, with a number of critics citing it as the best Shakespeare at the NT since the company moved to the South Bank in 1975. Ian also had a big success in the role and won Best Actor in the 1985 *Evening Standard* Awards. He is a very fine actor, a natural leader and a great "company man". By the latter I mean that he had not only his own interests at heart but the interests of the entire company. In the role he had a great command of the language and a physical and intellectual grip on the character which he played with effortless ease. He had that great actor's ability to switch from arrogance to contempt, from choleric rage to childish sulks in an instant. He found much sly humour in the part. Seeming to revel in a triumphal and garlanded entrance accompanied with blazing trumpets, he then got a very good laugh with his undercutting comment, "No more of this, it doth offend my heart". In his banishment he delivered the famous line in rejection of Rome, "There is a world elsewhere", from the wings, after he had exited the stage. When admonished by his mother, like a child he shifted from foot to foot and sulked. In the scenes and fights with his great enemy Aufidius, he and Greg Hicks brought a potent homoerotic edge to their relationship.

Although successful, there was an aspect of the production that was much derided. At the centre of John Bury's set was a circular sand pit. Around this on the upstage sides were two banks of raised seating. Peter Hall had decided that these should be filled with ninety audience members (at two pounds a seat). He wanted this onstage audience, urged on by actor/citizens in the play, to be brought into the action for a number of scenes involving "the people". On the first scene of the first performance it became absolutely clear to all the actors that this was a terrible idea.

"Enter a company of mutinous Citizens, with staves, clubs, and other weapons."

Some of these citizens then urged the onstage audience to leave their seats, descend to the sand pit and join in with the mutiny. Down they came. This long and crucial scene required an outraged and hungry crowd "resolved to die rather than famish" to do some acting. Disaster! What could they do? It was not their fault. Most of the press thought this idea a major miscalculation. One critic said these audience members "never for a second look more than patrons of the National Theatre doing the backstage tour". Another suggested that this was "Peter Hall's way of telling us that the NT is hard up". Within four days the journalist Tom Aitkin wrote a long piece in the *Guardian* recounting his "amateur debut at the National". He wrote of cynical mutterings in the two-pound seats on the NT's "acumen in persuading us to pay to be its extras".

On one or two occasions I noticed the chance to "appear" on the Olivier stage drew a number of obvious show-offs. I particularly remember a man onstage dressed completely in red. Red suit, red shirt, red tie, red shoes and red socks. And of course seeing the odd "mutinous citizen" in a flowered dress carrying a handbag was hugely funny if not very helpful.

All the actors felt that having these audience members "involved" in the action was proving a distraction and a comic one at that. After a few performances Ian wrote a memo to Peter Hall suggesting he get rid of the "crowd". Put them back where they belong – in the audience. Peter refused, accusing Ian of "undermining everything I think about the production".

The costumes for the production were an eclectic mix of ancient and modern. David Ryall and I, playing the Tribunes of the People, wore jackets and trousers. I remember in one scene I carried a briefcase. Although our performances were much admired, David and I tried hard but failed to find much sympathy for these two characters. In our dress we were described as "Leftist GLC councillors". David as "looking like Eric Heffer", a well-known left wing Labour MP and I was described as "sporting Tony Benn gear". But our clothes and performances were consonant with the political figures we represented. Ian was dressed throughout in Roman gear. On his first entrance he wore a knee-length tunic and sandals and held a ceremonial sword across his chest. During the tech, Ian mentioned to David and I that we looked "very good, very right". Next afternoon at a note session he whispered to me, 'Watch my first entrance tonight.'

On he came totally transformed from head to foot. Now, he wore an impeccable modern suit, a royal blue shirt, expensive tie and shiny black shoes. Over his shoulders was draped a big cream overcoat. His hair was pulled back in a tight ponytail and he wore sunglasses. He looked like a martial Marcello Mastroianni. The only remnant of the previous night's look was the ceremonial sword. Breathtaking. The historical and modern worlds conjoined.

I suspect Peter Hall and designer John Bury were as surprised as I was. Ian, telling nobody, had simply gone to the NT wardrobe and "designed" a new costume for himself. The overcoat he had bought in a sale in Bond Street.

Three years after our visit to Epidaurus, Peter again led an NT company to Greece. This time we went to Athens where we played *Coriolanus* in the Theatre of Herod Atticus, a Roman amphitheatre built on the side of the Acropolis. It held 6,000 people. The two full houses we played to were the equivalent of twelve performances at the Olivier. With only two mornings to restage the play, we had to work hard in the Athenian sun. Both shows went very well and were greeted with standing ovations. After the interval during the first performance, there was a genuinely breathtaking surprise, when in the middle of a scene, my eye was distracted by something at the top edge of my vision. Suddenly out of the surrounding darkness the illuminated Parthenon appeared above us.

It was a great privilege to have been lucky enough to play these ancient theatres. After the final performance at Epidaurus, as well as in Athens, I walked into the now empty amphitheatres and sat on the stone seats. I thought about the actors who had played there centuries before.

Obviously we took all the props, costumes etc to Athens. For some reason we had to bring our own sand for the onstage sandpit. That was thirty bags of sand. Coals to Newcastle. And because it was in the business manifest – a list of cargo in the shipment – the same sand had to be taken back to London.

FOUR PLAYS WITH
ALAN AYCKBOURN

A CHORUS OF DISAPPROVAL
ME, MYSELF AND I
TONS OF MONEY
A VIEW FROM THE BRIDGE

I can't remember how in 1985 I got to be cast in Alan Ayckbourn's production of his play *A Chorus Of Disapproval* but it led to a run of four hugely enjoyable projects with the man. The NT had already staged three earlier plays of his. Initally there had been much snobbish criticism at the idea of Alan's plays being allowed anywhere near this temple of the arts. Surely Ayckbourn was more suited to the down-market, commercial West End. But Peter Hall, struggling to establish and fill the new three-theatre building, was keen to offer the public a broad repertoire, especially plays that would bring in an audience who would normally run a mile from a temple of the arts. He famously remarked to Alan, 'No doubt you can do very well without the National Theatre, but can the National Theatre do without you?'

A Chorus Of Disapproval is set around the rehearsals by the Pendon Amateur Light Operatic Society (PALOS) of a production of Gay's *The Beggar's Opera* at the Joshua Pike Memorial Centre Complex. The plot of the *Opera* is mirrored in the action of the play. Alan had gathered together a terrific cast led by Michael Gambon, Bob Peck and Imelda Staunton.

The story of the play revolves around Guy Jones (Peck) an inconspicuous widower, a man who finds it hard to say no. He works in Pendon for a multinational company. He joins the local amateur theatre where he is soon involved in an affair with the director's unhappy wife (Staunton) as well as one with a local "swinger" (Gemma Craven). During rehearsals he is quizzed by various self-serving businessmen in the cast as to his company's expansion plans. They all have an interest in the surrounding land.

The play gives an unpatronising account of a group of enthusiasts who sing well and have a shot at acting. I played an unfortunate character called Ted Washbrook, who has a wife called Enid and a difficult daughter called Linda, who during the course of the play burns her mother's wardrobe.

Overseeing the rehearsals is the tyrannical director, Dafydd Ap Llewellyn (Gambon) – a character with the tyrannical qualities of John Dexter, but writ large. A shambling bear of a man, shirt hanging out of his trousers, whose life consists of imposing his will. There is a painfully funny scene where the company are re-rehearsing a section where some cuts have previously been made. On that evening Enid and I are supposed to attend the Co-op Dinner Dance, but Dafydd won't allow us the evening off. He insists we rehearse. With the company in jeans, tweeds and prints, Enid and I are in full evening dress, hoping to get away in time for the buffet. It was an Olivier production and Dafydd "directed" this scene with the new cuts from the back of the stalls. Unfortunately Ted hadn't put the cuts in his script and blithely ploughed on. As the other actors pause in confusion, a voice from the stalls would bark from the darkness, "That's cut, Ted." As we staggered on with the cast continually whispering, *"That's cut, Ted… That's cut too, Ted,'* a low strangled muttering began at the back the stalls. Then, out of the darkness this pent-up, hulking monster ran down the steps, on to the stage, pulled the script out of my hand and began to tear pages out of it, shouting in my face, *'That's cut! And that's cut! And that's cut!'* and finally in a silent rage tears the whole script apart and throws it in my face. Dumbfounded and deeply hurt I rush off into the wings – on many nights accompanied by sympathetic "Awws" from the audience.

"Dafydd: I used to be an actor, you know. Professional!
Guy: Really. Where did you work?
Dafydd: Oh, all over, all over – mainly in Minehead."

The play had many painful and funny scenes. In one scene during a rehearsal break, Dafydd alone onstage with Guy, pours his heart out about his unhappy marriage – *"I call her my Swiss Army wife"* – unaware that the tannoy is on and everyone backstage can hear the conversation. In another, during the "tech", Dafydd becomes increasingly annoyed while lighting the show. Shouting orders to the electrician he is entirely unaware that onstage under the roving lights his wife and Guy are having a blistering row as their relationship breaks up.

Alan had assembled a very strong cast. Michael, Imelda and Bob were very funny, but there were equally funny performances from David Ryall and Moira Redmond as the Huntley-Pikes, Jenny Galloway as the abrasive stage manager, Jane Wenham and Kelly Hunter as respectively my wife and daughter and Paul Bentall and Gemma Craven as the swinging Hubbards.

To be able to juggle such a disparate group of characters whose lives consist of disappointment, frustration, unhappiness and longing in the context of the rehearsals of an amateur drama group is a stunning skill. But the ability of the writer to bring a comic Chekhovian perception to their world is what makes Alan Ayckbourn special.

* * *

Towards the end of the run a large embossed invitation headed:

THE DIRECTORS OF PALOS
BERNARD LORNE-MESSITER ESQ., LORD SHYNE,
A. AYCKBOURN ESQ. AND MRS P CRODER

arrived inviting us all to a "soirée" at the Park Lane Hotel in Piccadilly **to celebrate the Society's highly acclaimed production of** *The Beggar's Opera.*

In a typically generous gesture Alan and his partner Heather had laid on a lavish spread in the hotel's Oak Room where the surrounding walls were covered with large production photographs of us all. A fabulous evening.

* * *

Soon after, Alan cast me in his short musical play *Me, Myself and I* with music by Paul Todd. It is the story of Mary Yately, a local "Mum of the Year". No ordinary housewife, she has three personalities, which are played by three actresses. One actor plays all the men in her life. Kelly Hunter, Jenny Galloway and Kate Dyson played Mary and I played the men. We did a short late-night run of it in the Lyttleton Terrace.

During 1985 Peter Hall divided the company into five acting companies under the direction of Bill Bryden, Richard Eyre and David Hare, Peter himself, Ian McKellen and Edward Petherbridge, and Peter Wood. In 1986 he invited Alan to run a company. Peter asked for three productions including a new Ayckbourn play. Alan chose *Tons of Money*, a 1922 Aldwych Farce, by Will Evans and Valentine; *A View From The Bridge* by Arthur Miller; and for the third play he wrote *A Small Family Business*. He invited me to join his company and I appeared in two of the plays.

* * *

Tons of Money I have very little memory of. The play had dated and Alan adapted it for a contemporary audience, taking out verbal gags that no longer worked etc. We played in the Lyttelton Theatre and the production received good but not outstanding reviews. The company's acting was praised, particularly the performances of Michael Gambon as the butler Sprules and Diane Bull as the bent-kneed myopic maid Simpson. These two created a very funny double act.

I remember Michael coming onstage during the costume parade in the tech, wearing an immaculate butler outfit. He wasn't happy with it. 'I don't like it, it's got no character,' he said to me. He had based Sprules on an old dresser we had had at the Old Vic, called Leslie. Leslie was a squat, bald, somewhat cantankerous man. He had a very distinctive gravelly, spluttery voice, and his movement was to say the least toad-like. He was very camp, often wore face powder and teased his sparse hair carefully around his face. He was famous for his malapropisms. He once told me he had redecorated his bedroom in contemptuous wallpaper. He warned Jane Lapotaire about her eating habits – 'You need to masturbate your food properly.'

Michael's Sprules, minus the camp and face powder, was Leslie personified. So, naturally, a well-cut suit and tails, not to mention an immaculately starched shirt did not suit his perception of the character. Coming back onstage for the tech an hour later, Michael had made some adjustments. As he shambled, Quasimodo-like, downstage, I noticed that the jacket had now taken on a tired, dusty and shapeless quality, the shirtfront was seriously stained, the crotch of the trousers had descended to somewhere in the region of his knees. Now, character and costume were as one. Witnessing this, I noticed that the designer's face had taken on a new and somewhat pained quality.

What had brought about this transformation? Well, Michael in his unhappy state, had retired to his dressing room, removed the costume and proceded to age it. Standing on the various garments he strenuously pulled, dragged, stretched, tore at the sleeves, the tails, the trouser legs and pockets etc . He soiled the shirt front with coffee stains and then trampled all over it in a dusty corridor. The shoes he rubbed vigorously against the many concrete surfaces in the building.

Nine months after Alan's party for *A Chorus of Disapproval* he threw an even more lavish spread at the Lancaster Ballroom of the Savoy Hotel. On that weekend he had, I think, either four or five productions of his plays running in London, an extraordinary achievement. He invited all the companies to a celebratory dinner and dance. The invitation was headed:

On behalf of
The Vaudeville Woman's National
Lyric Chorus Company

Lower down it said: "Dress: Elegant" – Golly, I'd have to hire a dinner suit and bow tie. Alan and Heather had invited about a hundred guests. We started with cocktails in the River Room and then processed into the ballroom for dinner followed by dancing. There were two bands. A swanky evening.

* * *

Rehearsals for *A View From The Bridge* started in December 1986 and for some reason, now forgotten, we rehearsed the play not at the National but in various rehearsal spaces all over the city. I particularly remember a couple of cold weeks in the crypt of a Hawksmoor church near Wapping.

A View From The Bridge is a small-scale modern tragedy. It is set in a cramped apartment in a tenement building near the docks in Brooklyn. It concerns an Italian-American longshoreman, Eddie Carbone who is unknowingly in love with his niece Catherine, who lives with him and his wife. Two illegal immigrants, relatives of his wife, come to live with the family. The younger brother, Rodolpho, falls for Catherine and she for him. This unleashes a furious jealousy in Eddie, which leads to his betrayal of the two brothers, breaking the ancient code of his society. The plot then inexorably slides into tragedy. Michael Gambon played Eddie Carbone, Liz Bell played his wife Beatrice, Suzan Sylvester played Eddie's niece Catherine and Adrian Rawlins and Michael Simkins played the two illegals. I played Alfieri, Eddie's lawyer, who is also the one-man Greek chorus – the man with a view from the bridge.

The production would be hailed as one of the National Theatre's greatest successes. My memories of the rehearsal period are of short days and lots of laughs. Alan directed the play with a very light but sure touch. He believed that afternoon rehearsals were often counter-productive with lower concentration and creativity in the room after lunch. He made a revolutionary suggestion. If we all agreed, we would take a short break for twenty minutes at 12:30pm, stay in the room, have a snack and then carry on rehearsing until around 3:30/4:00pm. And that's what we did. The cast were first rate. The work was intense and exciting. The strong emotions battered the room. Yet everything seemed to go so smoothly, so effortlessly. Late in December Alan said, 'Look, it's going very well. It's not a long play. We don't want to overcook it. Let's take a week off for Christmas.' So we did.

When we returned, rehearsals moved into third gear and quickly into fourth. Michael G now had a moustache, he greased his hair back, he began to motor. He used his height and bulk to make Eddie very intimidating. His voice had a gruff Brooklyn bite. His increasing dislike for the young Rodolpho took on a jeering menace. He had become a longshoreman, a man used to manhandling a ship's cargo. But his tenderness towards Catherine was very touching. He came to see me, his lawyer, in my office knotted with anger and frustration. Volcanic, torn. The tender courting of Catherine by Rodolpho upset Eddie: *"It's breaking my heart"*. He goads the boy, hinting that he is gay. There is a scene where the older Marco, angry at Eddie's treatment of his younger brother, challenges him to raise a chair in the air by gripping it at the bottom of one leg. Surprisingly, Eddie, furious with himself, can't do it. Marco then kneels, grips the chair leg and slowly, slowly, raises it. He stands up, towering above the kneeling Eddie with the chair above his head. He holds the pose looking down at him. It is a threat and a warning to Eddie. Michael Simkins gave a dangerous brooding intent to this seemingly inconsequential moment.

Both Liz Bell and Suzan Sylvester gave outstanding performances. Both the women's pain was tangible as Eddie's love for them became destructive. The final moment of the play as Eddie lies dying on the floor with his wife kneeling beside him was deeply moving. It is one of my favourite moments in the play. Great acting. The appalling realisation and sorrow for what he has done, especially to Beatrice, who so loves him, is expressed in four short words/sounds.

"Eddie: Oh, B. My B.

He dies."

This small, but powerful tragedy played in the Cottesloe Theatre. It shone like a jewel with a cast of outstanding actors. Peter Hall, I was told, had wanted Alan to do the play in the bigger Lyttelton Theatre. I presume this was for commercial reasons. But Alan felt very strongly that if we got the production right, the play had the capacity to give an audience a truly memorable experience, especially in such a small theatre. The watchers crowded around the stage would feel less like detached observers and more like fellow residents of the tenement gathered to witness the tragedy.

Many colleagues I encountered during the rehearsal period were surprised to hear that Alan Ayckbourn was directing this great American play. I presume they felt he should stick to lighter work. In my opinion no other director could have done a better production.

A View from The Bridge opened in February 1987 and was a massive success with audiences and critics and went on to win many awards.

Michael Billington wrote in the *Guardian*:

> *"In any critic's life there are certain red-letter nights. The new production of A View From The Bridge is emphatically one of them. In the first place it shows Michael Gambon unequivocally shaking hands with greatness."*

He then went on to lavish praise on Alan's production and on every member of the cast.

"It is hard to believe that there ever has been a better production of this play ... a definitive staging." – Sheridan Morley in *Punch*

"The National Theatre at its blazing best ... Miller has found his match in Michael Gambon." – *Sunday Times*

Arthur Miller came to see it and was very complimentary about the acting and the production. Talking to him in the stalls one day during previews, I mentioned how structurally tight I thought *A View* was. Also, given the scale of the tragedy, how short the play was, how there didn't seem to be an extraneous line or a spare moment in it. Miller smiled and said, 'Ah well, you know, I *squeezed* them all out.' A little later I enquired if he had seen any other theatre during his stay in London. He vaguely pointed his finger upwards towards the Olivier Theatre above us – 'I saw that *Antony and Cleopatra* play the other night'. (This was Peter Hall's production with Anthony Hopkins and Judi Dench.)

'Did you like it?' I asked.

'Yeah, yeah' he said 'But it was long, you know. Long. I felt I could have *squeezed* it a bit.'

After months of sold-out performances we eventually moved the production to the larger Aldwych Theatre in the West End. It had a very successful run there, but I felt the show lost the intimacy and intensity it had had at the Cottesloe. After the first performance we were given a little do in one of the bars at the Aldwych to welcome the production. As I entered I witnessed a remarkable tableau. Standing at the bar was Alan Ayckbourn talking to Arthur Miller and Harold Pinter.

When you do a run of a play in the West End with eight performances a week for a number of months – as opposed to three or four performances a week in repertoire – sometimes a little levity can creep into the odd performance. Michael Gambon is prone to a little levity. During the run at the Aldwych I made a terrible and extremely stupid mistake. Meeting him one night in the wings at "Beginners" I foolishly recounted a very embarrassing incident that had happened to me that morning. A day or two before, suffering from severe constipation I had foolishly managed to make my backside bleed. So, I went to the doctor. When called, I opened the door of his consulting room and in a mildly embarrassed mood walked in. Unfortunately, nobody had informed me that he was away that morning and another doctor was filling-in for him. So it was not until I reached out my hand to say, 'Good morning,' that I was confronted by a young female doctor. Not only a young female doctor – but an absolutely stunning female doctor. 'What can I do for you, Mr Hayes?' I *had* to tell her. God, the embarrassment, when soon after, she pulled on a rubber glove and asked me to drop my pants and lie face down on the table.

So, I had told Gambon. We laughed about it. The play started. I forgot about it. Fatal. Probably half an hour later I was onstage in my office when Eddie Carbone comes to seek my advice. It is a very serious scene. He enters, sits, we talk across a table, neither of us moves, at the end he stands and leaves.

Halfway through the scene Michael suddenly stood up. *What the hell is he doing?* He then in profile placed one of his large hands behind his back, bent a little, and pointed a finger to his arse, at the same time looking at me with a knowing open-mouthed horror. The bastard! Trying to corpse me. And succeeding.

PLATFORMS

"Platforms" at the NT in 2013 are "an eclectic programme of talks, discussions and interviews". In the eighties, they also included performances and readings of short plays, which gave a welcome opportunity to writers, actors, directors and designers working in the building. They were very popular. Staged on a tiny budget with much borrowing of costumes, furniture and props etc. from all departments of the NT, these small pre-evening performances were presented in the three theatres. Like much of the company I got involved in devising, performing and directing some of them.

Harrison Birtwistle's *Down By The Greenwood Side* – a

dramatic pastoral was one of the first Platforms I got involved with. The text is compiled from two folk-sources, which are interwoven: the traditional mummers play about the killing and resurrection of Saint George, and the ballad of the cruel mother who kills her children and meets them on her way home. The distinguished soprano Teresa Cahill sang the complicated role of Mrs Green, while five actors played St. George, Dr. Blood, etc. I played Bold Slasher. Harry directed the piece in the Cottesloe. Dominic Muldowney conducted the nine musicians. The instrumentation is taken from the Victorian ballad "The Floral Dance":

> *"We danced to the band with a curious tone*
> *Of the cornet, clarinet and big trombone,*
> *Fiddle, cello, big bass drum,*
> *Bassoon, flute and euphonium."*

* * *

"I guess I'm just an old mad scientist at bottom. Give me an underground laboratory, half a dozen atom-smashers, and a beautiful girl in a diaphanous veil waiting to be turned into a chimpanzee, and I care not who writes the nation's laws."

The actor David Baron and I shared a love for the great American humourist S. J. Perelman. A writer, alas, less read now than in the middle of the last century. At the age of twenty-six he went to Hollywood where he worked with the Marx Brothers and co-wrote two of their films – *Monkey Business* and *Horse Feathers*. Perelman didn't like Hollywood and returned to the East Coast. He developed his unique comic and satirical style writing for the *New Yorker* over many decades. His use of parody, ridicule, irony and wordplay was outstanding. He stated that he was heavily influenced by James Joyce and that other great humourist Flann O'Brien. In turn, Woody Allen admitted to being influenced by Perelman. David and I decided to compile a selection of his work and stage it at the NT. Many of his pieces are in the form of short playlets and lend themselves to performance.

One of the pieces we chose was titled *Send No Money, Honey.*

Perelman invents a 1940s advertising campaign for a very special necktie:

> *"Girls can't resist this 'Kiss Me Necktie' as it Glows in the dark! By day a lovely swank tie…by night a call to love in glowing words! 'Will you kiss me in the dark, baby?'"*

There then follows a short playlet illustrating the allure of said neckwear. It involved an "utterly lovely creature", Fern Replevin, her father Lafcadio, her soon-to-be ex-fiancé Fleetwood Rumsey and Rex Beeswanger, wearer of the seductive tie and "a thoroughbred from his saturnine eyebrow to the tip of his well-polished shoe". When Rex dims the light to reveal his glowing necktie she is his.

> *"FERN: Rex Beeswanger. I've always wanted to know someone named Rex Beeswanger. It's… it's instinctive with springtime and the song of larks."*

Another piece titled *The Idol's Eye* was a first-person narration of a very English country house story with a mystery involving a Muslim sect in Bombay and a mysterious idol, whose single eye was a flawless ruby:

> *"Four of us had cycled down from London together: Gossip Gabrilowitsch, the Polish pianist; Downey Couch, the Irish tenor; Frank Falcovsky, the Jewish prowler, and myself, Clay Modelling."*

David, Sarah Mortimer and I acted the pieces and Matthew Scott wrote the music. We played a few performances in the Olivier at 6:00pm. Unusually for Platforms, the *Guardian* came to review it and liked it, which helped sell some seats.

A HORDE OF UNEMPLOYED VENTRILOQUISTS

Around this time I decided to put together a project of my own. The other great humourist I loved was Flann O'Brien. So I compiled a one-man show based on his work.

The Irish writer Brian O'Nolan wrote under the pen names Flann O'Brien and Myles na Gopaleen. After a brilliant career in the civil service he became a full-time writer. He wrote four highly acclaimed novels under the name Flann O'Brien of which *At Swim-Two-Birds* and *The Third Policeman* are the best known. Myles na Gopaleen was the name he adopted for the very funny Cruiskeen Lawn column which he wrote for the *Irish Times*, from 1940-66. It was from these columns I chose the material for my show.

For my research I had the good fortune to be given access to the British Newspaper Library in Colindale. It housed three hundred years of national and local news. The oldest newspaper in the collection is French and dated 30th May 1631. Thought you'd like to know that! After filling in a few slips at the reception desk I was directed to a large high-ceilinged room. This contained rows of high wooden desks with sloped tops and tall stools with a lamp arched over each work space. Most had figures bent over them beavering away. Suddenly I was back in Dickens' London. Any moment I expected someone to open the door and call out, 'Mr Cratchit – a moment!' I went to the numbered desk I was assigned and waited. After about ten minutes a small man in a navy uniform entered, pushing a low rubber-wheeled trolley and approached my desk. He then reached down and hoisted three large leather-bound volumes onto it. I whispered a quiet, 'Thank you,' and he departed. I opened the first volume and was confronted with original bound copies of the *Irish Times* from 1940. It was exciting. Over the next few days I sifted through paper after paper, column after column, searching for material that would crucially not only be funny but would work theatrically. Much photocopying ensued. I eventually chose enough material for a one-hour show. Colindale is now closed and most of the collection has been digitised and made available online. All very marvellous but not quite the same as the physical experience.

Ireland in the forties had a strong censorship board and the Catholic Church exerted a control over all things moral. This small nation on the dark edge of Europe had great need of a satirist. Brian O'Nolan fitted the bill. He had a Byzantine love of complexity and ingenuity. Myles became the scourge of the pretenders to culture. Two of these pretenders he honed in on over a number of columns.

First was the man of great wealth and vulgarity who decided he needed a library: "Whether he can read or not I do not know, but some savage faculty for observation told him that most respectable and estimable people usually had a lot of books in their houses". The man buys some bookcases and fills them with all manner of new books. Myles noted on a visit that not one of the books had ever been opened or touched. So this set him thinking: "Why should a wealthy person like this be put to the trouble of pretending to read at all?" He decides to set up a "Book Handling Service" where professional book-handlers would go in and suitably maul the customer's library for so much per shelf. He offered four types of mauling from the cheapest at £1 7s 6d "where each volume would be well and truly handled, four leaves in each to be dog-eared, and a tram ticket, cloak-room docket or other comparable item to be inserted in each as a forgotten book-mark". The fourth class would be called "Le Traitement Superbe" where *"suitable passages in fifty per cent of the books would be underlined in red ink and appropriate phrases inserted in the margins, for instance – 'Rubbish!' –'How true , how true!' – 'Yes, but cf. Homer, Od. Iii, 151' etc etc.… Not less than six volumes to be inscribed with forged messages of affection and gratitude from the author of each work, e.g. 'From your devoted friend and follower, K. Marx.' – 'Your invaluable suggestions and assistance, not to mention your kindness, in entirely re-writing chapter three, entitles you, surely, to this first copy of "Tess". From your old friend T. Hardy'."*

The other pretenders to culture he assisted over a number of columns, were the people who owned no books but wanted to be thought educated; people who couldn't string a sentence together. Myles had access to a horde of unemployed ventriloquists. During theatre intervals these could be hired out to well-heeled dopes who would be ordered to keep their mouths shut. The "escort" would then carry on an erudite "conversation" with them to impress their neighbours. But soon blackmail is used and rogue ventriloquists demand financial reward otherwise they will ruin the customer: *"Empty everything in your handbag into my right-hand coat pocket! Otherwise you will spend the evening plying strangers with salacious conundrums, even in the middle of the play."*

Myles' invention of his Patent Ballet Pumps to help the ladies of the ballet achieve better "altitude" proved a huge success:

"Each shoe is fitted with three diminutive land mines…"

Myles invented a friendship between the poet Keats and Chapman, the great translator of Homer, to facilitate a long series of increasingly tortuous shaggy dog stories for the column. The first of these revolved around a meeting of the two great writers in Aalst, Belgium in 1814. Chapman, by way of a hobby, indulged in the cultivation and study of carrier pigeons and is first discovered by Keats trying to revive an ailing pigeon. It entails the translator using a portion of a toothpick to prop open the bird's beak and to study its throat with his magnifying glass. The story is long and convoluted, the carrier pigeon is healed. The poet then sat down and "according to report wrote the sonnet headed 'On First Looking Into Chapman's Homer'."

The Myles na Gopaleen columns were full of humorous, satirical, learned, grave-faced writing of the highest quality. Brian O'Nolan/ Flann O'Brien/ Myles na Gopaleen was a comic genius. Thurber and Perelman, James Joyce and Graham Greene heaped high praise upon him.

I titled my one-man show *A Horde Of Unemployed Ventriloquists*. Rod Langsford designed a simple set that would be easy to tour – a backcloth resembling a torn jagged-edged front page of the *Irish Times*, a desk, a hatstand.

I rehearsed it on my own at the NT Studio without a director. I invited Greg Hicks to come to see a late run-through and he was very encouraging. I opened it for a number of performances in the Cottesloe. On the first night I remember setting off from my dressing room, suddenly very nervous. What if this passion of mine for Myles na Gopaleen, for writing I thought hysterically funny, didn't make a successful journey from the newspaper to the stage? I was going to be standing up there for an hour on my own. Christ, I could die. Be greeted by gales of silence. I walked out onstage and began. It worked. The material worked. The audience laughed, really laughed. I dead-panned my way through the Keats and Chapman stories. Don't indicate funny. Suddenly it was over. The applause was strong. There were even some cheers.

I was asked to take *A Horde* to the Gate Theatre in Notting Hill for a three-week run. In the early eighties the configuration of that theatre was very different. To get to their seats the audience had to enter at the back of the stage. The bookings for my show were extremely good and the management put some large floor cushions along the front. I was asked if I could pause after the first couple of pieces and allow latecomers to get to their seats. I did this during every performance, moving a black curtain aside and calling the latecomers in. An unusual occurrence happened on the press night. As I moved the curtain aside and called, the one latecomer that evening, was Robert Cushman, the theatre critic of the *Observer*. Robert was mildly disabled and used a stick. With the little auditorium tightly packed I had to help him to his seat. On the following Sunday he gave the show a very good notice.

I took it to the Edinburgh Festival and in the following years I did over a hundred performances at various theatres – in Oxford, Bolton, Manchester, Bath, Essex University, on a ship in Bristol – all over the place.

RUSSELL OF THE TIMES

'Queen Victoria's reign has been an incessant record of bloodshed.' – William Howard Russell

Until the middle of the nineteenth century the British people waiting for news of foreign wars depended on army dispatches. Written by military men, these invariably contained biased material. In 1854, soon after the start of the Crimean War, John Delane, a legendary editor of The Times, sent the journalist William Howard Russell to cover events. Thus Russell became the first professional war correspondent.

He was born in Co. Dublin, in Ireland, but soon moved to London in 1842. Three years later he returned to Ireland to report on the Great Famine of 1845-1849 in which a million people died. A million people died in a country only a few hundred miles from London because the potato, and only the potato, the staple diet of the rural poor was blighted for four years. His description of a family of dead and dying people in a small house in Co. Clare is heartrending.

He travelled to the Crimea in 1854 to cover the Crimean War. What he saw there appalled him. In his dispatches he ruthlessly exposed the wretched conditions the soldiers had to endure, the badly equipped hospitals where huge numbers died from lack of food and water. He wrote of the incompetence of the commanding officers, their preoccupation with anachronistic regulations. Along with Lord Raglan and his staff he observed the disastrous Charge of the Light Brigade from a nearby ridge –"like looking down from the boxes of a theatre". Russell's despatches published in *The Times* shocked the public, led to immediate improvements in conditions for the troops, to the dispatch of Florence Nightingale to the Crimea and to the demise of the government of Lord Aberdeen. Russell went on to cover the Indian Mutiny and the American Civil War. He met Abraham Lincoln at the White House and then saw him across the street a few days later "striding like a crane in a bullrush swamp among the great blocks of marble, dressed in an oddly cut suit of grey, with a felt hat on the back of his head, wiping his face with a red pocket handkerchief". He travelled to the South and witnessed the sale of slaves on street-corners in Montgomery, Alabama. Russell was lucky to escape death during the retreat from the Battle of Bull Run.

Russell's life and adventures, his involvement in so many historic events, prompted me to put together another one-man show at the NT in 1988. *Russell of The Times* would be a longer and more ambitious project than *A Horde* and would run for ninety minutes with an interval. The development team at the theatre got *The Times* newspaper to put up a modest sum to help me stage the show. Once again I was back at the Newspaper Library in Colindale. *The Times* gave me access to their archives. It was very exciting when the archivist brought me Russell's leatherbound Crimean notebooks to examine. I was very moved to touch these books, to leaf through the pages crammed with descriptions and rough pencil sketches of his day-to-day life in Sebastopol and Balaclava.

Wearing white cotton gloves, I had spent days at the V&A Archives sifting through contemporary drawings, photographs and cartoons. I had slides made of dozens of these to be projected on to an onstage screen. During Russell's exciting description of the Charge of the Light Brigade I spoke before a montage of graphic images of the battle.

The designer Alison Chitty created a simple but stylish set, with an army tent, a folding campaign table and chair. I grew a huge beard and Alison had designed two wonderful and contrasting costumes. I was alloted a modest number of evening performances in the Cottesloe, which was very gratifying and exciting. Again I toured the show. This time the tour included three venues in Ireland including my home town, Limerick. While I was playing in Dublin, Laurence Foster head of drama at Radio Telefis Eireann came to see the show and asked me to do a radio adaptation of it for RTE. We did this some months later. I felt very proud of my little show. Laurence, a lovely, enthusiastic man, subsequently produced a number of my radio plays.

NOT THE NATIONAL THEATRE

In 1984 a group of ex-National Theatre actors set up a touring company (Not the National Theatre) with the intention of taking small-scale productions to venues around England and Wales. The company was the brainchild of three ex-NT actors, Roger Gartland, Tim Davies and Derek Hollis. They enlisted Harold Pinter and Ian McKellen as patrons. The repertoire over the next four years included *Waiting For Godot*, *The Caretaker*, an Orton double bill and D. H. Lawrence's *The Daughter-in-Law*. They employed no directors and their rigorous touring schedule earned them a £13,000 Arts Council grant.

In 1989 they invited me to play Lucio and Barnardine in *Measure For Measure,* the company's first Shakespeare production. Tim Davies would direct the play: 'We will do it in Victorian costumes in ironic reference to the Victorian values of our current government.' Margaret Thatcher was then coming to the end of her third term in office. Not before time. There would be eight actors doubling a number of parts. We were all paid £200 a week which was £43 above the Equity minimum. The production was speedy, the telling of the story was clear with sharp characterisations and with few cuts it came in at about two hours and twelve minutes.

The whole production, actors, and stage manager had to fit into a ten-seater minibus. Between April and July we played seventy-one performances in forty-four venues in sixteen weeks. We criss-crossed the country to venues in Cardiff, Burnley, Basildon, Shrewsbury, Bath, Aberystwyth, Yeovil, Builth Wells, Warrington, Buxton,

Truro, Telford etc. We played to enthusiastic audiences in small venues often unused to hosting a Shakespeare production.

Two highlights stand out for different reasons. In the middle of the tour we had the good fortune to go to Milan for a few performances where we had a chance to recharge the batteries. I remember a visit to Milan Cathedral, delicate and airy with its dozens of spires in bright white marble. The other highlight was a disastrous afternoon performance outdoors at the Glastonbury Festival. How this venue was booked I have no idea. We played on a high raised platform. Out front was an audience of at most fifty, most of them supine in the long grass. Large joints were being smoked. Strange pipes glistened in people's hands. In the distance a rock band were playing. Our hearts sank, but we got on with it. Towards the end of the first act a police helicopter arrived and for some unknown reason hovered very loudly above us. It didn't go away. I remember standing offstage waiting for my cue. The helicopter blotted out my fellow actors' voices. I entered ten lines too early. It was near the interval and I signalled to the other actors that we should stop immediately, which we did. After hurried talks with the organisers and presumably some contact with the police, the helicopter eventually departed. We then decided very swiftly to play only the crucial scenes of the second act and after forty minutes we took a swift curtain call to twenty pairs of vaguely clapping hands, got in the van and headed off the site. Down the road we stopped at a country pub, where we consumed a great deal of the local ale. I thought it was the tastiest beer I had ever drunk.

TOURING THE WORLD
WITH THE ESC

The English Shakespeare Company was formed in 1986 by Michael Bogdanov and Michael Pennington.

Their intention, Bogdanov wrote "was to portray Shakespeare not as an enduring classicist but as a writer of our and future times, an egalitarian with deeply held political convictions. Over the centuries Shakespeare has been culturally highjacked by a ruling elite to serve the purpose of shoring up the status quo. He has been used to support divine right, order, stability of government and to act as a warning and a deterrent to those who would question the validity and very essence of our western elite, capitalist society. Yet I believe that there is another Shakespeare at work, one who is not only subversive, but who morally and politically points the way to a better understanding of how we behave and lays down guidelines for radical change in the nature of our society and our method of government".

He wanted the company to look at the plays as pieces of living theatre, malleable, plastic, to be moulded in the shape of the present, not just holding the mirror up to nature, but cracking it and pointing the way forward into the future.

With very few resources, the two Michaels in a very short time established the ESC as an exciting new venture. In 1986/87 they staged the Henrys – *Henry IV Part I*, *Henry IV Part II* and *Henry V* and toured the UK, Europe and Canada, followed by a very successful season at the Old Vic.

In the autumn of 1987 they added four new productions to The Henrys – *Richard I1, HenryVI: House of Lancaster, Henry VI: House of York* and *Richard III* to create the Wars of the Roses. These productions toured extensively in Britain and abroad to huge success. Another hugely popular season at the Old Vic followed, where the productions won a handful of Olivier Awards. In two years the ESC was established as a classical company up there on a par with the RSC and the National Theatre.

CORIOLANUS III

In 1990 the Michaels asked me to join the company to play Autolycus in *The Winter's Tale* and Cominius in *Coriolanus*. This was my third *Coriolanus* and the first one where the name of the play and leading character was pronounced in the "traditional" way.

The production was aggressively topical. Bogdanov set it not in ancient Rome but in the dark metallic world of the Gdansk shipyards where a military autocracy is threatened by a popular uprising. He gave it a very Brechtian look with the rioting citizens carrying solidarity-style banners demanding democracy. The tribunes of the people had an office with busy typewriters and ringing telephones bringing news of Coriolanus' vengeful expedition. To tackle Shakespeare's most political play in this manner, initially seemed a brilliant idea and the early scenes with the citizens and the people's tribunes worked very well. Unfortunately there is the awkward fact that the play is in no way an endorsement of people power and the production made a nonsense of the wider imperial power of the play. The patrician Menenius and his friends, who lead an upper-class establishment, were an anachronism in Jaruzelski's Eastern European world.

Rome is not a democracy, but neither is it a totalitarian tyranny. All these differing elements led to a confusing and poorly received production.

In sharp contrast, the production of *The Winter's Tale* proved a much more successful project. It was very clear and direct. The Sicilia scenes were set in a cool formal Edwardian court with king and courtiers in dinner jackets, dark suits and wing collars. This suited the buttoned-up Leontes of Michael Pennington, his formal exterior masking the depth of his intemperate passion and irrational jealousy. Always regarded as one of the country's finest verse-speakers, Michael's work was sometimes accused of lacking feeling. As Leontes, his journey from jealousy, to paranoia, into a real madness with his threat to dash out his new baby's *"bastard brains"* and on into his shocked penitence and moving reconciliation with Hermione was excellent. All this, allied to his command and speaking of the verse was very fine. Lynn Farleigh's playing of Hermione was superb. It is never an easy task to play a good and loving person. In the trial scene, pregnant, humiliated and faced with a husband/judge who literally spat at her, I will never forget the quiet dignity she brought to her defence. Dressed in dirty prison clothes and handcuffed, her delivery of the line, "The Emperor of Russia was my father" was very moving. June Watson's implacable Paulina brought a savage rage to her defence of the innocent queen. In my opinion two definitive performances.

In contrast, the Bohemia scenes were set in a realistic Welsh world of county fairs, sheep-shearing, accordion music and country matters. The Old Shepherd and his son were very well played by the Welshmen Bernard Lloyd and Charlie Dale. Having doubled as a courtier in Sicilia I now donned the clothes of the travelling huckster and rogue Autolycus. Bodger asked me to play him Irish. And being Bodger – he couldn't resist it – he insisted I introduce myself to the audience as Aught O'Lucas. Cheap, but it got a good laugh. Autolycus is a very good part offering lots of opportunities for sly humour, role-playing, pickpocketing, raucous singing and serial flirting with the country girls.

We opened both shows in Swansea over four days. A few of us shared digs in the city, which were up an extremely steep hill. After long and hard days we dreaded the climb every night. But Robert Demeger, a very good Camillo/ Junius Brutus in the plays, devised an ingenious scheme to make the journey easier. We were each to imagine that on either side of us were two ropes at waist height running up the hill. If we 'pulled' ourselves up with alternate hands it would make the climb much easier. Being actors we tried it. And, you know, it worked. Sadly, Robert died during the writing of this book. He was a lovely man, a very good actor and a great bibliophile.

An extraordinary coincidence: there were two nights when I was playing Autolycus in Swansea and my daughter Abigail was also playing the role in a production at the University of East Anglia in Norwich where she was studying.

We toured England with both plays and then embarked on a world tour to Germany, Finland, India, Japan and Australia, followed by a season at the Aldwych Theatre in London.

Another digression. On the flight to India I was sitting next to the actor Vincent Franklin as we started down the runway at Heathrow. He had the window seat. He asked if I got nervous on flights. I said I used to but didn't any more. He told me he was very nervous. The plane built up speed. Vincent was looking out the window. 'What are those flames?' he suddenly asked. 'Oh, fuck off!' I said. Then I looked casually past him, to see large orange flames coming out of one of the engines. The plane began to brake heavily, the flames disappeared. Within seconds we were surrounded by flashing fire engines. The plane stopped, there was no great danger and we soon taxied back to the terminal where we had to disembark. Seven hours later once again we were back on the runway. I wasn't sitting next to Vincent this time. But apparently he coped very well.

* * *

INDIAN MEMORIES

MUMBAI – Eighteen million people rubbing along together; the pink stone Gateway to India on the waterfront overlooking the Arabian Sea, built during the Raj and through which the last British troops departed in 1947. The Victoria Train Terminus, an architectural mix of Victorian Gothic Revival with Indian features. The Mahalaxmi Dhobi Ghat – a massive open-air laundry with hundreds of concrete troughs where laundry from all over the city is handwashed by dozens of dhobis. The colours. An extraordinary sight: a street with maybe twenty plumbers looking for work, their bicycles encrusted with twisted soldered pipes, showing off their skills to potential customers. A barber cutting hair on the pavement, the customer seated on an old chair facing a large cracked mirror affixed to the wall. The poverty. Dusty, neglected, underfunded museums.

BANGALORE – Robert Demeger and I flout the warnings of our hosts and go for a meal in a poor part of the city. A large room with bare tables and strip-lighting. We are the only Westerners there. The customers look amazed to see us. We order some food. A young boy opens and places large green banana leaves before us. We realise these are the plates. Another boy arrives with a large galvinised bucket filled with rice and scoops portions of it on to the leaves. Curry follows. We eat with our hands. Delicious. I become very acquainted with a large number of lavatories over the next three weeks. Never missed a performance though.

DELHI – The Red Fort. The Jama Masjid, India's largest mosque. The Imperial sweeping architecture of Lutyens' New Delhi. A day trip to Agra and the Taj Mahal: – an astonishing sight. Built in 1652 by Shah Jahan in memory of his third wife Mumtaz. The white domed marble mausoleum is a structure of astonishing beauty. The tall minarets at each corner constructed, in the event of a collapse, to fall away from the tomb. On the way back to Delhi we left the coach and climbed up a steep rocky hill to visit the abandoned city of Fatehpur Sikri. It was founded in 1569 by the Mughal emperor Akbar and served as the capital of the Mughal Empire from 1571–1585. In many ways more impressive than the Taj, it is a walled city of beautifully ornate and delicate royal palaces, courts, mosques and tombs. There is a harem, a treasury, a mint, stables, private quarters and ornamental pools, all built of red sandstone. It literally takes your breath away. Sixteen years after it was built it was abandoned for two reasons: the difficulty of getting water to the site and the political turmoil in the neighbouring Rajputana areas. It sits on the hill, immaculate, unmarked, empty, magnificent and strangely sad. That trip was one of those great unforgettable days.

KOLKATA – A vast market with large inverted cones of multi-coloured spices. The well-dressed bodyguards who accompanied us on bus journeys to and from the theatre.

* * *

Here is a piece I wrote for the ESC Magazine when touring the two Shakespeare productions.

IT'S A TOUGH JOB BUT SOMEONE'S GOT TO DO IT.

Adelaide – 13th MARCH 1991

Sun in the high eighties, the sea beckoning, letters from family and friends in England littering the beach tell of cold, snow, flu etc. My heart goes out to them. Mind you, touring exotic countries during a bad English winter is not easy. Some of the company don't always enjoy the non-stop sunshine, or immersing themselves in Hockney-like swimming pools, or rubbing shoulders with film stars like Patrick Swayze, Greta Scacchi, Pauline Collins etc, or visiting Japanese temples, or the Taj Mahal, or sailing round Australian coral reefs in twin-masted schooners. Some confided in me that they would rather be doing Theatre in Education work in Rochdale. And believe me, it is very difficult to have a proper holiday when one has to perform two plays at inconvenient times.

So, here's a few tips to aspiring theatrical tourists.

JAPAN: In Japan when playing a line from *Coriolanus* – *"Our then dictator whom with all praise I point at"* – it is best not to point at a part of the balcony in which a crown prince of that country is seated.

At celebrations in Tokyo it is also best to let Michaels Bogdanov and Pennington crack the saki barrel open with the wooden mallet. Watching rice wine splash all over other people's clothing is a lot funnier.

FINLAND: Don't play comedy roles in this country. Hearing funny lines being greeted with gales of silence is not a comfortable way to spend your time. Being told that "audiences laugh a lot when they get home" may offer some small crumbs of comfort to comedy players.

INDIA: In *The Winter's Tale* if you have to "look upon the hedge", ie. urinate on stage, you will find that young Indian audiences do the best sound effects to go with this type of action. A few hundred mouths making hissing sounds is very impressive. Finnish audiences were disappointing in this respect.

When the attendance of Prince Charles and (gulp!) Princess Diana was cancelled at a gala performance in Delhi for obvious reasons, three strong men in the company broke down in tears and had to be put under sedation. No names, no pack drill, but the initials of one of them was J H.

In India always sit next to Roger Booth in the dressing

room. His ability to kill two-inch long cockroaches and scare the bats flying around above your head on stage is an obvious clue to the kind of military training this killing machine had back in the 1950s. Also best to visit this country when there is not a Gulf War going on. Then you don't have to bother with twenty-four-hour-a-day police and military protection and you won't have to sit on coaches next to men with strange bulges in their clothing.

THAILAND: Always visit Bangkok hours after there has been a military coup and the Prime Minister has been put in jail. Then, no curfews are imposed, the streets are quieter and it is easier to get a taxi to visit certain parts of this city where dubious practices are performed. Not that I visited these places. Only someone told me.

AUSTRALIA: After seeing the Taj Mahal, the Pearl Mosque and the Red Fort it is only slightly disappointing on a river trip in Perth to have one's attention drawn by the guide to Rolf Harris' mother's house.

Teeing off at the first hole of the beautiful Joondalup Country Golf Course is a daunting experience. As your ball drops inexorably into the lake, the snickering of the spectating kangaroos is hard to take. I look forward to eating one of these creatures in Adelaide.

Ludwigshafen, Delhi, Calcutta and Perth are cities to visit when you want to meet old friends – my brother and his family; a flatmate from drama school days; a director who gave me my first job in repertory in 1965; Mr Renouf, a teacher who had directed my children's school plays. I don't bump into these kind of people in the Charing Cross Road.

Right, that's it. Brush the sand off the page. Out of the corner of my eye I see Michael Pennington standing poised to whip this away, his lips mouthing, 'Deadline! Deadline!' Now it's time for a quick swim.

Yes, touring Shakespeare abroad – it's a tough job, but someone's got to…

* * *

Immediately after finishing *Coriolanus* and *The Winter's Tale* I began work on two further Shakespeare productions with the ESC. Michael P directed *Twelfth Night* and I played Sir Andrew Aguecheek in modern dress. I have a picture of myself as Aguecheek in sandals, socks, shorts, a flowered shirt and a long wig of blonde unfortunate hair. This was soon joined by Michael B directing Michael P in *Macbeth* in which I played Ross and the Porter. Again these toured the country, went to Chicago, Tokyo again, Seoul in South Korea and Hong Kong.

I have no strong abiding memories of either production, but remember a very good Malvolio from Tim Davies and a sparky Viola from Jenny Quayle. From the foreign tour I remember the big concrete underpasses in Seoul and being told these had been designed as civilian shelters in case of an attack from North Korea. In Tokyo, which I will return to later, I remember an incident when a young member of the company, Sean Gilder, perhaps a teeny bit drunk, "borrowed" a bicycle and ended up in police custody. Sean has gone on to do really good work in television and film and has become one of my best friends.

In Chicago I organised a surprise treat for Sean. One

Sunday a group of us hired a big American car and drove into Iowa. Sean's then favourite film was the baseball movie *Field Of Dreams*, a fantasy-drama about an Iowan farmer who hears a voice in his cornfields which whispers, 'If you build it they will come.' He ploughs up the field and builds a baseball diamond. The ghosts of the scandal-hit 1919 Chicago Black Sox turn up to play. I had found a tourist brochure advertising the farm location of *Field Of Dreams* in Dubuque County. So we drove to Dyersville in the middle of nowhere. Sean couldn't understand what we were doing in this flat uninteresting landscape and then he saw the sign, the cornfields and the baseball diamond. He was beyond moved. On the way back we got a bit carried away and forgot how low the speed limit was all over America. Behind us the unmistakable whine of a police motorcycle. It was classic. We pulled over. The cop parked behind us and approached the car. Yes, sunglasses, shiny helmet, brown jacket, jodphurs, high boots. 'Keep your hands in view!' we urgently whispered to each other.

'Licence and registration, please.'

'Sorry, officer, not used to your slower speed limits…Yes, from England… Forty dollars, yes, officer… Oh, a receipt, thank you, sir… *You* have a nice day!'

Back in the city we went to Buddy Guy's Chicago Blues Club, drank pitchers of mild American beer and marvelled at the music. Before we left for London I went on a pilgrimage to the Chicago setting of *The Front Page,* which I had done at the Old Vic in 1973. The Criminal Court Building is an attractive and imposing seven-storey brick structure with the classic black steel fire-escape ladders zig-zagging their way down the side of the building. It was the site of many legendary trials including the Leopold and Loeb murder case and the Black Sox Scandal. The building is now a listed historical site, has been refurbished and houses a big law firm and an advertising agency. But you can still get a sense of its former and more exciting life.

BRAVE NEW WORLD

THE ROYAL
SHAKESPEARE COMPANY

In 1993 my agent asked if I was interested in doing a season with the RSC in Stratford. Through the eighties I had turned down chances of working with the company because of my young family, but now I said yes. For the season, most actors had to commit to appearing in three plays. I was told that Michael Bogdanov wanted me to do Goldoni's *The Venetian Twins* and Di Trevis wanted to offer me a part in David Pownall's *Elgar's Rondo*. For the third play I was asked to travel up to Stratford the next day to meet the young director who would stage *The Tempest*.

His name was Sam Mendes, a golden boy if ever there was one. He had got a first in English at Cambridge, where, of course, he also played cricket for the university. Within minutes of leaving Cambridge he became an assistant director at Chichester Festival Theatre and in an emergency when the director of the play he was assisting on was taken ill, Sam was asked to take over and open the production. Need I say it was a big success and moved to the West End. Within days, it seems, and at the ripe old age of twenty-four he was directing Judi Dench in *The Cherry Orchard* in the West End.

Now at twenty-seven, he was Artistic Director of the

Donmar Warehouse and, with a handful of acclaimed productions behind him, was casting *The Tempest*. I met him in the Ashcroft Room high under the "tented" roof of the Swan Theatre. He was interested in me playing Antonio, Prospero's usurping and jealous brother. We had a very good meeting. He said he didn't want me to "read", just talk about the character and the play. All actors appreciate this.

At one point he said, 'You were in *The Front Page* at the Old Vic.'

'I was,' I said, 'Did you see it?'

'Ah, no. [pause] I think I was in Junior School then!'

I felt a right fool. You don't always think straight (or at least I don't) at casting meetings.

When I arrived back home from the meeting the phone rang. My agent. 'Sam Mendes wants you to do *The Tempest*. Do you want to do the season?'

'Bet your life I do!'

Working with the RSC had always been a big ambition of mine. I then casually enquired when rehearsals might begin. 'Monday!'

This was my first experience of the horse trading that can go on between the RSC directors up to the last minute when casting the season.

'I want so-and-so for such a part. Could you use him in your production?'

'Ahmm, well I, I – might. But I must have Jane Bloggs for my show. So is at all possible that you could find her something in your production?' And so on.

* * *

Over the next eighteen months I would rehearse and play George Bernard Shaw in *Elgar's Rondo*, Brighella in *The Venetian Twins* and Antonio in *The Tempest* with further projects along the way. In that 1993 RSC season we started rehearsals for all the plays in Stratford in March, played them in repertoire in the various theatres until the end of January '94. We then had a short holiday, followed by a five-week season of all the repertoire in three theatres in Newcastle. 1994 was the RSC's eighteenth consecutive season in that city. This was immediately followed by a further season of the plays at the Barbican Theatre in London until the end of 1994.

With *The Venetian Twins* Michael Bogdanov hit a rich vein. I have often felt that Michael is the biggest hit-or-miss director in England. When his productions work they are a joy to be in and to behold. Goldoni's glorious comedy gave him a wonderful opportunity to exercise his outrageous sense of fun and anarchic staging. *The Venetian Twins* written in 1747 was the first Commedia Dell'Arte play to be staged with the actors neither wearing masks nor improvising. The story, simply – two identical twins, separated many years before, coincidentally arrive in Verona on the same day. They are Zanetto, a bit of a bumpkin, not very bright, and his louche, self-satisfied urbane brother Tonino. Zanetto is to be married to Rosaura who he has never met. Tonino is being pursued by Beatrice his fiancée. Needless to say, the twins keep being mistaken for each other.

The production was staged in the Swan Theatre. David Troughton played both twins and differentiated the brothers very clearly with great wit and invention. He had a tremendous rapport with the audience and the priceless ability to improvise when anything unusual or unexpected happened. He and I on occasion did some outrageous improvising. I remember once miming, instead of speaking, a whole scene with him. He's a big man David, and he needed every shred of energy to get through the evening. He was as busy offstage as on, running behind and under the stage from entrance to entrance, often with frightening . quick changes. There were very funny performances from Sarah Woodward as Zanetto's unfortunate intended, and from Christopher Hunter, Guy Henry and Jonny Phillips.

Michael Bogdanov invented one truly great scene. In the script one of the twins, I can't remember which, is threatened by a rapier-wielding Guy Henry, a rival for Tonino's fiancée. Troughton grabbed a furled umbrella from a member of the audience in the front row to use as a weapon. During the fight he unfurled the umbrella and waved it to put Guy off. Then, when Guy's back was turned he jumped off the front of the stage, returned the open umbrella to the audience member and ran off. Guy ran downstage saw the open umbrella facing him and stabbed the owner through the silk. All the fun and frenzy came to a sudden stop. The owner, a man in a dark suit slowly stood up and took his hand away from the front of his blood-stained white shirt. The audience saw the blood on his hand. There was a horrified silence. Guy looked mortified, the stage manager ran on and asked if there was a doctor in the house. The houselights were turned on. All the company crept onstage, whispering, keen to find out what had stopped the show. In less than a minute actors from *The Merchant Of Venice* who were not onstage in their main house production also came on to the Swan stage, incongruously dressed in costumes from a different period. Soon, an ambulance siren was heard and the sound of brakes screeching and gravel being disturbed outside the theatre. Two uniformed St John's ambulancemen ran in with a stretcher. Slowly through all this, the audience began to realise they had been conned and the whole event was part of the show and had been stage-managed. A laugh began, grew, turned into a long burst of applause. Then the actors jumped back into position and the whirlwind production continued. Bodger at his very best. Anarchic, zany, nothing to do with the play, but very very funny.

Two particular memories of this scene, both on the press night. One, a member of the RSC Publicity Department, surprisingly not in the know, was totally taken in by the scene and clearly upset, began to admonish audience members around her for laughing at this potentially tragic event. The second, was watching the director of *The Merchant,* David Thacker, who was watching *our* press night and relaxing after *his* press night the evening before. When *his* actors walked on to the Swan stage his face took on a truly horrified expression. The world had turned upside down.

The Venetian Twins was a big success, truly funny, madly inventive, furiously and brilliantly directed and acted.

The Swan Theatre, a Jacobean-style playhouse, built inside the shell of the Victorian Gothic Memorial Theatre that survived the 1926 fire is a joy to play in. It was beautifully designed by the architect Michael Reardon in 1986. I have worked in many modern theatres and been often disappointed by the lack of theatrical nous in their design. Not to mention their unsympathetic acoustics. But the Swan with its thrust stage, its warm wooden balconies on three levels where the audience are closely wrapped around the action is a complete triumph. I have done many plays in the space and share my love of the theatre with many many actors.

* * *

Once we opened *Twins* we started on *The Tempest,* which would play in the main house, a fourteen-hundred seat pros-arch theatre not unlike many of the Odeon cinemas I had spent most of my life in. It was not an easy theatre to work in. The stalls were OK, the circle not too bad, but the distant balcony was a terrible place to watch a play from. Observing actors from up there was like viewing small lead soldiers on a stage no bigger than a paperback book. Terrible.

Anthony Ward was the designer of *The Tempest.* His set was simple and enabled the story to be told with minimal disruption. What the audience saw when they entered the theatre was a large planked wooden floor with a rich royal blue cyclorama at the back. Above a vast red sun. Alone in the middle of this floor stood a large wicker costume basket. As the houselights dimmed a pale figure with bleached hair wearing a blue high-collared Maoist uniform appeared from within it. A lamp descended from the flies. The figure grasped it and sent it swinging to and fro like a giant pendulum. Immediately a storm erupts. The sky darkens, lightning flashes, thunder rolls. The figure, Ariel, disappears as trapdoors open up in the floor and sailors in tarpaulins along with King Alonso and his compatriots emerge in panic from "below deck".

So began the production that John Peter in the *Sunday Times* hailed as a "brilliant, magical and magisterial new

Tempest". It had a loose Victorian look. Prospero wore a gold embroided floor-length dressing-gown, black waistcoat and white shirt. We members of the shipwrecked court wore starched high-collared shirts with white bow ties, velvet jackets with gold-buttoned waistcoats and knee breeches. There was gold decoration on collars and cuffs and much court regalia. I also had a long silk-lined cloak. Actors love wearing cloaks. Dressed like this we looked very ill at ease on the island.

Caliban was hairless, naked to the waist with long pointed talons on one hand. Stephano, the drunken butler, wore a heavily stained naval steward's outfit and Trinculo, the jester, was played as a Northern ventriloquist in a loud checked suit and ginger hair, his wooden dummy an exact replica of himself. Ariel had a group of androgynous scene-shifters in white tunics who helped him stage manage all the scene changes. These would glide onstage with plates of food, or appear with giant sunflowers and plant them in the floor.

In the difficult second scene, Prospero recounts at length to his daughter the reason for their sojourn on the island and tells her of the principal characters involved in his overthrow in Milan. He talks of the plot involving his treacherous brother Antonio and the King of Naples and of the help provided him by the kindly Gonzalo. Sam had a folding four-part Victorian screen set up behind the pair on the vast and empty floor. At the mention of each protagonist the character appeared as if by magic from behind the screen. Good, clear storytelling connecting the barely glimpsed characters from the shipwreck, to their appearance and recognition on the island in the next scene.

Prospero's cave was simply a couple of two metre-high piles of large books with a pair of lofty library steps beside them, from which he would observe some of the action. Miranda and Ferdinand played chess sitting on stools made of books.

For the masque, which Prospero, Miranda and Ferdinand watch, a beautifully ornate Pollock's Toy Theatre descended from the flies and the three goddesses appeared inside as life-size marionettes who spoke and sang. In the middle of this stunning masque, as the reapers enter and dance, Prospero suddenly stops the action, remembering "that foul conspiracy of the beast Caliban". Sam had a very good idea for this. He included Caliban in the scene, dressed as one of the reapers. Incongrous, dream-like, only in the head of Prospero.

Alec McCowen played Prospero as an urbane imperious figure, a Victorian master of ceremonies, who can confidently command the elements, but cannot control human behaviour. With fierce watchful eyes, he simmered rather than raged. The sense of revenge was controlled, muted. A proud, slightly tetchy father, full of a touching humanity but a man who lacks or possibly never wanted the skills of the politician. Simon Russell Beale played Ariel as an aloof, superior, never-smiling, steely malcontent. He does as commanded but never engages with his master. In no way airy (Sam didn't want the usual wimpy spirit) he glided at a stately pace around the stage in bare feet. In his blue high-collared suit and make-up he looked like a cross between Boy George and Pandit Nehru. When finally released at the end, he shockingly spat in Prospero's face, walked quietly upstage to the blue cyclorama, pulled open a disguised door to reveal a blindingly bright white inner world. He looked back at Prospero for a final time and stepped inside closing the door behind him. As a former chorister at St. Paul's Cathedral, Simon's singing of Ariel's songs was beautiful. The spit was controversial and was cut some performances later.

David Troughton's Caliban was brutish, vulnerable, savage and dreamy, a bulkier Gollum from *The Hobbit*. In turns dangerous and touching. Sarah Woodward, a wonderfully funny actor, played Miranda not as the often passive and dutiful daughter, but a feisty young girl, bubbling with curiosity. The double act of Stephano and Trinculo worked a treat. Mark Lockyer, with a set of large protruding teeth (which I would encounter again in other performances of his), played Stephano as a mock-genteel butler with strangled vowels and appalling lavatorial habits. David Bradley's Trinculo with red wig, Northern accent, ventriloquist's dummy and size twenty Little Titch boots was straight out of the City Variety Theatre, Leeds. A great pairing. As the two political plotters, that fine actor Christopher Hunter played Sebastian and I played Antonio, tormentors of the gentle Gonzalo, played by the wonderful Clifford Rose, an RSC stalwart and a member of the RSC company, on and off, from its inception in 1961. In the big reconciliation scene at the end I stood aloof from the group. Prospero looked across at me, his brother, offering forgiveness and friendship. I held his look, then turned away. Antonio wanted none of it, no reconciliation for him.

This final moment was just one of Sam's many inventions in a truly spellbinding production. His ability to come to each scene with new and fresh ideas was impressive. Also, being so young, he made me laugh when now and again he would reference a moment in *Star Wars* or Bugs Bunny to illustrate what he wanted in a scene at a particular moment.

In pre-RSC days the well-known actor manager Sir Robert Atkins ran the Shakespeare Memorial Theatre for a season or two in the 1930s. He was also the founder of the Open Air Theatre in Regent's Park. He liked a drink and was noted for his use of strong language. There were two incidents in his Stratford tenure. Over the years the theatre was heavily supported by Flowers Brewery. During Atkins' time as director, a distinguished member of the Flower's family was chairman of the theatre board. One day Atkins was summoned to a board meeting and informed that his services as director would terminate at the end of the season. Atkins gave no reaction to this shocking news. Asked if he had anything to say, he heaved himself out of his chair, strode imperiously to the door, opened it, turned, fixed Mr Flower with a beady eye and declared 'Flowers Ale is piss!' – and slammed the door behind him.

On another occasion he met the vicar of Holy Trinity Church in the street. There was an annual tradition where the director was invited to read the lesson at a particular church ceremony. No invitation had arrived. Atkins, a man with a deep stentorian voice addressed the cleric, 'Vicar, can you give me one cogent reason why I have not been asked to read the fucking lesson?' I particularly like his choice and use of the word "cogent".

* * *

In his Sussex garden, Elgar is hiding away from failure, troubled by the poor reception given to his *Second Symphony*.

He finds it hard to rise above the criticism of the one piece of music he has written that is quintessentially him. In Pownall's *Elgar's Rondo*, well directed by Di Trevis in the Swan, the composer is surrounded and visited by family and admirers, including King George V and George Bernard Shaw, while in the distance the guns of Flanders can be heard.

I don't have any particular memories of the production, but do remember working on how to not only look like Bernard Shaw, but how to play him. Shaw seemed to love being photographed and there are dozens and dozens of images of him. With that raised chin, questioning eyes, hair with the two curls on his forehead, the bushy eyebrows, the moustache with the upturned ends and square unruly beard he was instantly recognisable. To achieve this image was surprisingly easy, especially with the help of the RSC Wig Dept. Mark you, by the time I had stuck on a white toupee, false eyebrows, big moustache and full beard, it took some time to get over the feeling that I was looking out of a yak's arse. That said it worked a treat. The costume, all tweed plus-fours and hiking boots, was beautifully designed by Pamela Howard. Shaw took a big interest in his underwear and advocated the benefits of wearing wool next to the skin. With the help of the well-known clothing manufacturer Jaeger he designed his own underwear. So, in one scene I wore a long off-white one-piece woollen undergarment. It comprised a long sleeved vest and close-fitting ankle length underpants. My own father in the fifties wore a two-piece variation on this piece of clothing to see him through the long cold Irish winters. He referred to the lengthy pants as "long johns".

Then, of course one had to work on the voice. Recordings of Shaw's cultured Dublin accent were found, which I studied and copied. He had a wonderful sonorous and slightly affected theatrical delivery. When greeted in the play by a Catholic priest, *'Father John, of the Society of Jesus,'* Shaw replied, *'George Bernard Shaw, of the Society of Authors.'*

With all three of my plays now open and part of a nine–play season in the three Stratford theatres, there was time to do something else. So what did we do? More plays of course. For a few seasons in the nineties the actors and assistant directors organised a two-week Fringe Festival. In January 1994, eighteen small projects were presented in the Buzz Goodbody Studio at The Other Place, where a bank of about a hundred raked seats were installed. These were short performances of new plays, devised pieces and one-man shows and they played late nights and on Sundays. It was all great fun, very well attended, and provided a window for actors to write, direct and showcase projects they had hankered after or tinkered with over the years. For weeks any available space of any size on RSC property was fought over and commandeered for rehearsals. I played my Flann O'Brien show for a couple of performances and directed a play called *The Actor's Nightmare* by Christopher Durang. It is the story of an understudy who is about to go on and play the role he is covering. But, he has forgotten his lines, he doesn't know the play and thinks he is an accountant. A very funny play about the terrors of the stage and sweatingly close to all actors' nightmares. Unable to find a girl in the company free to play one of the roles, I cheekily conscripted my daughter Abigail, who had just finished a drama degree at UEA, to come up and play the part, which she did extremely well.

The RSC's season in Newcastle was always a treat. Audiences were always happy to have the RSC in town and turned out in large numbers. On days off we went on trips up the Northumberland coast and saw stunning castles (Dunstanburgh, Warkworth, Alnwick, and Bamburgh with its miles of deserted sands) and felt the strong blustery winds coming off the North Sea.

In April 1994 all the plays moved to the Barbican Theatre in London and in July I was asked by Michael Bogdanov to do a fourth play. It was Brendan Behan's 1958 play *The Hostage*. It covers events leading up to the execution of a young IRA member in Belfast Jail accused of killing an Ulster policeman. The play is set in a ramshackle house of ill-repute in Dublin. A young British soldier is taken as a hostage at the border in Northern Ireland and held in the brothel. A cast of prostitutes, revolutionaries and eccentric characters inhabit the house. The play is a mix of comedy, politics and tragedy, filled with many songs and heavily influenced in its music-hall structure by the work of Joan Littlewood and her Theatre Workshop, where it had its first English production. We opened to mixed reviews from the dailies. Two days later Adrian Noble, the artistic director, called a company meeting and to our amazement told us that the RSC were taking the production off. Someone suggested that he at least wait until the Sunday reviews came out. He replied that they would make no difference, as the bookings for the play were atrocious. I suspect that after many bloody and unfunny decades of the Irish troubles, very few English theatregoers were interested in seeing another and somewhat dated play on modern Irish history. I played Mr Mulleady described in the programme as "a decaying civil servant". With my bald head I asked the designer for a wig, a Bobby Charlton "comb-over". It worked rather well.

There was a famous and very successful Broadway producer called David Merrick who was renowned for the publicity stunts he used to help publicise his sometimes failing productions. In the sixties he brought a show to London, which was harshly criticised by the leading and most important English critic of the time, Harold Hobson, who wrote for the *Sunday Times*. Merrick was incensed. Then he came up with a plan. He searched all the English telephone directories until he found a Mr Harold Hobson living somewhere in the provinces. He contacted the man and invited him and his whole family to come to London for the weekend. Fares, flowers, hotel, restaurants, all expenses were paid by Merrick. The family then went to see the play. Best seats in the house, naturally. Afterwards, over champagne, Merrick asked Mr Hobson for his opinion on the play. Mr Harold Hobson heaped much praise on the work and then departed with his family. Next day Merrick put large advertisements in all the national newspapers quoting Mr Hobson's fulsome praise. "One of the funniest comedies I have ever seen" and had this plastered in large billboards outside the theatre.

Mr Merrick pulled the same stroke on Broadway in 1961. After all the New York critics had panned his new musical *Subways Are For Sleeping* he found seven citizens with the same names as the critics and elicited glowing quotes from them which he then had printed in the papers. No wonder he was often referred to as the Abominable Showman.

THE CHERRY ORCHARD

I had really enjoyed my first season with the RSC and fancied another. I heard that Adrian Noble was going to direct Chekhov's *The Cherry Orchard* in the Swan in the coming season. I have a great love, as many actors have, for Chekhov's plays. Never having had the good fortune to appear in one I now did something I had never done before. I knew Adrian's secretary Claire a little and found out when he would be alone in his office. I then popped my head round the door and asked if I could have a quick word. He looked mildly alarmed. 'Come in.' he said.

'Thank you.' I didn't sit down. 'I'll be very quick. I want to put a suggestion to you. I know you are going to do *The Cherry Orchard* in the new season. I would really like to play Semyonov-Pishchik. I really believe I could do something special with that part. Please consider me!'

'Right! I will,' he said.

'Thank you,' I said and left the office.

He offered me the part and I began rehearsals for the new season.

I did *The Taming Of The Shrew* directed by Gale Edwards with Josie Lawrence and Michael Siberry, Goethe's *Faust* in two parts directed by Michael Bogdanov, and *The Cherry Orchard* directed by Adrian Noble.

At the beginning of *The Cherry Orchard,* the household are awaiting the arrival of Mme Ranyevskaya, who is returning home after living in Paris for several years. Her daughter, Anya accompanied by her governess, has been to fetch her. The estate is hopelessly in debt and will have to be put up for sale. The Swan stage is bare. No furniture. Not a silver birch, not a branch of a cherry tree, not a samovar in sight. Simple wooden boards. Servants and family await the arrival of Madame. Carriages are heard. Everyone jumps into excited action. Characters dash to and fro bringing in the luggage. Case after case. Box after box. Very soon the upstage of the Swan thrust stage is piled two metres high with the baggage. Ranyevskaya has arrived. She enters in tears, excited to be home, to greet everybody. Soon the luggage disappears up the Swan stairs to the various wooden balconies. This will be a clear, uncluttered staging of the play to contrast with the rich imaginative lives of the characters. Furniture is kept to a minimum. A small table and some chairs, a simple wooden garden bench. All the dozens of pieces of luggage and the furniture are painted a pale shade of eau de nil. The party scene, with the guests dancing in couples or in a long mad swirling line on and off stage, is done on the bare stage with the Jewish band, seated on a long bench against the back wall. Interestingly some of Chekhov's letters to Stanislavsky reflect his exasperation with the director's attempts to overload the play with realistic stage and sound effects: "If you can get the train into the action without noise, without so much as a single sound – go ahead ..."

So this deeply atmospheric, compassionate and funny play unfolds. Self-absorbed and feckless Ranevskaya and her brother Gaev were magnificently played by Penelope Wilton and Alec McCowen, two of my favourite actors. She, charming, self-obsessed, funny and heartbreaking with fine moments of anguish and sudden candour, always true in performance, never going for the laughs. Subtle as the stroke of a feather. Alec, ineffectual, lost in the past, unaware of how much the world was changing around him, his plummy voice reducing the pushy servant Yasha (an excellent Mark Lockyer) to shake with silent laughter every time he opened his mouth. David Troughton's awkward thick-set Lopakhin veered from kneeling in awe of Ranevskaya to jiggling the estate's keys while he danced in drunken glee. Kate Dûchene's loneliness and unrequited love for Lopakhin was very moving. Peter Copley, who I used to watch in black and white films in Limerick in the fifties and who invariably played discreet and faithful civil servants, now played Firs, the doddery old retainer. His last scene as he came carefully, painfully, down the Swan staircases realising he'd been forgotten and locked alone in the house, alone with the past, was very touching. Lucy Whybrow's young, hopeful Anya, John Dougall's Yepikhodov, a walking disaster, Sean Murray's ardent, ageing, eternal student Trofimov, Josie Lawrence's vain, self-absorbed Dunyasha and Darlene Johnson's eccentric and melancholy Charlotta, all, all superb. How often can one say that?

Peter Gill's version of the play was excellent. Having been an actor he knows how to write great dialogue. Chekhov's writing and characters bring out the best in actors. Simyonov-Pishchik, the lonely, impoverished landowner, forever borrowing money from Ranevskaya and more than half in love with her, was a part I loved playing. Padded, rosy-cheeked and magnificently bearded I developed a great attachment to him. In the final scene when he enters, for once about to return some money, he is devastated to discover that the family are all leaving, forever. Chekhov's directions say "he cries". Soon he exits "deeply moved", but returns at once. "Dashenka sends her love", he says and goes.

Dashenka is his never-seen daughter. The man's loneliness, his attachment to this surrogate family and the deep sense of loss he feels at their departure I found extremely moving and emotionally easy to play. Ranevskaya puts her arm around him and kisses him. Adrian suggested to Penelope that as she did this she whispered something in my ear. 'Make it different every night.'

There was universal praise for Adrian's production. "Glorious" – "A magnificent RSC Chekhov production" – "RSC on top form" – "A uniformly superb cast" – "The finest RSC production of anything for several seasons" etc.

Eighteen months later we transferred the production to the Albery Theatre in the West End.

The Albery Theatre has had three names in the past fifty years. When I first played there it was the New Theatre. Then it reverted to its previous title the Albery Theatre, and now it is known as the Noël Coward Theatre. Other recent changes include the Novello Theatre, formerly the Strand Theatre – the Harold Pinter Theatre, formerly the Comedy Theatre, and the Dorfman Theatre, formerly the Cottesloe Theatre.

Following the run at the Albery *The Cherry Orchard* went on a short tour. Peter Copley, then aged eighty-two, felt that a tour in winter would be too difficult for him. So Charles Simon took over and was terrific. Charles was eighty-eight. He drove all over the country to each venue. He was a very heavy smoker. His inhalation of cigarette smoke was a sight to behold. His cheeks disappeared back into his face, the cigarette reddened frighteningly and lost about half an inch in length with each drag. After one performance in Aberystwyth in February we exited the stage door into a very strong wind coming off the sea. Charles, obviously a little frail at eighty-eight, was unable to force his way forward. Our hotel was about four hundred metres away. We eventually had to call a taxi to get him there. Actors – love 'em.

In January 1996 at the end of the Stratford season Sean Holmes, the assistant director on *The Cherry Orchard,* asked me to do a production of *Woyzeck* by Georg Buchner at The Other Place.

The Other Place, originally a small hut with a corrugated tin roof used by a scout troop, was acquired in 1974 and converted into a studio space for RSC experimental work. Actors often had to up the volume when heavy rain fell. It was demolished in 1989 and a new and better-equipped building with rehearsal rooms replaced it. This new theatre remained true to the spirit of the original and much-loved hut. Recently The Other Place was transformed into the foyer for the Courtyard Theatre, and now this is shortly to be remodelled and will contain a "new" Other Place.

Sean had a budget of about £100 to stage the production. This unfinished play, written in 1836 when Buchner was twenty–three, the year of his death, deals with the dehumanising effects of military life. Based on a true story of a young soldier who in 1821, in a jealous fit, murdered a young widow, the mother of his child, and walked into a watery suicide. She had grown tired of him and fallen for a handsome drum major. Sometimes seen as a working-class tragedy it is a powerful piece and Sean really caught the world of the play. He updated it to the 1930s and gave this brooding piece a hint of Nazi madness. I played the doctor who experiments on Woyzeck and sees him only as a scientific object: "You must eat nothing but peas!"

OTHELLO AT THE NT AND THE BEST TOUR, EVER

In 1997 I was asked by Sam Mendes to play Montana, the Governor of Cyprus in his production of *Othello* for the National. David Harewood would play Othello, Simon Russell Beale, Iago and Claire Skinner, Desdemona. It would open in the Cottesloe Theatre in August 1997 and would tour the world until June the following year. Although the part of Montano is not very big, the prospect of the proposed tour was mouthwatering, so I took it.

Sam wanted his *Othello* to be "a chamber piece, a domestic piece" so it would play in the Cottesloe. The period chosen was the 1930s. On a thrust stage there would be a cool tiled floor with a slightly raised walkway on either side and upstage, behind three thin pillars, a recessed wall with panels of large wooden louvred blinds. Above this a protruding upper level with the same wooden venetian blinds, which could be swivelled to reveal Brabantio's bedroom or provide a space for Othello to spy on Desdemona. Furniture would be kept to a minimum. Wicker tables, folding campaign chairs of wood and canvas for the Cyprus scenes. Large patterned Eastern rugs with floor cushions. The bed in the final scene, simply a large mattress on the floor with bright white sheets and an ornate lamp hanging above, providing a pool of light into which Othello would come in and out of as he paced the room.

The military costumes were cotton khaki with Sam Browne belts. Cyprus looked like a colonial outpost in a Somerset Maugham novel. Othello arrived in the senate in a dinner jacket with his bow tie undone and dress shirt unbuttoned. Later he wore jodphurs and knee-high polished boots. Desdemona in one scene wore a long green figure-hugging silk evening dress. A slight, vulnerable figure, like a piece of fine bone china.

In the opening scene between the desperate Roderigo (a very good Crispin Letts) and the scheming Iago, Sam tried different exercises to find the best way to stage the scene. He asked the actors to play the scene walking around the rehearsal room. Then to do it trotting round the space. He had Iago striding away from Roderigo who had to work hard to keep up and question him. He then asked them to reverse their positions and play the scene again.

> *"Rod: Never tell me, I take it much unkindly*
> *That thou, Iago, who hast had my purse*
> *As if the strings were thine, shouldst know of this –*
> *Iago: 'Sblood, but you will not hear me –*
> *If ever I did dream of such a matter*
> *Abhor me.*
> *Rod: Thou told'st me thou didst hold him in thy hate.*
> *Iago: Despise me if I do not."*

With Iago in pursuit it makes it look as if Roderigo is about to break their arrangement. Iago has to work very hard to persuade the gull. With Roderigo in pursuit Iago has the chance to appear detached and annoyed and in control. These exercises offered both actors options, which could then be used or rejected.

Seated alone at a table Iago tells the audience of his diabolical plan to destroy Othello. It is a complicated speech, but with the help of a pack of playing cards – using a picture card for each character, Cassio, Roderigo, Desdemona, Emilia and Othello – Simon made the speech simple and comprehensible.

In the scene where Iago deflects Cassio from going on watch and inveigles him into having a drink, a danger to someone with "very poor and unhappy brains for drinking", Sam set the scene in a military mess hall with sweaty hard-drinking soldiers and officers. Iago invents a drinking game, again with the use of playing cards, and easily cheats Cassio into downing tumblers of whisky. It finishes with Cassio's stabbing of Montano, the end of any hope of preferment in his career and crucially the sundering of his good relationship with Othello.

Soon after Iago plants the seed of jealousy in Othello's mind and the play takes on a truly dark foreboding, Desdemona enters and finds her lord distracted. He says he has a pain upon his forehead and borrows her handkerchief, which is then dropped. There was a very tiny but deeply touching moment as they exited.

"Othello: Let it alone. Come, I'll go in with you.

Desdemona: I am very sorry that you are not well."

Claire Skinner's delivery of this line, spoken very simply as she gently put her arm around her husband and leant into him was full of love. Tiny. Unforgettable.

David Harewood brought some fine qualities to the playing of Othello. Confidence, physical strength and power. He had the ability to move from volcanic rages to soft and tender expressions of love. His emotional outbursts led once or twice to the demolition of some rehearsal furniture. I remember his rage in one scene driving Claire Skinner to such emotional upset that she left the rehearsal room in tears and needed a little time to recover. Holding an army pistol to Iago's throat on "Be sure you prove my love a whore" you were very aware of the depth of his insecurity.

Sam had a strong dislike of bad stage deaths and wanted the murder of Desdemona to be horrendous. Suffocating a person with a pillow takes a long time. The audience should experience what it is like to be killed. Desdemona is a strong character and wants to stay alive. Claire struggled like hell. The killing took time.

Like *A View From The Bridge*, the tragedy played well in the intimate Cottesloe Theatre, with the audience virtually "in" the action and it had an overwhelming effect upon them. I believe the staging of Shakespeare plays in small theatres in the modern age began with Trevor Nunn's production of *Macbeth* with Ian McKellen and Judi Dench at The Other Place in Stratford in 1976. A great and hugely influential production that led the way to new, exciting discoveries in the direction and playing of classical plays.

Simon Russell Beale's Iago was a long way from his detached Mao-suited Ariel. Squat, lumpen, shaven-headed, a man jealous of the goodness and beauty of life around him. Sweaty, buttoned-up in a slightly too tight uniform, the Sam Browne belt holding him in. The jealousy he brought out in Othello was akin to his own. Iago had experience of it with his own wife, and knew which buttons to press and exactly when to do it. "Look to your wife" was brilliantly placed, his evil, precise and specific.

The scene where Desdemona prepares for bed, helped by Emilia, was full of a quiet melancholy. Played in soft light it was subtle playing of the highest quality. Claire, slim, fine-boned, quietly defending her husband, distracted by some fresh sheets for the bed – *"If I do die before thee, prithee shroud me in one of those same sheets"*. She remembers the song her mother's maid sang – *"she was in love; and he she lov'd prov'd mad, and did forsake her"*. As she remembers she crosses the room and puts a record on the wind-up gramophone and plays the song. The two discuss infidelity, with the older and more cynical Emilia sounding a warning.

"… And have we not affections,
Desires for sport, and frailty, as men have?
Then let them use us well: else let them know
The ills we do their ills instruct us to."

Maureen Beattie with those steely ice-blue eyes of hers brought a fierce implacable anger to the final scene. With Desdemona murdered, her own marriage a terrible failure, she unleashed all her frustration and bitterness on the two protagonists. She was electric.

This was a very, very good production and it was a keen pleasure to be a part of it. Yet, *Othello* is a deeply depressing play and affected the cast throughout its run more than any other tragedy I have been in. But the compensations were great and longlasting.

THE WORLD TOUR

SALZBURG, AUSTRIA

We did a few preview performances in the Cottesloe and then flew to the Salzburg Festival where we performed in an old converted salt mill in a village called Hallein a few miles outside the city. The great European director Peter Stein had turned it into a theatre. The show was very well received although the "auditorium" was vast compared to the Cottesloe. I remember for part of the journey to Salzburg we flew with a small airline owned and run by the former Formula One racing driver Niki Lauda. The interior fittings were first-class. The cabin crew wore stylish red jackets and jeans and the food and drink were served on proper crockery with metal cutlery and linen napkins. The drinks served in real glass. What an old colleague, Jonny Phillips, would call "a stylish conveyance".

PHOENIX, ARIZONA

The play opened to the press back at the Cottesloe and was received with extremely good reviews. The tour then began in earnest. We flew to Phoenix, Arizona and played at the Herberger Theatre. Phoenix is not a particularly attractive city. It was very hot. The streets were lined with large and beautiful palm trees. The pavements were deserted as everybody drove everywhere in huge air-conditioned cars.

Three events stood out. A couple of us out for a walk came across a large gun shop. We had to look inside. The choice of weaponry was staggering. Everything from small hand guns to 44 Magnums – the ones that even Clint Eastwood had to use both hands to control and fire. There were walls covered in Kalashnikovs and what looked to me like small machine guns. There were large glass cases filled with all kinds of pistols. We watched a young girl at the counter, supervised by her boyfriend and a shop assistant, try out a small pink-handled Derringer pistol. It was all strangely and disturbingly seductive. To purchase a new gun we were told, you had to fill in a form and wait a few days, but you could buy a secondhand gun and take it away immediately. There are *Guns R Us* stores in the US.

We had a couple of days off during our visit and we all chipped in, hired a minibus and went to visit the Grand Canyon. Photographs give no idea of the size and strangeness of the place. Staring across the yawning gap or down into the depths we sat for a long time mesmerised by the majesty of the place. That night we stayed in a motel on a Native American Reservation, which to our surprise had a strict no-alcohol law. Someone volunteered to drive out ten miles and bring some booze back, which we had to sneak into our rooms. On the way back to Phoenix, driving through the dry, red Sonoran desert, our driver/guide stopped and walked us over to look at a number of those high saguaro cacti we have all seen in numerous cowboy films, their arms always reaching skywards. He told us some of them were nearly two hundred years old. In the hot desert, birds bore into them and nest in the wet interior. For some reason these nests are called saguaro boots.

After one of our final performances in Phoenix we were all asked to line up backstage to meet Princess Anne. What she was doing in Phoenix I had no idea. Although not as enthralling as the Grand Canyon I found her heaped-up hairstyle strangely fascinating.

WARSAW, POLAND

Two weeks later we played the Dramatychry Theatre in Warsaw. The theatre is part of the Palace of Culture and

Science, a forty-storey classic example of the bombastic, social realist buildings of the Communist era. It was given as a 'gift' to the city by Stalin. The building is surrounded by many heroic statues of working men. During the Warsaw Uprising in 1944, eighty-five per cent of the city's historic centre was destroyed by the Nazis. Much of what replaced it I found grey and depressing, but the restoration of the Old Town with its palaces, churches and market square is very beautiful and it was here that we stayed. Returning to the hotel after a performance, one invariably noticed a number of not very attractive prostitutes disporting themselves around the lobby.

TOKYO, JAPAN

In January we embarked on the longest and most exciting section of the tour. I have found an old 1998 diary in an infrequently visited drawer. For some reason it is torn in two. But the front section from January to 5th April I had kept. On 18th January I started writing some intermittent entries about the tour. I will use these as an aide-mémoire for the following section.

Long twelve-hour flight to Hong Kong, then two hours later catch another three-hour flight to Tokyo. By coach into the city past Disneyworld with its glimmering towers. The old Metropolitan Crowne Plaza Hotel again. Stay up for another few hours then go to bed at 10:00pm. Been awake for twenty-four hours. Wake up four hours later. Can't get back to sleep. Read *Turn of the Screw* and 250 pages of *Left*

Foot Forward: A Year in the Life of a Journeyman Footballer by Garry Nelson. Four hours sleep in thirty-six hours. Crowne Plaza's hard beds win again. Go for breakfast on the twenty-fifth floor. Mount Fuji, snow-capped in the distance. By 9:30am it begins to disappear in the city smog. Get a train with some actors and a friend, who is in Tokyo studying paper-making, and go to Kamakura for the day. Thirty miles south of the city, it is the ancient capital of Japan, established in the twelfth century. It is a beautiful place with many shrines and temples, shinto priests and beautiful gardens. It is cold, with the remains of snow on the ground. Pass three punky girls with blue, green and red coloured hair – but wearing ornate kimonos. I help an old lady who fell over in the street and banged her head. I pick her up and sit her on a stone bench, but she is embarrassed and gets up and staggers away. We look at numerous temples, highly decorated with the corners of their roofs upturned – to ward off evil spirits. Some are set in woodland, some within groves of tall green and black bamboo, some with small lakes and water features. These are made of interconnecting bamboo pipes, which fill and then tip over, clicking, as they discharge the water. Quiet. A sense of peace. The most famous sight is the thirteen-metre-high bronze Buddha, which was made in 1252. Simon Russell Beale is very taken with its round-bellied shape and says it is the highlight of his day. I think he associates physically and spiritually with the Big B. To bed with three soft mattress pads and a sleeping pill. Does the trick.

Next day we open the play at the Ginza Saison Theatre. In the final scene, with Desdemona murdered and Iago stabbed, Othello is disarmed. So how, and with what, does he finally kill himself? Sir Laurence wore a wide metal bracelet on one wrist,which concealed a short spring-loaded dagger. David wore a chain with a large crucifix round his neck that concealed a knife. That night in the struggle to disarm him the chain breaks. David hasn't noticed. But I spot the vital crucifix entangled in the bed sheets, retrieve it and manage to sneak it to him for his stabbing. Saved the day. Otherwise we might have had to resort to the Wolfit Solution. The story goes that one night, in a play when Sir Donald Wolfit was to be shot onstage, the gun wouldn't go off. He quickly whispered to his opponent 'Kick me in the stomach!' The man obliged and the knight expired, gasping, 'The boot – was poisoned!'

Next day at the hotel I witness the departure of the St. Petersburg Ballet Company who had been performing in the city. The lobby is stacked high with large cardboard boxes. A massive pantechnicon arrives and is quickly filled with four fridge-freezers, aluminium car wheels, tyres, huge television sets and numerous electrical gadgets. Apparently one dancer had bought four small two-ringed electric cookers.

In the vast crowded Ikebukuru underground station I watch two geishas dancing to piped music, part of some promotion. On a small stage with a tatami mat they wear white make-up, hair piled high with flowers and decorations, kimonos to the floor. They dance with delicate flowing movements, making tiny gestures with their eyes and hands. It is beautiful. I clap loudly (not very Japanese) and gesture "thank you" when they finish.

There are small one-room police stations on street corners. People are very keen on cleanliness and order and

I notice shop staff often come out in the street and clean up any rubbish, even cigarette butts.

Notice a rather scruffy man in traditional Japanese costume – wide pantaloons, long cotton coat, obi, wearing wooden shoes. Unusually, instead of the two cross battens on each sole, his have only one, making balance very difficult for him as he wobbles along, picking his teeth with a bamboo toothpick.

A few of us go to see some Kabuki theatre. The plays go on all day with the audience taking a packed lunch to the performance. You can pay a smaller ticket price to watch part of the programme. The theatre is massive though not very attractive with a very wide shallow stage. The lighting is very basic. Musicians and singers sit and perform at the front by the pros arch. Nothing has changed in Kabuki for centuries. All female parts are played by men. Parts are often handed down from father to son. The first play is a tragedy about a samurai who has to sacrifice his son to a rival. It is all very slow and deliberate, each gesture studied, each move heavily symbolic. On a white set with white steps I watch a sword fight in which a man is beheaded and his head, trailing red ribbons of blood, rolls down the steps. Now and again a fearsome character, usually centre stage and in a crouched position, makes an extremely dramatic speech with much use of low, long, strangulated sounds. Invariably this sends part of the audience into a frenzy of both vocal and hand-clapping appreciation. Some of the actors are big stars and it is rumoured that they employ paid claques in the auditorium to show a fervent response to their work. No actors carry props, but when one is needed, a small figure dressed in the same colour as the set and with a gauze mask covering his face ghosts on and places the prop in the actor's hand from behind his back.

It took me a while to spot how another effect was achieved. Imagine if you will, a character dressed in a magnificent, wide, multi-fold red robe. He is crouched, with knees bent. There is a lot of bent-knee acting. Suddenly he straightens, making a most dramatic two-armed gesture as he stands upright. His whole costume swirls and magically changes colour before our eyes. He is now dressed in green! Fabulous! This is achieved by the "ghost" gliding on behind the actor's back and as the character is delivering a speech the ghost is quietly undoing lots of small bows in the costume folds. Pure theatre.

The second play we see is a comedy with a fat, jolly but cowardly warrior and ten soldiers in very colourful costumes. There is lots of stylised fighting and amazing somersaults. The men playing women are mesmerising. Gliding across the stage as if on wheels with high voices, their heads lowered, their gestures delicate and highly studied. The stringed accompanying music is not to my liking.

Organised a trip to Nikko National Park, north of Tokyo. At the station, as the second hand on the clock precisely touched the hour of three, the train moves off. Nikko is a magical place with many highly decorated Buddhist temples and Shinto shrines surrounded by majestic woodland. There is a beautiful red wooden bridge over the Daiya river. We have a great meal afterwards with the inevitable, 'Thanks, Dad,' from the younger members of our group, for the pains I have taken in organising the jaunt.

I go to look at the home, now a museum, of the famous sculptor Asakuro Choso. His studio is 1930s-style modern concrete, but the fascinating part is the living quarters at the back. A long, low wooden Japanese home overlooks a garden with large rocks and a quiet pool with grey, orange and white carp. Beautifully proportioned rooms have sliding doors with paper panels and are sparsely furnished with tatami mats on the floor. Walls slide back to reveal the garden a few feet away. It is quiet, peaceful, with soft honey-coloured light and the low sound of water flowing into the pond. It reminds me of some of the homes in my favourite film, Yasujiro Ozu's 1953 classic *Tokyo Story*.

At the end of the final performance in the Ginza there is a wonderful fall of silver squares of foil on the cast as we take the curtain call. I have loved each of my three visits to Japan.

SEOUL, KOREA

Two nights later we are in snowy Seoul. Trevor Peacock and I set off in the dark to have a look at the venue we will play in. We both like to strike out, not knowing where we will end up. We walk across the Panpo Bridge over the Han River. There are no other pedestrians and we soon realise how long and dangerous the walk is. The bridge is over 1000 metres long and entails much dashing into the traffic around various scaffolding contraptions. Eventually we reach the Seoul Arts Centre. There is a concert hall, an opera house, a calligraphy hall and of course a theatre. The theatre is OK, but the wings are vast and open. It will need a lot of vocal projection. Back at the hotel our waitress wears a traditional Korean outfit. A long rich blue dress with a pistachio-coloured top and her hair piled high. Outside the large dining room windows, what is usually a decorative high wide waterfall is now a high thick wall of ice. Trevor and I discuss laying our hands on some climbing gear and when the company assemble for breakfast we will appear and climb it.

iTaewan is the area to go for cheap electronic goods. I arrive early and watch the staff in a department store "exercise" before opening time. There are ten minutes of physical jerks, then some dance steps followed by the workers massaging each other. Finally a sensuous female voice speaks to them on the tannoy to which they reply, like at a prayer meeting. This is followed by some martial Western music and then they all stand to attention at their work station. The doors are then opened and as I enter the store they all smile and nod at me in a very friendly manner. On the final note of the music they relax and get down to business. As I leave the store a little later with my purchases I notice a black cab waiting. But these cost twice as much as the silver cabs. I spot a line of these behind some trees and get into the first one and using my map, point out to the driver where I want to go. The driver then gesticulates to the black cab saying, 'Taxi, Taxi!'

I reply, 'No, no, too expensive. Seoul Palace Hotel!' He gesticulates and protests in his own language, more strongly. I persist. To no avail. Eventually I get out thinking he was on some break, only to discover I had been in a private car. Silver, same colour as the cabs. Feel a right fool.

HONG KONG, CHINA

We arrive in Hong Kong on a Saturday in mid-February and have two days off. On Sunday evening Trevor Peacock and I walk down to the waterfront and board a ferry for the most stunning ride across the harbour to Kowloon to hear the Moscow Radio Symphony Orchestra play Mahler's Fourth Symphony in which a soprano sings in the fourth movement. As this singer, who is very attractive and wears a tight white dress, arrives onstage Trevor leans over to me and whispers, 'Great arse!' I am in a state of mild hysteria for the remainder of the concert.

The ferry ride back to Hong Kong Island is unforgettable. The skyline is dominated by crowded and spectacular glass and steel structures. In 1998 the two major bank buildings, designed by Norman Foster and I M Pei, are the outstanding features. Bright beacons against the dark rising hills behind.

Next day, we go to Aberdeen and bargain with a man who takes us on an hour-long tour of the harbour in a small boat. It is spectacular. Lots of sampans and junks – sadly none under sail – the famous and extremely large floating restaurants; a bustling water village with craft nose to tail, with small boats stuffed with vegetables and produce nosing their way through them. An old man wearing a wide-brimmed straw hat fishes quietly from the back of his boat. All this surrounded by high tower blocks.

At the Academy of Performing Arts we play to 1,200 people. But the response is disappointing. The acoustics are terrific, but half of the audience are too far back in the badly designed auditorium. Both balconies too far away.

I go to the China Exhibition in Kowloon with Clifford Rose. It is magnificent. The highlight is the terracotta warriors from Xi'an where 2,000 of an estimated 7,000 have been disinterred. There is an astonishing individuality to each one. Differences in their faces, close-cropped beards, topknots, tunics and armoured vests. A small part of one of the wonders of the world. On our return we go up to The Peak on a two-carriage funicular railway. A very steep journey but affording awesome views of the city.

Our penultimate performance in Hong Kong is plagued with an outburst of mobile phones. I count sixteen. One man whose phone rings answers it and then shuffles along the row talking loudly as he makes his way up the aisle. After the curtain call Maureen Beattie steps forward and makes a short brilliant speech pointing out how disrespectful it is, not only to the actors, but to the other members of the audience. There is loud applause. At the stage door an Englishwoman with tears in her eyes comes to apologise to us on behalf of Hong Kong.

BEIJING, CHINA

The day after we arrive we all go on a day trip to the Great Wall. The bus passes hundreds of labourers building a motorway. There are a small number of JCB-type diggers, but the majority of the work is done by hand with pickaxes, shovels and wheelbarrows. Labour they have in abundance. We stop at a cloisonné factory. Cloisonné is the ancient technique of decorating metalwork objects using vitreous enamel – but you already knew that! Here, we are led into a huge shop where many of the products are on show. It is all very impressive and tended by many girls at long counters. The lack of customers is slightly bizarre. We all buy small pieces. I buy a pair of rich blue enamelled balls. They are a little smaller than a billiard ball and decorated with bright red Chinese calligraphy, each symbol highlighted with inlaid gold wire. When rattled they give out the sound of a small metal bell. They are very beautiful, comforting to handle and come in a lovely red silk box with two thin bone slides that lock into little cloth sockets. I still have them.

As we drive through mountain gorges we catch glimpses of the Wall, snaking along the hilltops and up and down the valleys. It is a truly astonishing sight weaving its way into the distance, blistered with watch towers every few hundred metres. Eventually we walk/climb to the Wall, plagued by hawkers. Michael Owen, an *Evening Standard* writer travelling with us, takes a group photograph. We spend an hour walking and taking in the sights. Back in Beijing we go to the Chinese Opera, which is very commercial with an audience of tourists, drinking and taking flash photographs. Again, like in Kabuki, men play the women's parts with beautifully made-up faces, and exquisite rosy cheeks. Very colourful costumes with much waving of long willowy sleeves. A mix of high counter-tenor-type singing and chanting. Interesting to watch, but not sure if I will dash back to see it anytime soon.

Our theatre is unattractive with smelly toilets. Backstage is depressing. Audiences are huge and we add an extra matinee. Madame Wu comes to the evening performance. She is the most powerful female politician in China. During the performance as I am about to enter, Garth our ASM dashes past with a red fire extinguisher. There is the smell of burning electric cable.

Our visit is filled with extraordinary sights. Each evening outside the theatre, many bicycles with large aluminium boxes on their fronts gather. Their owners begin to prepare all kinds of food on them. On skewers – scorpions, silk worms, grass-hoppers and locusts. Restaurants with glass tanks outside, filled with weird fish and eels – one even with enormous squat toads. People having haircuts in the street. Bicycles, bicycles, thousands of bicycles. A man riding one with a sofa perched on the back. A reception at the British Ambassador's residence with large gin and tonics in a beautiful garden. Many old men flying kites, way, way up in the sky. A fish kite made of old plastic bags. The hutongs. Hutongs are small walled ancient neighbourhoods of narrow crowded streets and alleys. As China continues its whirlwind development, many of these small communities are being sacrificed in the name of progress.

We all make the obvious visits to the three great cultural landmarks in the city. Tiananmen Square is larger than I had expected. One hundred and nine acres to be precise. I am reminded of the white-shirted protester with those incongruous carrier bags halting the phalanx of tanks during the student-led protests in 1989. But the vast open space is incredibly boring. Huge Russian-style Communist Party buildings on all sides bedecked with red flags. Mao's mausoleum, a disappointing building with crowds queuing and being harangued with instructions by an official with a loud hailer. There are large group sculptures on each corner. Workers in heroic postures with resolute uplifted faces. I like these. Over the old Tiananmen Gate leading to the Forbidden City are the long viewing platforms for the politicos with the familiar portrait of the Great Helmsman and the banners proclaiming "Long Live The People's Republic Of China" on the red wall behind.

I visit the Forbidden City on my fifty-seventh birthday. Despite having watched Bertolucci's film *The Last Emperor* the year before, I am nonetheless blown away by the experience. The sheer scale of the site is astonishing. In this rectangular walled secretive place are hundreds of buildings. The Forbidden City is the Chinese Imperial Palace from the Ming Dynasty to the end of the Qing Dynasty. For five hundred years it was the home of emperors, their families and retinues. It was also the ceremonial and political centre of government. I spend hours wandering around majestic buildings with romantic names – the Gate of Divine Might, the Palace of Heavenly Purity, the Hall of Preserving Harmony, the Hall of Central Harmony, not to mention the Hall of Supreme Harmony. Huge gilded lions, glazed intricate carvings on walls, astonishing roof decorations, delicately coloured ceramics, red and gold pillars, beautifully carved wooden ceilings. On and on, wonder after wonder. One of my favourite buildings is the Palace of Tranquil Longevity – which I imagine as a home for self-satisfied aging aristocrats.

The Summer Palace on the northern outskirts of the city is another breathtaking delight. It is sited on the side of Longevity Hill on the banks of the Kunming Lake. The lake was man-made and the excavated soil used to make the hill. The slopes are now studded with beautiful palaces, trees and landscaped gardens. There is a large exquisite lakeside pavilion, made of white marble in the shape of a twin-decked boat, "floating" on the water. There is a graceful white bridge with seventeen arches over a river. There is the wonderfully named Cloud-Dispelling Hall and the Temple of Buddhist Virtue. There is a 287-metre-long covered walkway constructed for the emperor's mother to enjoy a walk through the gardens protected from the elements. It is a marvel with dozens and dozens of green pillars connected with red fretworked panels and rich blue crossbeams painted with hundreds of episodes from Chinese literature and folk tales.

SHANGHAI

As in Beijing one immediately notices the enormous amount of high-rise building going on in Shanghai. We go into the Bund, which is a waterfront area on the western bank of the Hangpu River. Astonishingly it looks exactly the same as the waterfront area in Liverpool. The architecture is eclectic with much Western-influenced, neo-classical and Gothic Revival buildings. The Peace Hotel is said to be where Noël Coward finished *Private Lives*. Across the wide river, where there is much to-ing and fro-ing of heavy shipping, tugs and cruise ships, it is another story. We can see dozens of high office buildings under construction. The contrast between the two river banks is extraordinary. Over there, new China at its most modern and progressive.

Shanghai feels like a much more cosmopolitan city than Beijing. That said, I am astonished to see the effect David Harewood has on its citizens as we walk along. Many people stare. Some people's jaws literally drop when they see him, their heads turning in astonishment as we pass. David seems to take it in his stride with no vocal or physical reaction to the people's rudeness.

We are invited to the Shanghai Academy of Drama. After welcoming speeches and little gifts, we watch some scenes from an operatic *Macbeth*. Very old-style. A well-known Chinese actor does a scene from *Antony and Cleopatra*. He is terrific, though the ancient Roman costumes are very worn. We are transfixed by the gusset of Eros' costume.

A very polite young man stops me in the street and in English asks me for a job. He says he doesn't want to work under Chinese "supervision".

I go to Jing'an Park. A small oasis away from the city noise. There are lots of old people there, many doing tai chi. I watch an old lady exercise with one leg placed on a railing level with her head. There are people playing draughts and mahjong, overlooked by spectators not averse to commenting on some of the players' dodgy moves.

The building of office blocks, high-rise flats goes on everywhere. In ten years the major cities in China will be indistinguisable from their Western counterparts.

The theatre we play in is freezing, dirty and run down. The lighting is dodgy. It is a barn of a place. It is so cold onstage the actors' breaths come out of their mouths like steam. We borrow military greatcoats to wear over our costumes in the wings. The stage management have to put a hot water bottle in Desdemona's bed. A cat walks across the stage during a scene. There is no hot water. Twenty-four-hour building noise can be heard loudly onstage. Mobiles and pagers go off. Touts pester us for tickets. A window is broken backstage by someone trying to get in to see the show. Apart from that everything is terrific.

I was sent a copy of a full-page article by Michael Owen from the *Evening Standard*. He had come out to Beijing to write about the visit. The headline read: *Othello* conquers China. In a slightly over-the-top piece, "National stuns Beijing", Owen pointed out that the visit coincided with the opening of the National People's Congress, at which the Chinese have to select a new prime minister and government. So all the political dignitaries were coming to the play. Seats in the thousand-seater theatre had to be individually labelled, observing proper protocol. The start of the performance was delayed as huge government cars arrived with camera crews in tow. When Othello spat at the feet of the Duke of Venice, "there were gasps of horror all round, a display of insubordination way beyond the comprehension of the high-profile guests". Owen then went on to describe the numerous curtain calls, standing ovations and cheers. "It was an emotionally charged moment, frozen in time as both the Westerners on stage and the Orientals in the audience were locked in common euphoria, and there were tears on the faces of dozens of Chinese whose culture normally dictates against public displays of such feeling". The top half of the *Standard* page had a wonderful photograph of the full company on The Great Wall.

WELLINGTON, NEW ZEALAND

On the coach in from the airport – Wellington looks a lovely place. Clapboard colonial houses, a bay surrounded by hills, small skyscrapers. Looks like a cross between Torquay and Hong Kong. Hotel room is excellent with big windows and my own balcony overlooking the harbour. Eat lamb shank with local red wine. Surprisingly moving to be eating Western food again. I remember my difficulty attempting to eat a duck's foot, at an official banquet in Beijing – a prized delicacy.

The week flashes by. At a British Council reception I meet and talk with the novelist Arundhati Roy. Dressed in a simple cotton sari, she is very beautiful. She won the Booker Prize in 1997 for *The God of Small Things* When I tell her I have been waiting for it to come out in paperback, she urges me with great charm but much persistence to, 'Buy it now. It's out here in New Zealand. It's cheaper!' I promise I will.

I open my curtains one morning to see the Greenpeace ship *Rainbow Warrior* docked in the harbour. I go to look at it. There are five big rubber dinghies with outboard motors on deck, all ready for immediate action. I think this is the replacement ship for the original, bombed and sunk by French secret agents in Auckland Harbour in 1985.

We play a matinee to 1,400 school children who laugh a lot in all the wrong places.

I walk to Katherine Mansfield's birthplace, a lovely old wooden house on the side of a hill. Impressively laid out inside, though now backed by a six-lane motorway.

I get the bus round the harbour to Eastbourne. The commercial buildings of the 1910s look straight out of an Edward Hopper painting. I lie in some sand dunes. The sea like beaten silver, the smell of pine trees. Perched in the hills small one-storey houses with verandahs and red tin corrugated roofs. I get the ferry back to the city. Calm, wonderful day.

ADELAIDE, AUSTRALIA

Glad to be back here. The city is laid out in a grid system. The centre is about one mile square, surrounded on four sides by parkland with the suburbs beyond. This is my third visit. The tram ride to the sea at Glenelg is terrific. The Art Gallery of South Australia is full of fascinating early

Aborigine pictures as well as twentieth century English works – Duncan Grant, Vanessa Bell, Gwen John, Harold Gilman and Stanley Spencer. There are also good pictures by Freud, Kosoff and Hodgkin. At a wildlife park, I see Tasmanian devils, dingos, kangaroos, koalas, snakes and emus, who have feet like dinosaurs. We go on a trip to the McLaren Vale and visit a couple of wineries. D'Arenburg wines delicious. Luckily, no show this evening. Hire some clubs and play golf with Dave Mullaly, our props man. At a tricky par three, hit a good tee shot across a deep wooded valley to the green on the bank at the other side. Made it. The "paper" money here is made of plastic.

SAN FRANCISCO, USA

Up at six am to fly from Adelaide to Sydney, which in time is half an hour ahead of us, then on round the world eastwards on a fourteen-hour flight to San Francisco where we are having a forty-eight-hour stopover. How many miles have we travelled on this tour? Haven't a clue. We arrive at nine am. Later that day we all go to see the sights and have a drink at the Fairmount Hotel. The glass lift that takes us to the top is on the outside of the building – truly vertigo-inducing but stunning views over the city: the Golden Gate Bridge, Alcatraz, the sea on three sides around us. Afterwards we go to Pier 39 to the Bubba Gump Fish Shrimp Restaurant. The film *Forrest Gump* is playing on a large screen and the staff wear Gump costumes. There are *Run Forrest, Run* signs on the tables to summon the waitresses. We wear huge paper napkins round our necks. The food is excellent, the portions very large. Yes, we're in the USA.

In the next twenty-four hours I am in film-buff heaven. I visit the Wells Fargo Museum, where there are old stage coaches, morse machines, wooden prospectors' sifting troughs, gold nuggets, Pony Express saddles and mail bags. I am thrilled by the place. I go down to the bay and get a ferry that goes out into the harbour. We go close to the Golden Gate Bridge and I am yards from the spot where in *Vertigo* Kim Novak jumps into the sea to be 'rescued' by James Stewart. Fifteen minutes later we are skirting the rocky and forbidding Alcatraz Prison, the location of many memorable films. I go for a spin in an old manually controlled cable car, used in so many films – a Buster Keaton short, *The Birds*, *What's Up Doc*, *Pal Joey*. I go to John's Grill where a scene from *The Maltese Falcon* was shot. I climb up and down steep streets where Steve McQueen shot a great car chase in *Bullitt.* By the way, I never liked that *Forrest Gump* film.

NEW YORK CITY

The torn diary finished on the 5th April the day we flew on to New York. So from now on I'll have to rely on memory.

We stayed in a hotel in Lower Manhatten near the World Trade Centre and travelled every day by coach across to Brooklyn where we played at BAM, the Brooklyn Academy of Music – a very classy venue. Sam arrived from London and restaged and refreshed the production. *Othello* was a huge hit in New York. My son Séamus flew over to visit and stayed with me. I have two vivid memories of his stay. One was the evening when he came to see the play. The wonderful actor James Earl Jones came into the dressing room after the performance. I asked him if he would meet my son who was at the stage door.

'Of course,' he said. I dashed to get Séamus and told him there was someone I wanted him to meet. I brought him back to the room and said, 'Séamus, please say hello to James Earl Jones.' Séamus was speechless. James said in that unmistakable bass voice what a pleasure it was to meet him. Séamus found his voice and had a lovely chat with the actor during which he told James what an unbelievable thrill it was to meet the actor who had played Darth Vader. Séamus had seen the first *Star Wars* film in 1978 when he was six and has been obsessed with the series ever since.

The second memory of Séamus' visit is the morning I took him up to the top of one of the World Trade Centre buildings where we spent a wonderful half hour looking at the great views of New York. Just three short years later they would be destroyed with such great loss of life.

New York was a wonderful end to the world tour of *Othello*. My kind of town.

During our stay rumours circulated that Sam's work had come to the attention of Steven Spielberg and that film scripts were being sent to him. Within a year he had made his first film from one of those scripts. There is a story that after shooting for two days Sam realised that the film wasn't working. Some of the sets were wrong, his perception of the characters and direction of the actors was all wrong. With heart in mouth he met with the producers and said he would like to scrap the footage and start again. What guts. They had faith in him and said OK. Of course the film was *American Beauty*, which would go on to win five Oscars, including Best Director for Sam. His Oscar was presented by... Steven Spielberg.

BACK TO STRATFORD

EDDIE IZZARD AND PETER HALL
POLONIUS WITH MARK RYLANCE

THE LION, THE WITCH
AND THE WARDROBE
THE WINTER'S TALE

In the autumn of 1998 I returned to the RSC to appear in Adrian Noble's production of *The Lion, The Witch and The Wardrobe*. The audiences and the press loved it and the production stayed in the repertoire for four years, although I only did the first season. In one scene I played Father Christmas, entering upstage in the full red and white outfit, the big white beard, singing the song 'Always Winter'. At each performance I was greeted with hysterical cheering and loud applause from the young playgoers. I now know what it is like to be a member of One Direction. Despite the adoration I never let it go to my head and remained the modest professional.

We rehearsed *The Lion* and *The Winter's Tale* at the same time and it was somewhat weird to go from the world of Narnia to Sicilia and Bohemia. From a world of innocence to one of jealousy, revenge, repentance and redemption. Greg Doran directed *The Winter's Tale* with Tony Sher as Leontes.

It was the first time I had worked with both of them and a very satisfying experience it turned out to be. The production had a buttoned-up Edwardian/Romanov look to the court scenes and a bucolic, pastoral look to the country scenes. I played that lovely part, the Old Shepherd, who finds the abandoned baby Perdita and brings her up as his own child. He has one of my favourite lines in Shakespeare. Having rescued the baby he meets his son who has witnessed both the bear's attack on Antigonus and the shipwreck with the loss of all on board:

"Shepherd: Heavy matter, heavy matters! But look thee here, boy. Now bless thyself: thou met'st with things dying, I with things new-born."

The part of Leontes is notoriously difficult. The character's descent into the most bitter jealousy of his wife Hermione erupts out of the blue within the first few minutes of the play and there seems to be no rational reason for it. Tony Sher thought that the writing "felt very personal, as if Shakespeare had experienced or witnessed the same terrible brainstorm". He consulted a number of experts, a neurologist, a professor of psychiatry, a psycho-analyst and in the end decided that Leontes suffered from a malady called morbid jealousy. He then created a detailed characterisation with none of his noted flamboyance but a deeply troubled, insular study in psychological realism. His rages were frightening and the change brought about by his subsequent guilt and loss, over sixteen years, into humility and tenderness was very moving.

Initially, because Leontes doesn't appear in a long section in the middle of the play, Tony was going to double Leontes with the rogue Autolycus. But in the first few days of rehearsal he changed his mind. I thought this was a good decision. I'm not sure the audience would have been prepared to accept the heartbroken Leontes if they had been watching the same actor cavorting in the Bohemia scenes minutes before.

Greg came up with a wonderful and speedy transformation from the world of Sicilia to the world of Bohemia, which also incorporated a very good solution to Shakespeare's most famous stage direction, "Exit pursued by a bear". Above the panelled rooms of the court, large billowing "clouds" of white parachute silk flew. As Leontes is told of the "death" of his wife, repents his sins, and departs to pray, a loud thunder storm breaks out and the silk drops and drapes itself over the furniture creating a snowy landscape. We are now in Bohemia. Immediately, Antigonus appears in the middle of the storm with the baby in his arms. As he places the child on the ground about to leave it to its fate, a new sound is heard, the roar of a bear. Upstage through the white silk a huge threatening shape is seen and a head and two massive bear paws with long spiky claws press into the cloth and move forward. Blackout.

Greg had worked as an actor and as an assistant director with the RSC back in the late eighties. As I write this he is embarking on his first season as the new RSC artistic director. The man is steeped in Elizabethan and Jacobean theatre and history and has a profound love for the RSC.

EDDIE IZZARD AND PETER HALL

In 1999 Peter Hall asked me to do a play about the great American comic Lenny Bruce in the West End. Titled *Lenny* it was written by Julian Barry. Dustin Hoffman had starred in a film version of the play in 1974, directed by Bob Fosse. Bruce was the founder of "alternative comedy". Throughout the fifties and sixties, until his death in 1966 from a drug overdose, he did a form of stand-up, which incorporated politics, religion, sex, race, abortion, drugs – you name it. He saw himself as an oral jazz man who could walk onstage and talk on anything that came into his head. Two of his most memorable riffs were 'How to Relax Your Coloured Friends at Parties', which was a parody of stupid white people and their condescension towards blacks, and 'Christ and Moses' which involved these venerated figures in a debate with Cardinals Spelman and Sheen in St. Patrick's Cathedral in New York. A number of lepers also featured with Spelman interjecting, *"Look, you lepers, no offence, but just don't touch anything, OK"*. This kind of material shocked the bland conformist America of the fifties.

He was arrested for obscenity on countless occasions, banned from several US cities and blacklisted by nearly every nightclub in America where the owners feared prosecution. He played in London in 1962 and on a return was arrested and deported back to America. In Sydney, Australia he went on stage, declared,'What a fucking wonderful audience,' and was promptly arrested.

The cast of *Lenny* was strong, with David Ryall, Stephen Noonan, Annette McLaughlin, all of us doubling and trebling parts. To play the stripper Rusty Blaine, who became Lenny's wife, Peter Hall had brought over from America the actress Elizabeth Berkley.

Rehearsals were interesting. Eddie Izzard, playing Lenny Bruce, was charming, friendly and obviously very funny.

He didn't play status, which always goes down well with other members of the cast. Although renowned as a comic, he had done a number of plays and was very comfortable in the rehearsal room. However, he did something I had never come across before in the theatre. He maintained his American accent at all times, even during coffee and lunch breaks.

Peter tends to direct from a seated position, usually with the script on a lectern in front of him. After lunch he invariably dozes off for a few minutes. Nothing unusual, we all carry on. Then one day, Peter came to rehearsal wearing an extremely nice suit and tie. That lunchtime his wife, the beautiful Nicki, turned up to have lunch with him. After lunch we continued rehearsing. Twenty minutes in, when we were running a big scene, Peter stood up. Watching us, he backed up to the wall behind him and leant against it observing the action intently. *Golly*, I thought, *he's really on the ball today*. The scene played on. Next time I looked, Peter had left the room. *Lavatory*, I thought. We eventually finished the scene. Peter did not return. Mystified we waited. No Peter. We didn't see him again that afternoon. The assistant director took over. Eventually we found out that Peter had joined Nicki outside and departed to Glyndebourne with her to see an opera. Next day I asked Peter what the opera was like. 'It was marvellous,' he said. No apology, no mention of his discreet departure from the rehearsal room.

Thirty-three years after Lenny Bruce's death, the play opened at the Queen's Theatre in the West End. But in the intervening years the world of comedy had changed radically and was now crowded with comedians who had taken up the Bruce banner. The play, which was basically a cursory run through Bruce's life and career, got a mixed reception from the press. It was a mix of short scenes covering Bruce's life story, his stand-up acts and an obscenity trial. The many characters we played were not very rounded. For instance I played a bailiff, an old-style comic, a district attorney, a head tribesman and a Chinese waiter. The latter now obviously very un-PC.

There were three or four scenes in the play where Lenny, in a tight spotlight, stood at a mic and did stand-up. During these all the cast were sat at the sides of the stage. Peter had given Eddie licence to depart from the script, to improvise in these segments, as long as it was in the style of Lenny Bruce. So for instance on a Monday Eddie might suddenly start a funny riff on the Lone Ranger and Tonto. Over the next few performances he would effortlessly extend and embellish the story. Soon it would be full of mad invention and strange logic. The Lone Ranger became a closet homosexual. To watch him work close-up like this over a week was a real lesson. Now any actor would "lock" this story off and repeat it for the whole run. Not Eddie. With such a great gift he could afford to be profligate. The following Monday he would ditch the Lone Ranger completely and begin and develop a whole new riff. Some of Eddie's gentle flights of surreal fantasy lacked the frisson of danger that inhabited Lenny's work. For instance, there was a section when Lenny asked for the houselights to be turned on when he was talking about racism and asked, 'Are there any niggers in the audience, tonight?' He then went through the auctioneer routine: 'Five niggers, eight micks, two yids, three kikes, four spics and two Polacks…' The whole atmosphere in the theatre changed and the laughter became tense and tentative. Lenny's material still had the power to shock.

Elizabeth Berkley had achieved massive notoriety as

the star of one of the biggest disasters in American cinema. It was called *Showgirls*. The 1995 film follows the path of a gorgeous young girl to Las Vegas, who climbs the ladder from stripper to showgirl. Often ranked as one of the worst films ever made, it has now become a cult classic renowned for its gratuitous nudity and simulated sex. Elizabeth was very attractive, very tall, very sexy, a good actress and a really nice person. Here she was in London, again playing a stripper, a part not well-written, but one she brought a very vulnerable quality to. She was totally uninhibited about her body. Passing her backstage with barely a stitch on, was at first, shall we say, disconcerting. I remember knocking on her dressing-room door and being invited in to find her sitting at the mirror naked except for a pair of knickers. She was totally relaxed. I on the other hand nearly dislocated my neck trying to avoid looking at her – or her reflection in the bright mirror, while at the same time trying to appear a man of the world as we talked. After performances strange men haunted the stage door. During the run, and for a couple of years after, many actors and male friends would salaciously question me about what it was like working with the lovely Elizabeth Berkley.

I remember Eddie turning up at the stage door for some performances wearing make-up and red high heels. I remember when he was ill and his understudy, Matt Devereaux, had to go on for him – a daunting prospect. Matt did very well. But without the improvised sections the performance was twenty minutes shorter. Eddie had a little "club", a couple of rooms he used to invite us to after the show. It was in a little side street in Soho. We would go there, meet his girlfriend, drink some beer and sometimes watch a film.

POLONIUS WITH MARK RYLANCE

In 2000, three years after its opening, I went to Shakespeare's Globe to play Polonius to Mark Rylance's Hamlet . I also did a little-known and underrated 1638 comedy *The Antipodes* by Richard Brome. Mark was then the Globe's artistic director. The production was directed by Giles Block whom I had worked with on *The Fawn* at the National. The Globe, which receives no government subsidy has, from its inception, been a huge success. Initially people in the business tended to sneer and see the place as somewhere where heritage theatre was staged for the entertainment of tourists. I enjoyed my season there and can only say that though the productions were "traditional" in look, the exploration of text, the rigour of the work in the rehearsal period, the care taken, the passion of all concerned differed in no way from an RSC or NT production.

The rehearsal period was generous and included a weekend when Giles and Mark arranged for the full company to go and stay at a Jacobean manor near Ipswich. This beautiful moated timbered house had a number of other buildings where the company stayed and where we cooked our meals. The days were spent exploring the play, staging scenes, improvising imagined scenes around the main action etc. Even the moat came in handy. Giles Block would set up a basic scene and actors would, with whispered instructions, enter and join the action. I remember one where, as Polonius, I came into a bedroom where Ophelia and Laertes were quietly talking and quizzed them on what they were doing, suggesting there were better ways for them to make use of their time. The gravediggers dug an actual grave and one evening when the rest of us were eating, Mark went and lay in it for a couple of hours. Can't remember if they put earth on top of him or not. He's a bit spiritual, Mark, a bit New Age. It was a very productive weekend and helped us explore the characters and situations in a new and exciting way.

We also went on an outing to Hatfield House in Hertfordshire, the home of Robert Cecil, Chief Minister to James I and son of Lord Burghley, Chief Advisor to Elizabeth I. Polonius is often said to be a satire of Burghley who, I discovered, wrote a set of precepts to his son. So, when I played the precepts scene with Laertes I had them written on a large sheet of paper, which I then quoted from. It worked well. We had a tour of the house and met the archivist who brought out some fascinating documents to show us. I remember a handwritten poem by Ben Jonson dedicated to Cecil. I have always been struck by the similarity in face and career between Robert Cecil and Peter Mandelson. There is a group painting in the National Portrait Gallery of the 1604 Somerset House Conference with Cecil sitting at the front on the right. The resemblance is striking.

There were some eccentricities at the Globe. For instance, Giles was not the "director", his title was "master of play". The costume designer, Jenny Tiramani – or Tiramisu as I called her – was "master of clothing". Jenny was excellent and a stickler for authenticity. Shirts could not have buttons. All the fastenings had to be tied with little strings. Doing one's cuffs up demanded a newfound skill, which entailed the combined use of fingertips and teeth. There were buttons on the richer characters' doublets and I had to do up twenty-six of these from the neck to the waist every performance. No velcro, no jumping into costume at the last minute.

Giles wanted the production to play like a thriller with each scene tumbling into the next. His intelligence and understanding of the text, as well as how the verse should be delivered, was impressive. "Trippingly on the tongue" was the catchword. Mark has a strange otherwordly quality that makes him very watchable. His Hamlet was witty, mischievous, nimble and deeply troubled. His soliloquies were delivered superbly. He seemed to new-mint each word. I remember him starting his first soliloquy, "O, that this too too solid flesh…" with his back to the audience. His mastery of the Globe groundlings was supreme. Some would call it shameless. On the advice to the players, he looked the audience in the eye when he came to "– the groundlings who, for the most part, are capable of nothing but inexplicable dumb shows" which got cheers. Then when the laughter died down he completed the sentence – "and noise." A belter, of course.

Playing in the open air in daylight threw up surprising discoveries. Mark had mentioned that Elizabethan audiences always spoke of going to *hear* a play. *Hamlet* opens at night with the watch on the battlements, soon followed by the entrance of the Ghost. For an audience on a bright Southwark afternoon Shakespeare had to conjure the scene, the time and the weather with words. The opening line is, "Who's there?" followed by much reference to *the time* – "Tis now struck twelve, get thee to bed". By the end of the twentieth line, night has been mentioned five times.

In Act 3 Scene 2 there is a very funny exchange between the "mad" Hamlet and Polonius.

"Hamlet: Do you see yonder cloud that's almost in shape of a
    camel?
Polonius: By th' mass and 'tis: like a camel, indeed.
Hamlet: Methinks it is like a weasel.
Polonius: It is backed like a weasel.
Hamlet: Or like a whale?
Polonius: Very like a whale."

On an indoor stage this works well. But on the Globe stage open to the sky, it works really well. Mark and I had a lot of fun twisting and turning to study the real sky above us, with many of the audience turning upwards to follow our observations.

Polonius is an exceedingly good part. There are many sides to the character that the actor can explore. He is an important and respected minister of the state. He is a controlling and insensitive father. He is long-winded and dull. He is wily. In the end he loses his way politically. which ends in the deaths of himself and both his children. Yet, along the way there are many moments where the actor playing him can find truly comic moments.

I have a love/hate relationship with the Globe. On certain evenings it is the most magical place to perform in. When the production is working and the rapport between the players and the active and enthusiastic audience is palpable, there is no finer experience for the actor. All this in an always packed auditorium. But sometimes it rains, or there is noise from planes, helicopters or from traffic on the Thames, or invasions by small flocks of pigeons, or some of the audience in the "yard" are moving around. Then, selfishly, it can be doubly annoying if any of the above happens during one's "best bits".

We took the production to the Teatro Olimpico in Vicenza. Designed by the great Palladio and built in 1585 it is one of only three remaining Renaissance theatres. The back of the shallow stage has a permanent white "marble" colannade, made of wood and plaster and decorated with high Corinthian pillars, cornices and niches with life-sized statues. At the centre is a large triumphal arch and on either side of this two further openings. Through these three entrances are the most wonderful trompe l'oeil Roman street scenes giving the illusion of a town stretching beyond into the distance. These were installed in the sixteenth century. We had to fit our production around all this, which was not difficult. It was moving to play *Hamlet* in a theatre that had been built seventeen years before Shakespeare wrote his play.

I took some of the company on a day trip to Padua to visit the Scrovegni Chapel. Originally, it was a small private place of worship attached to a palace. The exterior is unimpressive but the high walls of the interior are completely covered with a cycle of frescos painted by Giotto in 1305. There are three tiers of narrative images focusing on the life of Christ and the life of the Virgin Mary. Above, there is a barrel vault ceiling beautifully painted with a star-studded rich blue sky. This is one of the most important masterpieces of Western art. It is extraordinary. It is breathtaking. It brings tears to the eyes. It was one of the finest, most uplifting, most joyous half-hours I have spent in my life.

* * *

From the Globe I went to the tiny Gate Theatre in Notting Hill to do a metaphysical mystery play *Tear From A Glass*

Eye by the talented Australian writer Matt Cameron. We rehearsed at the NT Studio and for our time there and for the first week of the run we were paid a modest wage. For the three further weeks of playing our wage consisted of a daily travel card. The play was extremely well directed by Erica Whyman, who took over as director of the Gate soon after. One of her provisos in taking the job was that the actors should receive a salary. Erica made it happen.

Playing a one-armed man in that small space took some ingenuity. Playing a one-armed man in a drunken stupor wearing his wife's dress and lipstick while aggressively dancing with his grown-up son took a bit more.

THREE MORE AT THE NATIONAL

2001 – 2002

In early 2001 I had a meeting with Trevor Nunn who was running the National at that time. He was about to do a production of Vanbrugh's *The Relapse* and asked me to play Lory, servant to Tom Fashion, brother to Sir Novelty Fashion, the newly created Lord Foppington. Lory is a droll, impertinent and funny character. Trevor asked me if I would mind doing a little fight in the production. 'Of course not,' I replied, though a small question mark appeared at the back of my mind. The production was one of the events to mark the twenty-fifth anniversary of the National Theatre's permanent home.

The vast open space of the Olivier Theatre does not lend itself to the rapier wit of Restoration comedy. Trevor and designer Sue Blane offset this by creating a false eighteenth century theatre with pros arch and side boxes inhabited by chattering beaux.

A study of unhappy marriage, the main plot concerns the "reformed" rake Loveless and his naïve wife Amanda. He pursues her widowed cousin Berinthia, while Amanda is wooed by the cynical Worthy. In the sub-plot, the penniless Tom Fashion moves to the country in the guise of his brother Lord Foppington to woo his sibling's intended, a rural heiress.

Trevor had gathered a large and impressive cast of twenty-six including Alex Jennings as Foppington, Imogen Stubbs as Amanda, Claire Price as Berinthia, James Purefoy as Loveless, Adrian Lukis as Worthy – along with Janine Duvitski, Edward Petherbridge, Brian Blessed, Maxine Peake and Ray Coulthard.

Foppington, of course, is one of the great scene-stealing, play-stealing roles and Alex Jennings had a ball playing him. He gave us a total narcissist, a man who finishes everyone's sentences. He was camp, flamboyant, with a drawling voice. He had a *number* of costumes. He wore clothes to suit all occasions. When he descended into the country to woo his rural heiress he looked like one of those specially designed gardens at the Chelsea Flower Show. He wore the largest and highest periwigs ever seen on a stage, with a pampered and powdered face, a sequin star on his forehead, a moon on his cheek. He was in love with mirrors. Through all this came a performance of great style, superb comic timing and the cleverness to also make Foppington a red-blooded womaniser.

Trevor's staging was terrific, his handling of the many scenes with such a large cast seemed effortless. He was never unfazed, always a mile ahead of us. The production was a stylish hit. His inquiry at our first meeting as to whether I would mind doing a fight had sent me back to the text. I had not remembered any mention of one when I read the play. On rereading it I was correct, there was no fight. But Trevor had decided that the scene in which Tom Fashion and Lory flee from the country mansion needed a boost, that the play could benefit from a surge of adrenalin at that point. So, instead of a discreet departure Trevor inserted a big rustic scrap where Ray

Coulthard and I fought the entire household of Sir Tunbelly Clumsey. This was further complicated by a suggestion of mine that the pair of us should effect our escape dressed as women. Fighting with swords, pitchforks and cudgels while clothed in long dresses, wigs and shawls was, shall we say, complicated.

Towards the end of the rehearsal period we were all called to a company meeting. As Trevor was about to address us, the actor sitting next to me whispered, 'Here comes the mike speech!' He was right. Trevor spoke about the problems some audience members have in hearing the actors' voices in the Olivier. There is already discreet use of amplification in the auditorium for all productions. Usually the Voice Department works with the company on audibility and very good they are too. Trevor however, spoke of the many letters of complaint he received on the subject. 'So, you will all wear microphones.' And so we did, even Alex Jennings who has the biggest voice in Equity. At each performance this entailed the actors being fitted with battery/transmitter packs with a wire/microphone which is then attached to shirt fronts, foreheads, wigs etc. Actors hate these being used in a straight play. They feel, rightly, that control of their performances is being taken away from them. I was miked in the most recent play I did in the Olivier.

This was the first time I had worked with Trevor and the beginning of the denim mystery which for a short time led to my obsession with his wardrobe.

* * *

Soon after the finish of *The Relapse,* Max Stafford-Clark asked me to do a new play which would be a co-production between his company Out of Joint, the National Theatre and the Abbey Theatre in Dublin – Ireland's National Theatre. It was titled *Hinterland* and was written by Sebastian Barry, one of Ireland's finest writers. *Hinterland* is about a disgraced Irish elder statesman facing a tribunal on charges of corruption. It is also about his complex private life. We rehearsed the play at Out of Joint's rehearsal rooms, opened it in Bolton, then took it to Dublin and then into the Cottesloe Theatre.

As we rehearsed we little knew the fury this play would eventually engender. More of that later.

Max Stafford-Clark is a very successful director who uses a rehearsal technique called "actioning". Some people credit him with its invention. Basically it is a method where the actor and director take every line in the play and describe it, using a transitive verb – an action one character can do to another. What we say and what we mean don't always correspond. Max would say that what we are feeling or thinking is less important than what we are *doing* to another person. An apparently innocent line like, 'Can I get you a coffee?' can be played/actioned in many ways. If the actor places a transitive verb between the "I" and the "you" then he can for instance, play "I welcome you" or "I seduce you" or "I placate you" etc. as well as offering a cup of coffee.

In the early days of rehearsal the company spent many hours actioning every line of the play. Max is a little anal about all this and meticulously notes down every choice the actor makes. He would also question many of the choices. If occasionally, perhaps out of devilment, you offered a fancy verb, Max would have none of it. 'Keep it simple,' he would exhort. I remember when we began to run the play he reminded me that I had not played the action on a particular line. I agreed I had not, but had decided to play the line in a different way. He demanded the new action/verb and when I gave it him he was quite happy, erasing the earlier choice and writing in the new verb in his notebook. Doing this with the full text can at times be tiring, not to say tiresome. But if the actor applies himself fully to the technique it can prove truly rewarding. You think deeper about every line of the part. You make active decisions on every nuance and when it comes to performance, you feel mightily supported by a kind of internal scaffolding.

Max was suspicious and surprised when in rehearsal the other actors laughed at some of my lines. He seemed to think I was up to something. I had to tell him that humour was one of the legitimate facets of my character.

In *Hinterland,* the disgraced elder statesman, Johnny Silvester, facing a tribunal on charges of corruption is on the whole a lightly disguised portrait of Charles Haughey, three-time Taoiseach of Ireland and the most controvertial politician of his generation. Like Silvio Berlusconi, his career faltered over a number of allegations and revelations about his public and private conduct. Yet he always managed to survive, even triumph. Two tribunals set up to investigate his private finances uncovered large cash gifts amounting to millions of pounds from successful businessmen. Despite modest beginnings and modest salaries earned throughout his life he ended up owning an island, living the high life, dispensing lavish hospitality and residing in a Georgian mansion on a two-hundred-and-eighty-acre estate. Despite all the charges of corruption, a large section of the Irish population continued to have a sneaking regard for the man.

So, after opening the play in Bolton, we took it to

Dublin and that is where the aforementioned fury erupted. It was very obvious to Irish audiences that the play's main protagonist was a thinly veiled portrait of Haughey. This was compounded by the decision of Patrick Malahide who played "Silvester" to affect, with the help of a wig, make-up and vocal characterisation a striking resemblance to Haughey.

On our battered departure from Dublin a few weeks later, the theatre presented us with a very attractive folder holding all the photocopied press reactions to the play. There is a lot of it. I have spread it on the floor below my laptop. There is not much carpet showing. Apart from the reviews of the play there are articles from virtually every national newspaper. There are comment pieces, there are editorials, there are profiles, there are political pieces, there are articles commenting on radio phone-in reactions, there are many large photographs. There is a cartoon, there is even a review in Gaelic for a magazine titled *Foinse*. It is all on a scale with *The Romans in Britain* broadsides.

Here's a few examples:

- *"Haughey Fury at Abbey Play"*– Front-page headline of the *Irish Independent*
- *"Poor Drama and Bad Manners"*– Half-page feature from the *Irish Times*
- *"Portrait of Haughey as Macbeth at Bay"* – Half-page feature/review from the *Irish Times*
- "Hinterland *has Made Charlies of Us All*" – Large comment piece in the *Sunday Times* (Irish Edition)
- *"Haughey's Lawyers Studying* Hinterland *Script"*– Front page of the *Irish Independent*

Did I mention that C. Haughey was forced to resign from politics in 1992, was still living in his Georgian mansion with its many acres in Kinsealy, Co. Dublin, and awaiting the deliberations of the Moriarty Tribunal? Eventually he agreed a settlement with the revenue and paid a total of over six million euros in back taxes. He was also accused by the tribunal of "devaluing democracy".

The play was received with lukewarm reviews. Fintan O'Toole in the *Irish Times* was most insightful. "This is Haughey as the Macbeth of Shakespeare's last act: abandoned, at bay, holed up in his fortress waiting for the last encirclement, yet fascinating in his awareness that the price of political power has been a hollowing-out of his very humanity". He called the play "deeply flawed but utterly compelling". Emer O'Kelly writing in the *Irish Independent* said, "Barry comes up with a chilling conclusion, that those guilty of corruption are irredeemable, because they are rooted in *amorality* and are incapable of recognising right from wrong". She added that "the play combines farcical elements with edges of melodrama, but the two sit uneasily at times". She wrote that Patrick played Silvester magnificently and admired Dearbhla Molloy as the wronged wife, Anna Healy as the mistress and myself as a "'foxy aide/manservant who bows subserviently while silently despising his master".

The not very popular artistic director of the Abbey, Ben Barnes, gave an interview defending the play. He stated that the theatre was often criticised for not reflecting contemporary life. Soon things escalated. An article in the *Sunday Independent* stated "Charlie Haughey's four children are this weekend separately studying the script of a controversial new play at the Abbey Theatre and, with their parents, will next week take a final decision on whether to sue for defamation... their legal advisor, the barrister Eoin McGonigal, attended the play on Tuesday night and carefully scrutinised it from the front row'. And on it went. Meanwhile we acted the play and I enjoyed my time back in Ireland. No one sued. We took the play to the Cottesloe where it received moderate reviews.

* * *

The third play was Sheila Stephenson's *Mappa Mundi* at the Cottesloe. This production also had problems, but of a different kind.

The play concerns an old man, Jack, who is dying. He has a fascination with old maps and, as a premature birthday present, his two children give him a map of his life, showing his school, the houses he has lived in, the company he has worked in for forty years and so on: "Is that it? I thought it would look more than that". Death, acceptance, memory, family discord, and faith are the main themes. The rehearsal process started with the director, Bill Alexander, and a strong cast led by Ian Holm as Jack, Lia Williams and Tim McInnerny playing his children, Patrick Robinson as the daughter's partner and myself as Father Ryan, a friend of Jack's. As I write this Patrick is disporting himself as a contestant on *Strictly Come Dancing* – and very good he is too.

We were all excited to be working with Ian, one of the best actors in the business. In rehearsals he was compelling to watch. Subtle and detailed in preparation. As a character, Jack offered the actor many facets to explore. There was his indulgence of his daughter, which contrasted with his resentment towards his unsuccessful son, an actor. There was his own sense of failure, the anguish of approaching death, the secret guilt that has contaminated his life connected to an incident in his past. I personally enjoyed a very funny scene where Jack and I explored rival philosophies in which he peppered the dialogue with all the well-known swear words. So, in other words, Jack was a very good part.

But, sadly, when we began to put the scripts down, Ian had some difficulties. Recently recovered from a cancer scare and seventy-one years old, he had problems remembering some of the lines. Many actors have heard of his famous nervous breakdown in 1976; when playing Hickey in O'Neill's *The Iceman Cometh* he suffered from stage fright, left the stage and could not return. When he "dried" in our rehearsals it was very distressing to watch. It is something that every actor dreads. On a few occasions, Ian, visibly distressed, left the rehearsal room and did not return for fifteen minutes. A day or so after an incident where in deep frustration Ian banged his head against a wall, he decided to leave the production. Understandably everyone was upset for the actor, but now with the production about to tech in a week, there was a dilemma. Should the production be cancelled? Bill Alexander and the cast were determined that the show must go on. So, enquiries were made and within a couple of days that lovely actor Alun Armstrong took over the role. Although nowhere near Jack's age he soon inhabited the part very convincingly. The opening had to be postponed for a number of days while Alun, with ferocious speed, learned the lines and rehearsed. On the night with the aid of some hair dye, a moustache and make-up he was absolutely terrific in the role. He had managed, in little more than a week, to not only learn a large part, but to create a character that embodied all the many sides of Jack's character. It was a joy to work with him. In the middle of the whirlwind, he was funny, self-depecating and always calm. The critics, were fulsome in their praise of his performance.

* * *

PLAYING THE MOST POWERFUL MAN IN THE WORLD, WORKING WITH PATRICK STEWART AND DOING SOME DISCO MOVES IN A 400-YEAR-OLD PLAY

Between 2003 and 2006 I did five and a bit Shakespeare plays, a Ben Jonson tragedy and a Middleton and Rowley black comedy with the RSC. I also went to the Bristol Old Vic to do Sheridan's *The Rivals*.

The five Shakespeare plays were *Measure for Measure, Richard III, Julius Caesar, Antony and Cleopatra* and *The Tempest*. The 'bit' was a three-page contribution Shakespeare is said to have made to *Thomas More* written by Anthony Munday, Henry Chettle and others. The Ben Jonson play was *Sejanus: His Fall,* the Middleton and Rowley comedy was *A New Way To Please You* – both little-known and rarely performed in the previous four hundred years.

For *Measure for Measure* the director, Sean Holmes decided to set the play in the 1940s Vienna of Harry Lime. The cast included Paul Higgins as the Duke, Daniel Evans as Angelo and Emma Fielding as Isabella. The opening scene, in which the Duke hands over power, was set in the Wien Westbahnof railway station where, under a large clock and amid the sound of hissing steam trains, a throng of busy porters, hurrying travellers, prostitutes and black-marketeers mill about. The Duke enters hatted and overcoated with a suitcase. He is closely followed by the older of his two deputies, Escalus – the part I played – and soon after by his other deputy Angelo. He surprises both by the announcement of his sudden decision to leave the city and his placing of the temporary running of the state into Angelo's hands. The scene was played with great urgency followed by the swift departure of the Duke on his train. Given that the Duke never actually leaves Vienna but stays to spy on Angelo, Sean's setting of the scene at the station was a clever choice.

In a previous production of the play, by Adrian Noble at Stratford, this first scene was played in the Duke's quarters, where Escalus and Angelo had to listen to the Duke's instructions pour out of a prominent tape recorder, the ruler having already departed the city. I thought this was a poor decision, yet the rest of the production was excellent, with a very good performance by Robert Glenister as the Duke.

Measure for Measure is not one of my favourite Shakespeare plays. I find it hard to like or care for many of the central characters. The Duke, who decides to leave Vienna in a somewhat parlous state and then return in disguise as a friar to spy on his deputy Angelo, can come across as a deceitful and interfering hypocrite. Angelo, though "well-seeming" is duplicitous and untrustworthy. Isabella can seem a prig and her brother Claudio weak and unlikeable. Our inability to engage with these characters makes it a difficult play to bring off. Despite the size of the role, the fifth biggest part in Shakespeare, the Duke is not a very exciting part. Interestingly none of the theatrical "greats" of the twentieth century played the role, though John Gielgud played Angelo in Peter Brook's 1950 RSC production.

The production was greeted with mixed reviews.

"... it has pace and energy and a fine performance by Emma Fielding... Holmes' boldest stroke is to set it in 1940s Vienna... but although this gives the action a social context, it does little to illuminate the central debate between justice and mercy...' –Michael Billington in the *Guardian*.

* * *

Richard III, again directed by Sean Holmes, soon followed. During this period I was juggling rehearsals with studying for an Open University Arts degree and wrote the following piece for *Sesame*, the OU Magazine.

DIARY OF AN ACTOR
By James Hayes, Royal Shakespeare Company

9:40am *Stratford upon Avon. Out with the laptop, transfer TMA 05 to disc. Gulp down some tea, and toast in hand, dash out the door. Rehearsals for* Richard III *at the RSC at ten am. As I arrive, the director is discussing the murder of Clarence in a tub of Malmsey – which reminds me immediately of the murder of Marat in his bath, given that the subjects of the TMA I was still typing at one am this morning were the French Revolution, the philosopher Rousseau and the painter*

David. But 'A103 An Introduction to the Humanities' fades from my mind as I rehearse the role of Lord Stanley for the rest of the morning.

1:45pm *Dash up to the roof room (a space where staff can relax, with terrific views out to the countryside, but, more importantly for me, a computer for the use of all.) Quick check over last night's OU work, a bit of a rewrite and a spellcheck. Back to rehearsals where Richard III (Henry Goodman) is acting not unlike M. Robespierre.*

6:15pm *Back to the roof to email the assignment to the excellent Hamish Johnson, my tutor in Richmond upon Thames, where I started this course. As I am performing here most nights until November, I have to miss the summer school part of the course, which is a pity as I was looking forward to it.*

7:30pm *Standing in the wings of the Royal Shakespeare Theatre in a linen three-piece suit and broad-brimmed hat, about to go onstage to play Escalus in* Measure For Measure *– a production set in the 1940s Vienna of Harry Lime. Escalus is deputy to Angelo who is charged with governing the state while the Duke is "away". The puritan Angelo (the very talented Daniel Evans) seems to have no time at all for the general will of the people – unlike M. Rousseau. During a break, in my dressing room, I sneak a gawp at Units 16 and 17 on the Victorian naturalist Alfred Russel Wallace – the next TMA. With his huge beard he looks like a character I once played in* The Cherry Orchard.

10:35pm *Out of costume, I dash to The Dirty Duck for a pint. I've got TMA 05 in on time, so, will I do some work on Wallace when I get back to my flat? Will I ****! 'Another pint, landlord!' and on with the noisy banter of actors in post-show mode. I'm sixty-two, and have been meaning to do the OU for years but wondered if I could fit it round my work. Now I know I can, and I'm enjoying it tremendously. Best decision I've made for years I decide, as I get to my bed at 1:15am again.*

Over the next four years, with much help from a new tutor, the knowledgable and enthusiastic Owen Gunnell, and following exams in Birmingham and London I got my degree. Impressed by my enthusiasm, Daniel Evans decided to do an OU degree. And look at him now, not only acting, but artistic director of the Crucible Theatre, Sheffield.

* * *

I love Restoration comedies. I love the ornate costumes and wigs. I love the dialogue, the sharp edgy wit and flashing repartee. I love the clearly defined characters, the romance, the infidelities, the disguises, the asides to the audience, the seeming effortless style of it all. So I was very happy when invited to play Sir Lucius O'Trigger in *The Rivals* at the Bristol Old Vic by director Rachel Kavanaugh. The Vic was built in 1766, nine years before Sheridan wrote his comedy. The play was written when he was twenty-three and drew extensively from his own romantic experiences in nearby Bath where he had fought two near-fatal duels over the woman he later married – Elizabeth Ann Linley.

In Bath, the fashionable resort of the rich, you have Jack

Absolute pretending to be a penniless ensign to win Lydia Languish, a young woman who through her obsession with cheap romantic fiction has decided to only love an impoverished soldier. You also have her friend Julia who is pursued by Falkland, a neurotic lover consumed with self-inflicted doubts and who becomes hysterical at the news that his estranged love has apparently been perfectly happy without him. Then you have the great Mrs Malaprop with her "nice derangements of epitaphs", the choleric Sir Anthony Absolute, the bumpkin Bob Acres oozing terror at the prospect of a duel and urged on by the "blood-thirsty Philistine Sir Lucius O'Trigger". It's a rich brew. All played on a set that created a wonderful vista of Bath's orderly crescents topped by a soft Gainsborough sky and delivered to an audience in the beautiful golden horseshoe-shaped auditorium.

Mrs Malaprop, a plum part very easy to caricature, was beautifully played by Selina Cadell. She gave us a woman not just inadvertently funny but also vulnerable and longing for love. I enjoyed playing the red-blooded Sir Lucius and had a lot of fun tormenting Dylan Charles' Bob Acres. Martin Hudson, contorted and twisted in love's agony, was an excellent Falkland. Rachel Kavanaugh's production was stylish and intelligent. In rehearsal one day she told me that, when a student, she had spent a few days doing work experience at the National and had sat in on a play in which I was rehearsing. She told me that I had been kind to her. So there, a small act of kindness led to a very happy job for me.

In 1809, Drury Lane Theatre, which Sheridan owned and had insured for only a fraction of its worth, burned down. The writer was famously reported to have sat in a tavern opposite,watching the conflagration. When questioned about his calm demeanour he replied, 'A man may surely take a glass of wine by his own fireside.'

* * *

Greg Doran has an abiding enthusiasm for the neglected plays of Shakespeare's contemporaries. In 2005 he chose four of these plays for the RSC's Gunpowder Season – *A New Way To Please You* by Middleton and Rowley, *Sejanus: His Fall* by Ben Jonson, *Thomas More* by Munday, Cheetle and Shakespeare and *Believe What You Will* by Massinger, all performed in the Swan Theatre. I appeared in the first three. It was refreshing to work on plays by these lesser-known figures. Playing in, let alone watching, your fifth *Twelfth Night* or any of the Bard's overperformed favourites can on occasion be wearisome.

* * *

A New Way To Please You is actually the subtitle of the play. The main title is *The Old Law*. Personally I prefer the shorter one, as it gives a better indication of the story of the play. A black tragi-comedy, the savage premise of the piece is that all men at the age of eighty and all women at the age of sixty should be put down by law for having no further use to society. So, in 2005, with euthanasia, collapsing pension schemes and burgeoning tax burdens on the young, what better time to revive this 1618 play? Following the Duke's decree, there is a complete breakdown of the social and moral order as young men plot to rid themselves of wealthy, aging fathers, and, young wives of aging husbands. Trophy wives are the new order, the "hags" are to be disposed of.

Sean Holmes' much admired modern-dress production peopled the stage with sharp-suited lawyers – "Here's a good age now for those that have old parents and rich inheritance", strutting baroque punks, femme-fatales, Marilyn look-alikes and stoic old men. I played one of the latter, Lysander, an aged husband with a gorgeous flame-haired young wife (Eugenia) in the Rita Hayworth mould, the delicious, malicious Miranda Colchester. Eugenia is much admired and lusted after by three young layabouts led by the abrasive Simonedes, played by the brilliantly louche Jonjo O'Neill. Hearing of my imminent demise, they come to woo her. With a white beard, long straggly hair sticking out of a knitted nightcap and dressed in a grey, floor-length, shaggy dressing-gown, which made me look like an old Old English sheepdog, I enter and confront them. Insults fly.

"Monsters unnatural! You that have been covetous
Of your own fathers' deaths, gape ye for mine now?
Cannot a poor old man that now can reckon
Even all the hours he has to live, live quiet
From such wild beasts as these?"

They taunt him. I curse them roundly and exit.

Two scenes later, the bucks are back and the flirting Eugenia tells them her husband *"takes counsel/ With the secrets of all art to make himself/ Youthful again."*

Then – "Enter Lysander looking in a mirror". Eugenia and the young men hide and laugh at him in his new guise.

On the surface Lysander looks the same as in the

previous scene. Still in the long shaggy dressing-gown, but the nightcap and straggly hair are gone. He has cut his hair and dyed the hair and beard an inky black. The mirror is a full-length pier glass on wheels. Lysander proceeds to psych himself up in the mirror.

> *"Ah sirrah! My young boys, I shall be for you.*
> *This little mangy tuft takes up more time*
> *Than all the beard beside! Come you a-wooing*
> *And I alive and lusty? You shall find*
> *An alteration, jack-boys!"*

Messing about with the mirror in rehearsal one day I was reminded of the scene in Scorsese's *Taxi Driver* where Robert DeNiro also psychs himself up with a mirror: "Are you talkin' to me? Are you talkin' to me?" so I Jacobeanised his dialogue:

> *"Art thou talking to me? Art thou talking to me?*
> *Methinks there's no one else in the chamber!"*

It made Sean Holmes and the other actors laugh – so we kept it in. Audiences recognised the allusion and also laughed.

The designer Kandis Cook came up with an inspired physical transformation for Lysander on the line, "You shall find an alteration, jack-boys". When rehearsing at the RSC rehearsal rooms in Clapham she found a "youthful" outfit for him in a local charity shop. Something to make him look young and hip. So on the line, I dramatically threw off the long dressing gown to reveal an eighties hip-hop outfit, a gold shirt and trousers of inordinate awfulness. A garish ensemble covered in huge multicoloured letters of the alphabet. This, enhanced with an amount of gold bling around my neck and the clunkiest red-laced trainers on my feet made me look like an over-dressed Grandmaster Flash.

There soon followed a contest between Lysander and the three bucks entailing dancing, drinking and fighting, in which Lysander wipes the floor with the young men. The "dancing" competition involved disco moves on a squared, electronic Dance Mat to a pounding techno soundtrack. The drinking involved downing disgusting colourful cocktails.

Lysander is one of those tour-de-force parts that rarely come my way. I grabbed it with both hands.

* * *

Ben Jonson's *Sejanus: His Fall* was performed in 1603 and published in 1605, the year of the Gunpowder Plot. Jonson used the Roman Empire as a metaphor for his own age. The story of Sejanus' violent rise to power and subsequent overthrow under the emperor Tiberius did not mirror any contemporary events, but its analysis of power politics brought Jonson before the Privy Council where he was accused of "popery and treason". There had been the Essex Rebellion in 1601. Surveillance was a fact of life and much of the play dealt with spies, informers, and entrapment and related to Elizabethan and Jacobean experience. The part I played, Sabinus, a principled man and senator, is betrayed by his nephew. In a very well-written scene the nephew Latiaris hides two spies under a grille in his villa and with much manoeuvring proceeds to entice his careful uncle into speaking ill of Tiberius.

Apart from a single performance in 1928 and a couple of

amateur productions, this was the play's first staging since 1603.

In his *Address to the Readers,* Jonson states that the text published is "not the same with that which was acted". Its 3,250 lines would have lasted over four hours. Greg Doran, who directed the production had skilfully filleted over 800 lines. He retained the scene structure and some of the less central characters were telescoped. He excited the company with his deep enthusiasm for the play and his staging of it in the Swan Theatre made for a very satisfying evening. All this along with a very strong cast made the revival of this play an exciting "discovery".

The Gunpowder Season was well received and we later transferred the plays to the Trafalgar Studios in London.

* * *

In 2006 Sean Holmes phoned me and asked if I would like to play Julius Caesar in *Julius Caesar* at the RSC. I told him this was a ludicrous idea.

'Why?' he asked.

'Because, Sean, Julius Caesar was one of the most powerful men the world has ever known and I never play characters like that. I'm the character man, the comedy man, the player of quirky roles. I don't know how to play powerful men.'

'Of course you do. You'd be great.'

I asked for time to study the play and think the offer over.

'No rush. Let me know tomorrow – Oh, by the way, I'd also like you to play the Cobbler in the first scene as well.'

Bells began to ring in my head. If I was right, the short first scene consists of a confrontation between two Tribunes and a crowd of lowly celebrating citizens in which the Cobbler cheekily jests with the tribunes. Also, if I was right, once the citizens have been dismissed, the tribunes have only a short scene before the magisterial arrival of Julius Caesar accompanied by a group of the main protagonists of the play. So, I pulled down my trusty, spineless and well-thumbed *Complete Works* and went to page 860. Yes, Julius Caesar enters fifteen lines after the crowd exit. Intriguing. How could this transformation from craftsman to great general and soon-to-be-dictator be achieved. Worry about that later. I read the play through, and then, read the Caesar scenes a number of times. Then I sat and thought about Sean's offer. Could I spurn such a challenge? Dammit, I hate saying no. I did some more thinking and a lot more reading. Then I said yes.

Sean decided to do the production in the traditional way. Togas, swords etc. No contemporary cliches with fascist uniforms, cameras, helicopters, machine guns etc.

Before the start of rehearsals I read a lot of Roman history. I found Tom Holland's *Rubicon* very useful. In my rehearsal script I have found pages of notes I had made on Caesar's history: "He shamelessly exploited his own personal enrichment in Gaul. He was famous among Romans for his clemency, but resolved to make an example of a rebellious city in 51BC by chopping off the hands of everyone who had borne arms against him. Brutus' mother Servilia had been the great love of Caesar's life. It was claimed that Brutus himself was their love child. He achieved the goal of his life – a fame akin to immortality. Is Caesar an ill man? Is he a danger to

347

the state? Is he a colossus, a great man with extraordinary abilities?"

The important thing for the actor is to soak up all this information, but remember that in performance most of it, true or false, is not contained in the play. Use what is useful from the research, discard the rest. Make him a rounded individual. Cassius' great speech in which he denigrates Caesar's character is full of bitterness and thwarted ambition. How much, if any of it, is true? Decide.

I soon learned how to play power. This came about in accidental as well as in structured ways. For instance, in the opening scene Sean filled the large RST stage with revellers. The full cast singing and dancing and in multicoloured muslin –their "best apparel" – came tumbling on (with me as the Cobbler) "to see Caesar, and to rejoice in his triumph". At the end of the scene when we are herded away we all moved upstage. Here in the semi-darkness and in sight of the audience we changed costumes, while the tribunes finished the scene downstage. Then the entrance of Caesar is heralded with martial music. Out of the darkness, way up at the back of the big RST stage, a thrilling sight: a wide phalanx of senators in white togas begin to march downstage. In front, leading them, is Julius Caesar dressed in imperial purple. The music rises, they march forward. As they reach the front of the stage, Caesar, with his wife Calpurnia at his side but slightly behind him, raises his arm and stops. They all stop. Pause. Caesar speaks.

There, before I opened my mouth was power and status manifest. In retrospect, I reckon that first entrance gave me twenty per cent of my performance.

Power can be structured. Having spent most of my

career playing "supporting" roles, where you are often placed in subservient positions, it takes a little while to become accustomed to being the main focus in every scene. Centre stage. Initially I found it slightly embarrassing. But you soon get used to it. Not only get used to it, but *demand* it. You *must* have the best position onstage. Look what you have done for the republic. You are the most important and powerful man in the world. A certain imperiousness steals into one's bones.

It was interesting to see actors I have spent years working with, treat me in a new way. Well, for a few weeks anyway!

Exploring the complexity of Shakespeare's Caesar was fascinating. The conflict between arrogance and unease, power and paranoia, between public and private. In the assassination, I was determined not to die without a fight. I stabbed one of the conspiritors and watched them back away, then all the fight and will are drained as I realise the loyal Brutus is among the killers: "*Et tu*, Brute?" In the text Caesar appears as a ghost to Brutus in Act 4 Scene 3, the tent scene. Sean decided to also place me in a number of other scenes as Caesar's ghost, observing the action. Caesar dead is as potent as Caesar living.

The production received moderate notices. Some reviewers felt it didn't explore the mixed motives of the plotters and, unlike the Peter Stein production, lacked the civic chaos that should have followed the murder. Of course, Herr Stein had half the Austrian army to help him with this. There were very good performances by Finbar Lynch (Cassius), John Light (Brutus), Golda Roseuvel (Calphurnia) and Maria Gale (Portia).

I was keen to know if my playing of the mighty Caesar

had worked. Had I been powerful, commanding? So I read the notices. Apart from one sniffy review for the production, where my performance was noted as "imperious, but in a schoolmasterly way", the others were very good: "Above all James Hayes' excellent Caesar suitably dominates the action: Hayes, shooting voracious sidelong glances at the mention of another crown, conveys Caesar's imperial vanity...' – Michael Billington in the *Guardian*. Others noted, "a commanding presence", "ever the military leader", "catches this self-regarding man's soul". Pleased.

The dressing rooms at the National Theatre have a tannoy feed controlled by a dial on the actors' dressing table. It has three setting – for the Olivier, the Lyttelton or the Cottesloe theatres – and relays the performances of each play, depending on which setting is chosen. When Sir John Gielgud played Caesar in the Olivier Theatre at the National, the story goes that he was "off" for an important scene. With no sign of him as his entrance approached, a stage manager hared off to his dressing room to fetch him. They quickly knocked and entered. 'Sir John, Sir John, you're off, you're off!'

'Nonsense!' declared the knight, 'I haven't heard the Portia scene yet!'

The stage manager cocked her head. 'Sir John, you're listening to the Ayckbourn in the Lyttelton'.

That Stratford season was titled "The Complete Works Festival". Michael Boyd, the RSC Artistic Director, and Deborah Shaw, Associate Director, with great vision and planning, arranged for productions of all Shakespeare's plays to be staged in Stratford. Twenty-three RSC productions were presented throughout the year. There were visiting companies from Germany, Japan, Poland, South Africa, India, Russia, South America, USA, Italy, China and the Middle East. There were also visits from The Peter Hall Company, Cornwall's Kneehigh, Propeller etc etc. Some came for one performance, others for five, ten. Of the few I managed to see I liked best the company of Indian and Sri Lankan multilingual actors who brought a new, strange, visually exciting and sexy interpetation of *A Midsummer Night's Dream.*

The production I most wanted to see but missed was the Tiny Ninja Theater from New York. They work with "Tiny Ninjas" –plastic figures found in vending machines across the city, along with "other dime-store figures". They present tiny versions of Shakespeare's plays to small audiences. "In Stratford for two performances, Ninja takes the title role for the first time in Shakespeare's great tragedy *Hamlet,* which sees new and innovative effects for the inch-high cast – No small parts, only small actors'.

I played in two other Shakespeare productions in that season. Rupert Goold's very original *Tempest* in the RST and Greg Doran's storming *Antony and Cleopatra* in the Swan.

Rupert chose to set *The Tempest* in an Arctic, snow-dusted landscape, where Prospero's cell is a rough wooden hut that Captain Scott would have recognised. The *Guardian* called it "a startling production... a blend of Beckett, Shockheaded Peter, *Edward Scissorhands* and polar exploration movie". Patrick Stewart brought tremendous power and depth of feeling to his Prospero. He had the bitterness and cruelty that is essential for great swathes of what is, for much of its length, a revenge play. But there was tenderness too, as when he spat on his hanky and wiped some smudges from his daughter's face as she was about to meet Ferdinand. Mariah Gale brought a very disconcerting quality to the playing of Miranda, automaton-like, innocent, astonished at the wonder of other human beings. As Ariel, Julian Bleach was unnervingly eerie and otherwordly, truly disturbing as that character should be. But, as ever with innovative interpretations, there are for the actor various problems to be surmounted. *The Tempest,* as written by Shakespeare, is set in a Mediterranean island where some of the main protagonists are returning from Africa to Italy when the tempest shipwrecks them. How they end up on an Arctic wasteland shows enormous incompetence by the ship's crew. Sympathy must be extended to the actors who then have to utter the following lines: "The air breathes upon us here most sweetly... Here is everything advantageous to life". Or in my case, playing the kindly old Gonzalo – "How lush and lusty the grass looks! How green!" I have to tell you that the delivery of this line took ingenious invention, which necessitated my brushing away some "snow" on the grey icy ground before me. Invariably the director is totally unconcerned by these conundrums. Whether they unsettle the audience I have no idea.

Antony and Cleopatra threw up no such problems. Playing Shakespeare in smaller theatres where speed and intimacy take precedence over spectacle is always satisfying. Greg Doran decided that this is a very intimate play, set on an international scale. His production was outstanding. Before that excellent designer Stephen Brimson Lewis' impressionistic relief map of the ancient world, the politics of the ruling triumvirate is run by two men who detest each other, Antony and Octavius, and despise their partner,

Lepidus – the part I played. Antony and Cleopatra were played by Patrick Stewart and Harriet Walter. Both actors brought infinite variety to their playing. He, flawed, volatile, dangerous, torn between his feelings for her and his duty as a Roman and a soldier. She, seductive, full of wit, vivacity and narcissism. I remember a great moment when she appeared in an early scene wearing a classic, though clichéd Cleopatra wig, the full Elizabeth Taylor black bob. Suddenly she reached up pulled it off and threw it away revealing her own short hair beneath. This would be a different Cleopatra. Two powerful performances.

At the end of the season we took the three plays to the university town of Ann Arbor in Michigan where they were well received and where we were given tremendous hospitality. It was disconcerting to be recognised in the street by students, who would shout out from passing vehicles, 'Hey, Julius Caesar! Good job!'

SAINT JOAN
ROMEO AND JULIET MEETS
QUENTIN TARENTINO
KISS ME KATE

In 2007 Marianne Elliott directed Bernard Shaw's *Saint Joan* in the Olivier Theatre with Anne-Marie Duff in the title role. She asked me to play the Archbishop of Rheims.

Back in the sixties when I first came to London there seemed to be a major Shaw production in the West End every week. In the intervening years his plays have been staged less and less often. John Osborne dismissed his work as "posturing wind and rubbish". Shaw had few champions. This *Saint Joan* was the first Shaw presented at the NT in thirteen years. The revival proved surprisingly topical. Joan could be seen as a religious fundamentalist who with her "voices" claims a direct connection to God. They tell her to drive the English out of France. The play deals with faith, nationalism, authority and the freedom of the individual. It has much debate and discourse but little physical action. In her production, Elliott, with the writer Samuel Adamson, trimmed the dialogue. She then added a strong element of physical theatre. Not very Shavian. The first image designer Rae Smith presented the audience with was a raised wooden platform with a towering pyramid of rough sturdy wooden chairs. In the gloom behind, through swirling smoke, could be glimpsed some scorched and jagged trees like the aftermath of a war. Actors came on and in slow motion removed the chairs and lined them in rows at the side of the stage, sat on them and watched the action. These chairs featured throughout the production. In the stylised battle scenes, brilliantly staged by the choreographer Hofesh Schechter, they were raised, swung in the air, smashed against the floor, accompanied with the loud banging and screeching of staves against corrugated iron panels and the waving of tattered flags. At the end, for the burning of Joan, the chairs were symbolically piled in a mound, on top of which she is placed. As the flames rise and consume her she falls backwards into the arms of the soldiers. Blazing theatricality.

Some of the long wordy static scenes were enhanced by the use of a large revolve on the raised platform. For my first entrance in rich red as the Archbishop, I entered from the left wing, mounted the revolve at say nine o'clock and travelling round through nine hours to six o'clock I spoke my first line downstage centre. It took much skill in staging when, in a long scene, the actors, even when standing still, were in continuous motion. But the resulting moving pictures and character groupings proved very watchable. Mind you there was no way all this could be achieved without having the luxury of a permanent revolve in the floor of Rehearsal Room 1.

Marianne's production, conceived and executed in great detail, was a triumph. She was terrific to work with. Rigorous in her approach to every detail, she was imaginative, effortlessly inventive and – crucially for me – the possessor of a great sense of humour. Most directors like to keep a little distance between themselves and the actor. Understandable. Marianne certainly surprised me, and I suspect most of the company on the first day of rehearsal by asking us to write something down. It was her telephone number. If we were ever concerned about anything we should call her. This went down well with the company. Anyone who saw *Saint Joan, War Horse* or her production of Simon Stephens' fine, bleak, Northern play *Port,* will know what a talent Marianne is.

Anne-Marie Duff, slight of frame, luminous of character, whose face and body so beautifully convey deep emotion was a very fine Joan. Her transformation from a simple, stubborn country girl with a soft Irish accent to a courageous, difficult woman of iron-strong faith, challenging the intellectual might of Church and State, was fiercely done. Among all these bullying men, her playing was deeply moving and unforgettable.

The lowering forces of Church and State were very well represented by Paterson Joseph, Angus Wright and Oliver Ford Davies.

MILLER, WILDE, ORTON

In 2008, I was lucky to be involved in three very different plays: a production of Arthur Miller's first play, *The Man Who Had All The Luck,* was my first appearance at the Donmar; Joe Orton's *Loot* my first at the Tricycle; and Oscar Wilde's *An Ideal Husband* took me back to the Abbey Theatre in Dublin.

Arthur Miller had first written *The Man Who…* as a novel, then as a play. It's 1944 production, his first on Broadway, lasted four performances and then disappeared. Little known for decades, Sean Holmes chose it for his first production at the Donmar. That building has had a chequered history. In the 1870s it served as a vat store and hop warehouse for a local brewery in Covent Garden. In 1961 it was bought by the impresario Donald Albery and converted into a rehearsal space for the London Festival Ballet, which he formed with the great ballerina Margot Fonteyn. The combination of their Christian names gives the theatre its current name. In the mid-seventies the RSC used it for studio productions. It was then titled The Warehouse. In 1990 under new management Sam Mendes became artistic director, followed in 2002 by Michael Grandage. Both men made that small theatre a hugely successful and internationally admired venue.

Set in a rural community in the Midwest, *The Man Who* "wrestled with the unanswerable – the question of the justice of fate, how it was that one man failed and another, no more or less capable, achieved some glory in life". As the hero David Beeves, cursed with good luck, reaps success after success, all around him fail. Many of the themes contained in the play were to reappear in Miller's later and greater works. The favoured and unfavoured sons' relationship in *Death of a Salesman* is echoed here in the rejection of the hero's talented baseball-pitcher brother, Amos, who is turned down by a big-time talent scout. A favourite of his father and a victim of the parent's obsessive fantasies, this massive and unexpected disappointment seals the boy's fate. Meanwhile David's inexorable success almost drives him to madness, watched uncomprehendingly by his pregnant wife. The play comes across as an early work but was nevertheless worthy of this exciting revival.

The small stage of the Donmar threw up some interesting technical problems for the director and designer. The opening scene is set in an old barn where the hero works as a motor mechanic. He is asked to mend the car of a rich but measly mink farmer Dan Dibble – the part I played – which, if he succeeds, will lead to further and lucrative work from the farmer. Dibble's car has then to appear and be worked on in a couple of scenes. The vehicle model mentioned in the text was a Marmon, way too big for the Donmar stage, so a smaller 1930s vehicle was found, resprayed and refurbished to its former glory for the production. With little wing space, there was the problem of how to get it on and off stage for the scenes. An ingenious solution was found. Although not a high stage the crew made a large oblong "skirt" of black woollen material and fixed it above the playing area. They then "flew" the car inside shrouding the vehicle from the audience's view. It was lowered into position in a blackout and flown out the same way. When playing scenes I found it best not to think about what was hanging ten feet above my head.

Sean, with the casting director Anne McNulty, assembled a very talented cast and created, with the ensemble, a strong sense of the rising and waning fortunes of a small-town Midwest community. The production was a big success and toured after the Donmar run. This was without exception one of the most talented group of actors I have worked with. They were Andrew Buchan, Michelle Terry, Felix Scott, Sandra Voe, Aidan Kelly, Nigel Cooke, Shaun Dingwall, Mark Lewis Jones, Roy Sampson and Gary Lilburn.

Later that June, Neil Bartlett asked me to play Lord Caversham in Wilde's *An Ideal Husband* at the Abbey in

Dublin. It was ironic to return to my homeland to play a quintessential upper-class Englishman in an Irishman's play. I very quickly decided that the voice I needed for this member of the aristocracy was that of Edward Fox, when he famously played Edward VIII in *Edward & Mrs Simpson*. I went out and bought the complete series and spent many hours listening to him. The posh, clipped tones soon seeped into my head. I noticed that all vowels were severely compacted. If one used the same voice for Hamlet, the famous soliloqy would sound like this: "T b, 'r n't t b, – tht's th quest'n".

Unlike my previous visit with *Hinterland*, no anger or controversy greeted this production. With *St Joan* designer Rae Smith's classy set and costumes, Neil's production was very stylish and the press loved it. At the start of every day he welcomed the company with the considered greeting, 'Good morning, colleagues!' Vastly experienced he staged large and small scenes with consummate ease. With his black clothes, tightly cut black hair, dark eyebrows, piercing eyes, moustache and small chinbeard he looked like a ruminating cleric in an El Greco painting. I really enjoyed working with him. Rehearsing a two-hander scene with my "son" Viscount Goring, played by Mark O'Halloran, where father and son find communication both embarrassing and frustrating, Neil decided that the scene would be best played in a small study. Consequently, three narrow walls flew in and shrunk the large acting area. The contentious scene then played very well in this tight space. Wearing evening dress, white tie and tails with a blue sash, while delivering razor-sharp witty dialogue what more could you ask for? Mark O'Halloran is ludicrously talented both as an actor and as a screenwriter. He lent me copies of his two Irish films, *Adam and Paul* and *Garage.* They were funny, achingly touching and extremely well written. Apart from the English Simon Wilson, who played Sir Robert Chiltern extremely well, the cast were all Irish. I was fascinated after all my years of exile, by some of the actors' names. Caitriona Ni Mhurchu, Aoibheann O'Hara, Deirdre Donnelly, Diarmaid Murtagh, Derbhle Crotty, Susannah De Wrixon. I loved saying them out loud. They were a great group of actors and tremendous socialisers. Playing in Dublin meant many old friends and family came to see the play. It was a great job.

* * *

"Mr McCleavy: I'm not interested in doing good. There are organisations devoted to that purpose.

Fay: The British police force used to be run by men of integrity. Inspector Truscott: That is a mistake which has been rectified!"

At the end of the year I was reunited with Sean Holmes for a production of Joe Orton's black comedy *Loot* at the Tricycle Theatre, where it was scheduled for a very unseasonal run at Christmas. Almost fifty years after its first performance, the play, although still a very funny work, was beginning to show its age. Sean was very aware of this, so set it in a realistic suburban sitting-room, fronted by a false procenium arch with velvet curtains. With a box set and the playing of the national anthem as the house lights dimmed I felt I was back in Barrow in 1965.

Actors love Orton, once dubbed the Oscar Wilde of welfare-state gentility. We love his satire, his irreverence, his disregard for any taboos about sex, death and figures of authority. But most of all we love his talent for writing great quirky characters and laugh-out-loud razor-sharp dialogue.

A play that contains a scene where the body of a recently deceased mother is unceremoniously ousted from her coffin by her son to accommodate the swag from a bank robbery is, of course, shocking. To see said body then dumped in a nearby wardrobe is likewise shocking.

"You have been a widower for three days. Have you considered a second marriage yet?" – A scene where a mourning father, Mr McLeavy, is harangued by his dead wife's nurse, who has probably killed the woman. This is abhorrent.

A man from the Metropolitan Water Board turns out to be a police inspector. With a display of psychotic savagery he administers a beating to a young man: *"Under any other political system I'd have you on the floor in tears."* To which the boy replies, *"You've got me on the floor in tears!"* Shameful.

But within the confines of a farce, these incidents are also blackly funny. At the heart of the play is one of the great comic creations, Inspector Truscott. We were lucky to have David Haig to play the role. "Right up his street" would be an understatement. Suppressed rage, smug self-satisfaction, frothing frustration, physical contortion, dumb deductions, you name it, David delivered. His comic timing was, of course, brilliant, the laughs he elicited were massive, but what I admired most was his ability to portray all the contradictory aspects of Truscott's character. He could be as chilling as he could be funny.

In a world where everyone is corrupt or on the make, the only innocent character in the play is led away in handcuffs at the end. This is the bewildered, victimised husband Mr McLeavy, the part I played. The press on the whole admired the production and praised the playing, but felt that Orton's cynicism now lacked shock value. Michael Billington in the Guardian hit the nail on the head: "Great satire always implies a moral positive, but Orton's stance never expands beyond nihilistic contempt, which, in the end, is not quite enough".

FRANK MCGUINNESS AND YET ANOTHER ARTHUR MILLER

In 1959, inspired by working in a neighbourhood theatre in New York, the director James Roose-Evans created the Hampstead Theatre Club in a small church hall in north London. This was fringe before fringe existed. He decided that Hampstead's cosmopolitan inhabitants would be interested in seeing a repertoire of new and exciting plays. His first season included two short plays *The Room* and *The Dumb Waiter* by a writer Harold Pinter whose *The Birthday Party* had been savaged by critics and closed after eight performances at the Lyric Hammersmith the previous year. Fifty years later in 2009, in its purpose-built third home, the current artistic director, Tony Clark, decided on a year-long celebration, which would include new productions of some of the theatre's past triumphs. One of these was Frank McGuinness' *Observe the Sons of Ulster Marching Towards the Somme*. It was directed by John Dove, had an all-male cast of nine in which I played the Older Pyper, a survivor of that First World War conflict and whose haunted reveries frame the action.

Observe the Sons... follows the progress of eight young men from the 36th Ulster Division who bring to the battlefields of France their own cultural, tribal and religious antagonisms. McGuinness probes the motivations and beliefs of these young men; he dissects their patriotism, their faith, their narrow superstitions. At the end, to keep their spirits up on the eve of battle, they re-enact with much humour the Battle of the Boyne. Then, donning orange sashes they go into battle. As the play progresses there is the slow realisation that they owe their allegiance not to king, country or Ulster, but to one another. The 36th Ulster Division famously suffered huge losses at the Somme.

An upper-crust Protestant, Old Pyper, starts the play with a long soliloquy recalling his lost comrades. He remembers his rebellious younger self, his refusal to join the army as an officer. He slowly, painfully remembers a fellow Ulster comrade, a young blacksmith he fell in love with. Old now, alone and full of self-loathing and anger at his younger self, he rails against a God who allowed such atrocities. He is visited by the ghosts of the dead. This Beckettian monologue I delivered seated on an old high-backed kitchen chair. It took me a while to learn it. Following a run-through of the play, the stage manager complimented me on the speech – or rather on the timing of the speech – 'Very good, Jimmy, sixteen minutes!' *Sixteen minutes!* Those five words put the wind up me. With the days of the prompter long gone I knew I would have no one to turn to for help if I "dried".

Later, before every performance I stood just offstage in

the wings, very close to the audience, waiting for the house lights to dim. The company manager standing beside me in the silence would then give me the cue to creep on in the darkness to my chair. He did this by touching me gently on the arm. I remembered thinking that this soft sympathetic touch, could have been given to any poor soldier about to leave the trenches – 'Good luck, you poor bastard.'

My memories of the production are of:

The eight talented actors who brought a true sense of ensemble to this disparate group of characters. Their playing was outstanding.

Of the support and affection of Frank McGuinness for all concerned with the project. His rosy, bearded, lived-in face topped with curly greying red hair radiated warmth, admiration and affection.

Of director John Dove, whose preparation and deeply studied knowledge of the period could be witnessed every day in his talk and especially his script, in which it was hard to determine the dialogue surrounded as it was by myriad notes, ideas and observations. John is a very incisive director and also one of the funniest men I have ever known. He loves actors. You can't say that of every director.

Talking one day to Richard Dormer who played the Young Pyper in *Observe the Sons...* I mentioned that I would like to play Krapp in Beckett's *Krapp's Last Tape*. It is a one-man play where the sixty-nine-year-old Krapp intersperses his reminiscenses with recordings he has made of himself three decades before. These recordings he listens to during the action.

'I want to play Krapp as well,' Richard replied. 'In fact, I've already recorded the young voice.' I told him I thought that was ingenious and very clever. As ingenious and clever as his fine performance in our play.

In mentioning earlier the cosmopolitan Hampstead audiences I was reminded of the story of the actor Jim Broadbent falling ill during a performance of Mike Leigh's *Ecstasy* at Hampstead Theatre. When the SM asked if there was a doctor in the house, fourteen men and women stood up.

Walking along the Royal Mile in Edinburgh on a snowy December morning is bracing. With the castle proud on the hill to one's right, the road curves downhill and the ice on the cobbles can be treacherous. The journey warms one's cheeks but freezes one's fingers. Luckily the full beard I was growing helped. At the bottom of the hill it was a short walk to the beautiful Lyceum Theatre where I was rehearsing. I enjoyed that walk every morning, it set me up for the day.

The play was Arthur Miller's *The Price*. Having played in and deeply enjoyed three other Miller plays over the years I felt very lucky to be tackling another. The director was John Dove, who I was delighted to be working with again so soon. *The Price* was the fourth Miller play John had directed at the Lyceum in five years.

In *The Price*, set in 1968, two estranged brothers meet in a cluttered room to discuss what to do with their deceased parents' furniture, now that the building in which they once lived is to be demolished. One, a policeman, Victor, who sacrificed his career as a promising science student to care for the dying father who had lost everything in the 1929 Wall Street Crash. The other, Walter, abandoned the family and went on to make a very successful career for himself as a surgeon. The play mirrors Miller's own life, when he chose to pursue his own creative career, while his brother Kermit sacrificed all to support their parents. The other characters are Esther, Victor's resentful and frustrated wife and Gregory Soloman, the part I played, an eighty-nine-year-old Russian Jewish furniture appraiser and dealer who comes to put a price on the contents of the apartment.

The sacrifices, the hopes, the disappointments, the resentments and the guilt within the family, slowly emerge as we come to know the characters. Soloman's efforts to put a price on the furniture becomes the most complex of metaphors for the price both brothers have paid for the loss of love, contentment and emotional fulfilment. What are things worth? What value do we place on our relationships with other people? The price is something we all have to pay for our choices and actions.

In the space where dying father and son eked out the old man's last days, Michael Taylor created a large neglected room overwhelmed with grand antique cabinets, a rocking horse, a giant oar, a handmade radio, bulky outdated once-valued wardrobes, old lumpy armchairs, an old harp, two beds and a number of chairs hanging from the ceiling. In this cramped world John Dove crafted a production full of fine detail. He worked to great effect on the bruised complexities of the four characters in the drama. Greg Powrie's Victor was full of hurt, disappointment, unfulfilled dreams, a thoroughly decent man. Sally Edwards' Esther, was long-suffering, sometimes bitter, but doggedly hopeful: a wife still wanting to dream. Aden Gillett's Walter, smooth-talking, reeking of success; a prodigal son, resilient then suddenly vulnerable. Pitch-perfect performances.

Eighty-nine years old, and one of the great talkers, Gregory Soloman was a big challenge but a huge delight to play. He was both eccentric and dignified. He had a cunning blend of down-to-the-bone honesty and wily pragmatism. He was persuasive, he was manipulative. He had the wisdom of Solomon – Gregory Solomon – a man who cannot set a price without first having a prolonged philosophic conversation. He had a fund of acute observations that have stood the test of time:

> *"Solomon: You see, it's also this particular furniture – the average person he'll take one look, it'll make him very nervous … he knows it's never gonna break... You're laughing, I'm telling you the factual situation. What is the key word today? –Disposable. The more you can throw it away the more it's beautiful. The car, the furniture, the wife, the children – everything has to be disposable. Because you see the main thing today is – shopping. Years ago a person, he was unhappy, didn't know what to do with himself – he'd go to church, start a revolution – something. Today you're unhappy? Can't figure it out? What is the salvation? Go shopping."*

With writing of that quality the character comes bursting, fully-formed off the page. It makes the job of acting exciting and a lot easier. Well, actually, trying to play an eighty-nine-year-old Russian Jewish man is not easy at all. You grow the full white beard, you put some more lines on your face, you do some doddery acting – and *then* you have to work on the Russian/Jewish/New York accent.

"The old Jewish valuer (an enjoyable James Hayes, even if his accent wanders from Brooklyn to Bethnal Green...)" – The Times

'In James Hayes, director Dove has a fine Solomon. It is not an easy feat to render a character both eccentric and dignified, but Hayes achieves this with a delightful combination of skill and moral authority" – Sunday Herald

Aden Gillett had an unusual method of learning lines. Not for him the quiet room, going over the words again and again. His preferred location for this time-consuming and frustrating task? – a public house, preferably crowded with chattering customers.

'TIS PITY SHE'S A WHORE

Romeo and Juliet meet Quentin Tarantino

Outside the theatre, the large six-metre poster shows a sculpture, a Pieta, the Virgin Mary holding the body of the crucified Christ surrounded by candles. On the wall beside the two figures is a 1950s framed photograph of two young children, a brother and sister holding hands. On the left of the poster is the title of the play *'Tis Pity She's a Whore*. At the heart of John Ford's 1633 revenge tragedy is the forbidden love between a brother, Giovanni and his sister, Annabella. The theatre is the West Yorkshire Playhouse. The director is Jonathan Munby and he has cast me as the father of these young siblings.

I arrive in Leeds in 2011 to find controversy surrounding the project. After receiving a number of complaints from outraged parishioners who had been "distressed and outraged" by the poster, the Roman Catholic Bishop of Leeds wrote a letter of complaint to the theatre. Essentially it was felt that the juxtaposition of Our Lady and the crucified Christ with the title of the play was offensive, crass and a marketing ploy. The theatre apologised, pointing out that "the religious faith of the characters is integral to the development of their stories and we felt it was important that this is reflected in any image to promote the production". The offending poster was taken down and replaced by a stark black and white statement: "Judge the play, not the poster". Incidentally, the Church comes out of the play surprisingly well, with the kindly Friar Bonaventura warning the brother what lies ahead if he persists in his love for his sister, "Death waits on thy lust", and warning them both of hellfire and damnation.

Having played the father of an incestuous child in Marianne Elliott's production of Middleton's *Women Beware Women* at the NT in 2010, here I was in Leeds nine months later playing the father of *two* incestuous children. Perhaps a new career path was opening up for me.

Jonathan Munby decided to update the play from its setting in the Parma of 1633 to the Italy of the sixties. It was a world of inter-generational conflict, student activism, anti-authoritarianism and church reform with Pope John XXIII and the Second Vatican Council. There were the films of Fellini and Antonioni and the new American and British pop music. This was the world Giovanni and Annabella inhabited. With its incest, doomed young couple, revengeful scorned mistress, murderous servants, cynical manipulative parents, together with murders, poisonings, and a final bloodbath when the young hero arrives with the heart of his sister skewered on a knife, the play seemed at times like a *Romeo and Juliet* reimagined by Quentin Tarantino.

The director's "stylish, sexy, fiendishly sixties makeover" – the *Telegraph* – had very evocative settings by Mike Britton combining dark candle-lit churches, their confessionals overlooked by a massive Christ on the Cross, with upmarket hotel lounges with lemon-coloured low-backed sofas, and soft lighting. In a street scene, a very sixties Vespa scooter. For the men, the costumes were a mix of sharp Italian-tailored suits and dinner jackets. For the women, acid-blue and green silk dresses with wide flounced skirts and high heels.

Good and witty use was made of contemporary music. At a party to celebrate the cynical betrothal of the unhappy Annabella to the rich nobleman Soranzo, the young girl stepped up to the microphone and sang the old Doris Day song "Secret Love", throwing furtive glances across to her unhappy brother. At the wedding, Soranzo's spurned mistress, Hippolita, played by the comely Sally Dexter, comes on disguised and masked, wearing a long tight black satin dress with elbow-length gloves flanked by two backing singers and performs an accusatory rendition of Burt Bacharach's "Anyone Who Had a Heart". This before she tries to poison her lover and is forced to take her own medicine.

The success of the production rested on the young shoulders of the actors playing Giovanni and Annabella. Jonathan had chosen two actors at the very beginning of their careers. In fact, Damien Molony who played Giovanni, hadn't even started his career. He was still at drama school with one term to go. He brought a sharp intelligence to Giovanni and spoke the verse with great ease, pace and fluidity. His playing of the fiendishly difficult final scene where he has to enter with his sister's heart on a knife was exceptional. The beautiful Sara Vickers, whose experience amounted to one production at the Manchester Royal Exchange, brought a tenderness, a bruised innocence, a deep, doom-laden devotion to her Annabella. *'Tis Pity* is a fiercely difficult play to bring off for a modern audience but Jonathan Munby was equal to the task and delivered a thrilling, innovative production.

* * *

SEPTEMBER 2015

I start these final pages having just embarked, somewhat belatedly, on my first *musical*. It is Cole Porter's *Kiss me, Kate* and is being given a big, lavish production by Opera North in Leeds. I am writing a blog for their website. I thought it would be interesting to write about the staging of a great musical from the point of view of a complete newcomer to the genre.

Here are a few short extracts from the blog.

I enter the large rehearsal room and am confronted by about fifty people. (The last play I did had a cast of four.) Apart from Jo Davies, the director, whom I have worked with at the RSC and the actor Peter Harding, who I worked with on *The*

Romans in Britain, I don't know a soul. There is a bewildering mix of professionals. There are singers and dancers. There is the American conductor David Charles Abell and his assistant Oliver. We have *two* assistant directors, Ed and Matthew. There is the choreographer Will Tuckett and his assistant David. There is the chief repetiteur, Catriona Beveridge, seated at a grand piano. Note, *chief* repetiteur – apparantly there are five repetiteurs with Opera North. I'm so green, I can't even pronounce repetiteur!

* * *

This morning we are joined by the twenty-four members of the chorus who will be heavily involved in the opening scene of the play-within-the-play where the musical company are putting the final touches to the production before the opening night. They will play various members of the crew, stage management, wardrobe, dressers and lighting staff. The director, the unflappable Jo Davies, now has nearly fifty performers to work with. She is suggesting dozens of complex entrances and exits, bits of business, moves, sketching in character traits and relationships, lining up the curtain calls etc. Suddenly Cole Porter's thrilling music leads into the first song. Out of a tight huddle of performers, the lovely Katie Kerr, fizzing with energy, bursts forward and launches into "Another Op'nin"

"Another op'nin', another show
In Philly, Boston or Baltimo'e,
A chance for stage-folk to say 'hello',
Another op'nin', of another show."
She is swiftly joined by three more voices. *Then,* forty more

voices come in. The sound they make is astonishing. It is big, full-bodied, thrilling. The song builds to a tremendous climax.

There is nothing in theatre, *nothing* to beat a great musical number. Joyful, uplifting – it makes you glad to be alive. It certainly makes *me* glad to be here and involved in this show. And this is with piano accompaniment. 'Wait 'til we are joined by the forty-eight-piece orchestra,' Jo says to me. Now, *that*, I am looking forward to.

* * *

On top of this we have, of course, our two opera stars, Jeni Bern and Quirijn de Lang – playing Lili/Kate and Fred/Petruchio. Watching both singers cope with the many physical battles Kate and Petruchio inflict on each other is impressive – but way, way more impressive is their ability and talent to *then* open their mouths and pour forth the most beautiful sounds imaginable.

* * *

All *I* have to do, in a number of short funny scenes, is play the actor Harry Trevor, who plays Baptista, the brow-beaten father to two difficult daughters, Kate and Bianca, utter some Shakespearean lines and, when forty singers are in full flow, add my voice to one or two of the numbers.

* * *

I am watching sixteen dancers working on a fiendishly complicated dance sequence. I marvel at their extraordinary ability to incorporate any changes, instantly and effortlessly. They are all highly talented. They have been working for two hours on what will be a seven-minute sequence. One section is balletic, with much sweeping, swirling movement, the boys lifting the girls gracefully into the air. They then leave the stage, and in what seems like five seconds, are back – now wearing tap shoes! A comic "tap battle" begins between two rival groups. There is much showing-off. The movement with the syncopated sound of the shoes on the wooden floor is wonderful to watch. They are all working flat out. The room smells of sweat and effort. In the short breaks many energy drinks, nuts and bananas are consumed.

* * *

EPILOGUE

That's it. My fifty years in the theatre – so far.

I'm still working. Much of 2016 I'll spend performing in Sean O'Casey's great play *The Plough and the Stars* at the Abbey Theatre in Dublin, as part of the commemorations to celebrate the centenary of the Easter Rising. It will play at the Abbey, tour Ireland, including a visit to my home town Limerick, followed by more touring to the USA.

The older I get, the more I enjoy working with young actors, young directors. For a short time they display a deference to my age and experience, and then move swiftly on to challenge and stretch me in all the best ways. They also take the mickey out of me. I like that and give as good as I get.

Some things are harder. No longer can I turn up on the first day, secure in the knowledge that I can blithely learn the role during rehearsals. The day after the offer comes through, I go into learning mode. Knocking the words in before rehearsals start is paramount. It is extremely hard and on some days, slow and dispiriting work. Panic can set in. But then, suddenly, the brain kicks in, confidence builds and hey presto, you have only two more pages to learn! I believe Noël Coward, when directing, insisted that the cast knew all their lines on the first day of rehearsal. I suspect this method would be secretly welcomed by many directors.

I look back with warmth to the days of fortnightly rep and mourn the closure of so many provincial theatres, along with the training and opportunities they gave to new performers, directors and designers. But, those that have survived, have blossomed and in some cases expanded, moving to newer and better venues with brave and adventurous programming. Budgets are tight. Funding is, as ever, fluid and Arts Council support cannot always be relied upon.

From their relatively modest beginnings in the early sixties, the National Theatre and the Royal Shakespeare Company are now unrecognisable. Their growth and expansion have bred fertile, joyous, often phenomenal work in all their differing and flexible spaces. A permanent London venue for the RSC is badly needed and will hopefully soon be found or created.

The "new" unsubsidised Shakespeare's Globe is now no longer perceived as a Disney outpost and goes from strength to strength. The term 'fringe' can no longer be used to describe the 'off-West End' theatres. From the well-established Donmar, Almeida, Tricycle, Orange Tree and others, we now have attractive new spaces producing exciting work. The relocated and bigger Bush Theatre, the Park Theatre, the Print Room, the Arcola, the Rose in Kingston etc. The rise in projects presented outside the conventional theatre spaces in "site-specific" or "immersive" work is adventurous and expanding. Whether performed in underground car parks, hotel rooms, office buildings or Edwardian swimming pools they enrich the theatre-making and theatre-going experience.

The West End rolls on with a largely unchanging diet of musicals, much as it did when I arrived in London in 1963, when *The Sound of Music* played 2385 performance at the Palace Theatre and *Oliver* played 2618 performances at the New Theatre. But the smaller West End theatres have been revitalised by successful transfers from the subsidised sector.

The quantity and diversity of today's theatre is immeasurably more exciting, ambitious and satisfying than when I became an actor. The changes I have experienced along the way have been profound, surprising, sometimes uncomfortable, but always challenging.

From Limerick to London, from Barrow to Beijing, from Stoke to Salzburg, from Newcastle to New York, from Chester to Chicago, from Edinburgh to Epidavros, from Waterloo to Warsaw, from Stratford to Shanghai.

I look around the room before I start this final page. There are mementos of my theatrical travels: some framed production posters; a small, snub-nosed, blue-green tea pot, covered in exquisite gold calligraphy from Beijing; a pair of small square pine boxes I drank saki from in Tokyo; an old, delicate painting on paper of an Indian potentate, surrounded by servants, with a hawk on his wrist, seated below a beautiful awning, bought in Delhi; a soft cotton throw with delicate sky-blue and brown hand-printed flowers and decoration bought at a village fair deep in the Indian countryside near Bangalore; a Picasso lithograph of a young woman with the most soulful eyes you could imagine, bought in Dublin; a wooden Aborigine egg decorated with hundreds of blue, white and orange dots in sinuous patterns bought in Perth, Australia. These along with handfuls of guide books, postcards, photographs, gallery catalogues from all over the world are the tangible reminders of how enriching my theatrical journey has been.

The less tangible proofs of that progress are the unforgettable experiences I have been lucky enough to enjoy with hundreds of fine actors, directors, designers, composers, musicians, stage management teams, technicians, theatre people and audiences over the past half century and which I have endeavoured to recount in this memoir.